AF574624

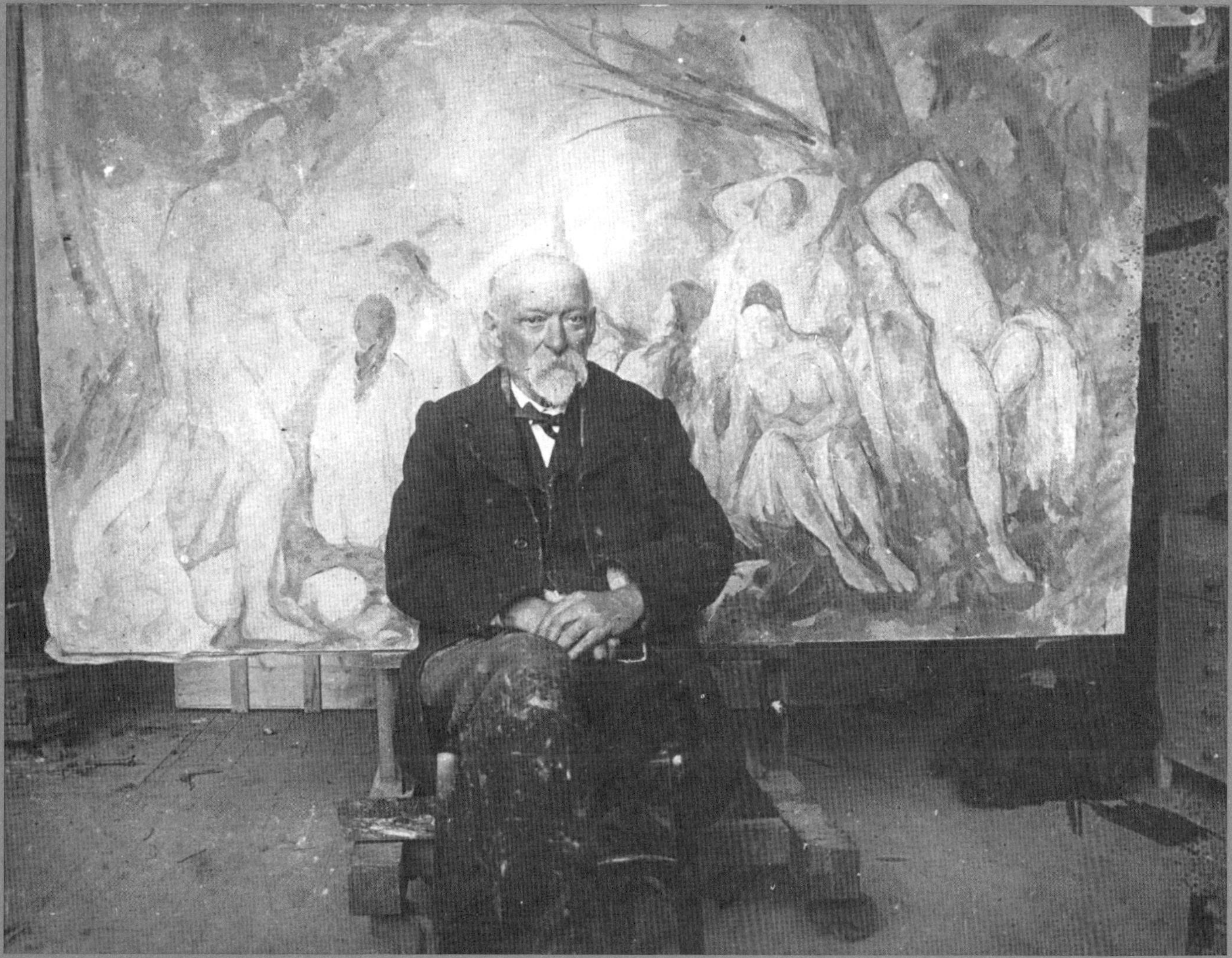

CÉZANNE'S BATHERS

Aruna D'Souza

CÉZANNE'S BATHERS

Biography and the Erotics of Paint

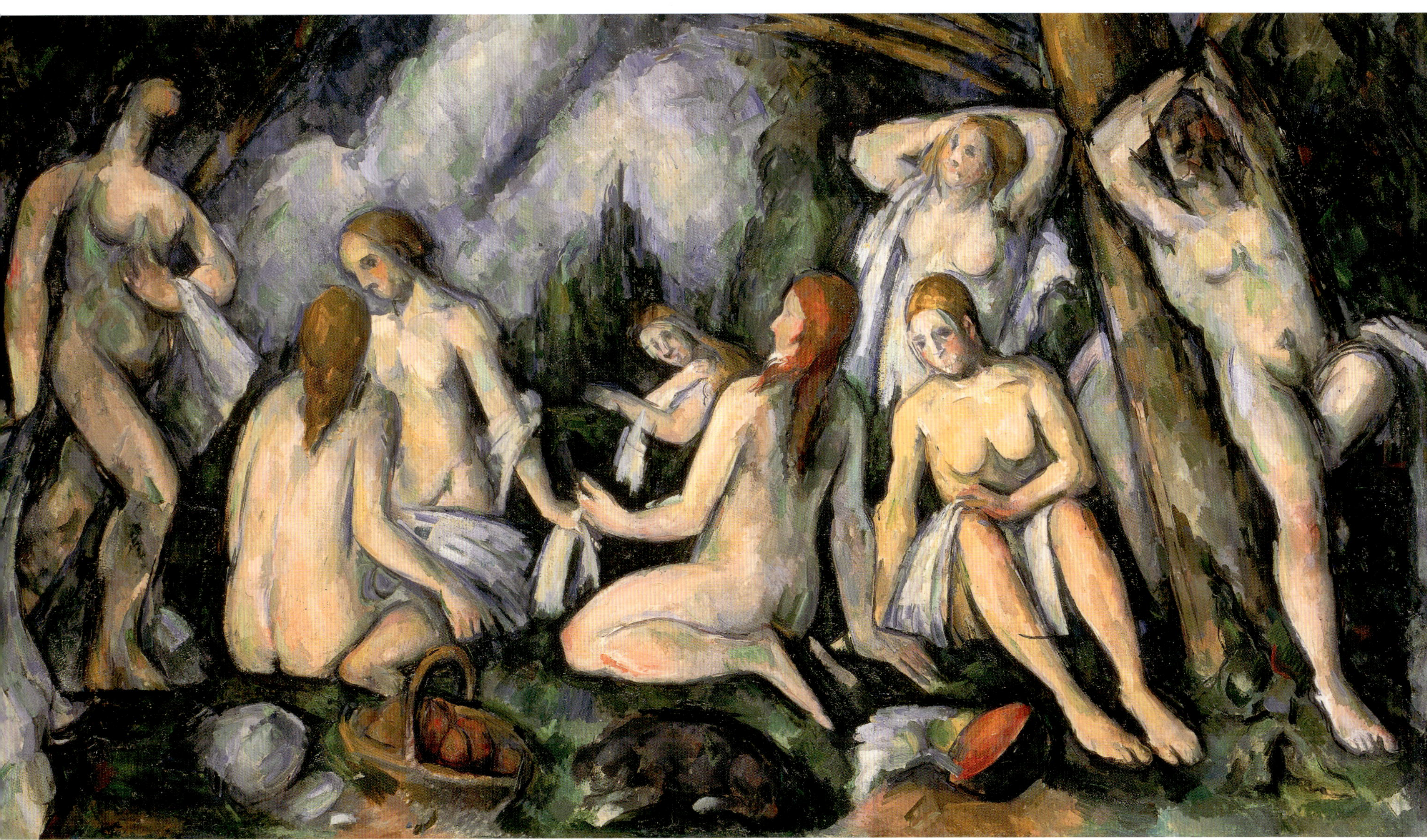

THE PENNSYLVANIA STATE UNIVERSITY PRESS · UNIVERSITY PARK, PENNSYLVANIA

Published with the assistance of the Getty Foundation.

Library of Congress Cataloging-in-Publication Data

D'Souza, Aruna.
Cézanne's bathers : biography and the erotics of paint / Aruna D'Souza.
p. cm. — (Refiguring Modernism)
Includes bibliographical references and index.
ISBN-13: 978-0-271-03214-6 (pbk. : alk. paper)
1. Cézanne, Paul, 1839–1906—Critisim and interpretation.
2. Female nude in art.
I. Title.

ND553.C33D78 2008
759.4—dc22
2007025805

Designed by Bessas & Ackerman
Printed in China by Everbest Printing Co.
through Four Colour Imports, Louisville, KY
Published by The Pennsylvania State University Press,
University Park, PA 16802-1003

The Pennsylvania State University Press is a member of the Association of American University Presses.

It is the policy of The Pennsylvania State University Press to use acid-free paper. Publications on uncoated stock satisfy the minimum requirements of American National Standard for Information Sciences—Permanence of Paper for Printed Library Material, ANSI Z39.48–1992.

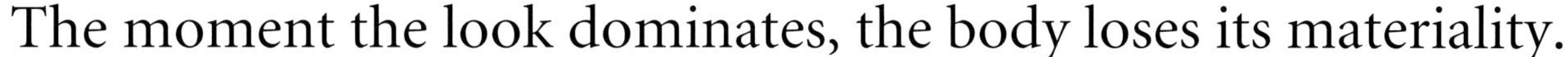

The moment the look dominates, the body loses its materiality.

LUCE IRIGARAY (1978)

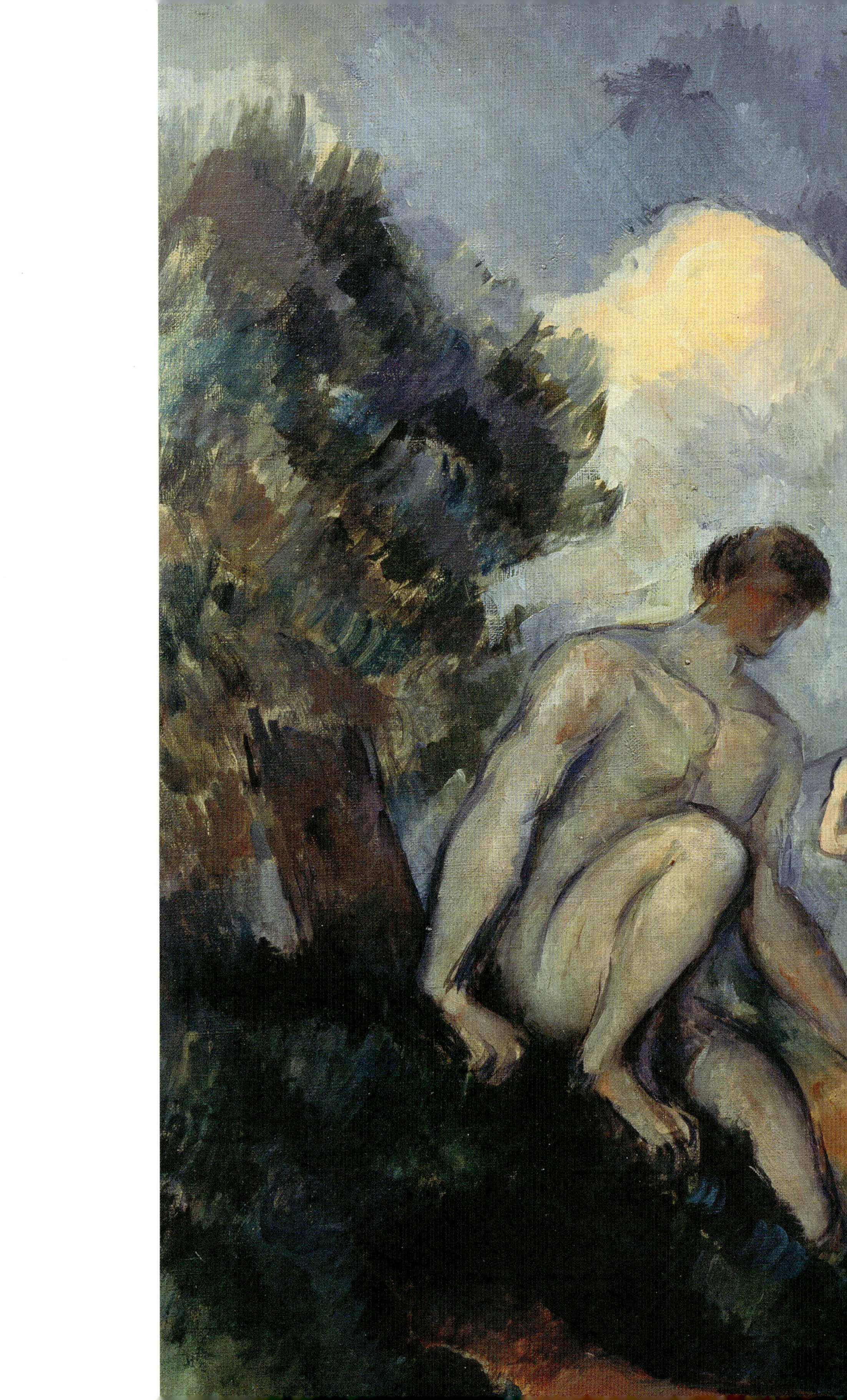

CONTENTS

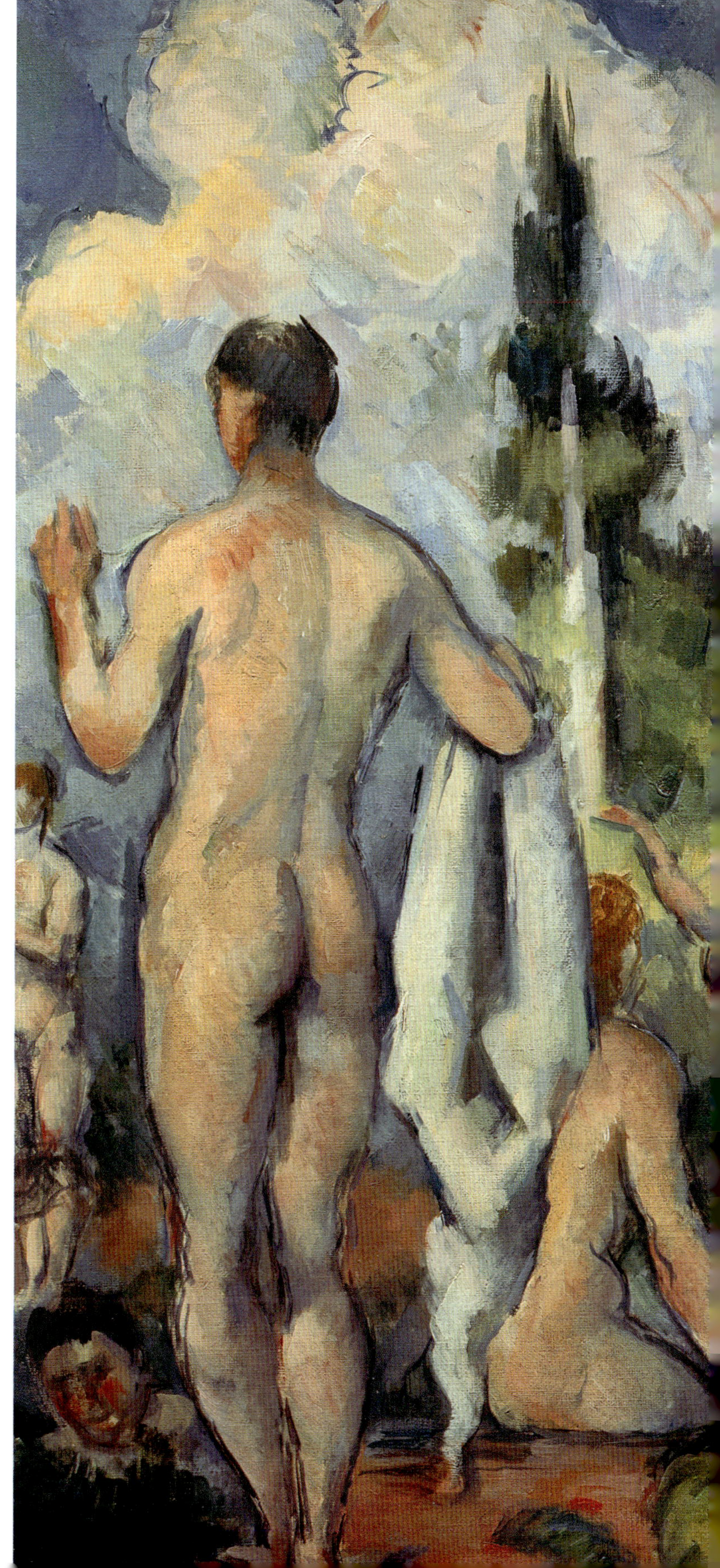

ILLUSTRATIONS

FIGURES

PLATES

ACKNOWLEDGMENTS

I would like to thank a number of individuals and institutions for their support, moral and financial by turns, of this project. This book started out as my doctoral dissertation, and I am grateful to the Social Sciences and Humanities Research Council of Canada as well as to the Institute of Fine Arts, New York University, and the Institute of Fine Arts Alumni Association for funding my research. In the subsequent transformation of dissertation to book, the Union of University Professionals and the dean's offices at Purchase College and Binghamton University generously underwrote both research and reproduction costs. I benefited tremendously, as well, from research leaves offered by Binghamton University. Jean-Pierre Mileur, dean of Harpur College of Arts and Sciences at Binghamton University, has been particularly generous, and I thank him heartily for it.

The moral support offered by a number of mentors, colleagues, and students has been no less valuable, though it is perhaps less quantifiable. First, my former teacher, mentor, and dear friend, Linda Nochlin, has encouraged me—and even needled me, when the occasion presented itself—over the time that it took to see this project through. As an advisor, she had the confidence in me to let me run with my intuition and to rein me in when necessary; as a friend and a mentor, she has set an example for me in both her professionalism and her zest for life and love of her subject. The other members of my dissertation committee, Robert Lubar, and especially Abigail Solomon-Godeau, provided useful and thought-provoking feedback. Though he was not an official advisor, the late Kirk Varnedoe certainly provided me with wise counsel during my time as a graduate student, and though I suspect that the end product would not exactly jibe with his own views of the subject, my understanding of Cézanne and of the process of writing about modern art was enriched immeasurably by my good fortune of being his student. In the subsequent process of writing a book, I have received valuable advice from Tamar Garb, Ann Wagner, and Tom Gretton. Gloria Kury, my former editor at Penn State University Press, was a constant pillar of support, treating my delays with the greatest of tact and imagining the project in the most generous possible ways. Subsequent to her departure from the press, her colleagues, most notably Sandy Thatcher, Cali Buckley, Laura Reed-Morrisson, Cherene Holland, Patricia Mitchell, and Jennifer Norton, have been most helpful.

Audiences at the University of Toronto, Wesleyan University, Barnard College and Columbia University, and Harvard University asked challenging questions and opened up new paths for me; I would particularly like to thank Benjamin Buchloh, Yve-Alain Bois, and Ewa Lajer-Burcharth for inviting me to their institutions and for each in their own way changing the direction of this project, sometimes dramatically and hopefully for the better. Nina Athanassoglou-Kallmyer, whose work on Cézanne has proven extremely useful for my own, invited me very early on to take part in a CAA panel she organized; the paper I presented there, which was subsequently published in *Nineteenth-Century Art Worldwide,* forms the core of chapter 1 of the present volume. Even more importantly, she has been a helpful and enthusiastic colleague and mentor. The same can be said of Susan Sidlauskas, who included me in a CAA panel that she convened in 2006, on the occasion of the centenary of the artist's death. The opportunity allowed me to clarify my ideas at a late stage in the process.

At Sotheby's, Charles Moffett and his colleague Jeremiah Evarts were most gracious in helping me secure permission to reproduce a number of images. The librarians at the Musée d'Orsay and the Bibliothèque d'Art et Architecture in Paris as well as at the Binghamton University Library and the Institute of Fine Arts at New York University also offered help at various stages of the project. Marcia Focht, curator of the Visual Resources Collection at Binghamton University, generously assisted me with reproductions.

I am so lucky to be surrounded by a group of friends who have been excited about and engaged with my project. George Baker, who was once my colleague at Purchase College and remains the dearest of friends, was an unflagging supporter and a deeply critical reader in the best possible way. Helen Molesworth has been my reality check, in both intellectual terms and professional ones. Martha Lucy and Ellen McBreen, deeply respected classmates from graduate school, read the manuscript and provided extremely useful feedback; Ellen's work on Matisse, in particular, has guided my own at certain points, and our dialogue on the subject of the material conditions of the erotic has been a most treasured one. André Dombrowski was kind enough to read parts of the manuscript and provided generous and useful feedback. Conversations with a number of abstract painters, including Michael Brennan, Richard Tsao, and John Zinsser, provided a wonderful backdrop to looking at Cézanne's paintings.

My family and inner circle of friends have offered diversion and encouragement by turn, although I suspect they wondered what I could possibly be doing with Cézanne that would take so long. My parents' pride in my work as a writer has been hugely motivating to me. My dear friends in Paris, Steven Melemis and Louise Van Winkle, have done more than their fair share of diverting me from the sometimes lonely task of sifting through archives and were always ready with a good meal and a good bottle of wine to remind me of the pleasures of my work. And though I could not really say in all seriousness that my daughter's birth in 2003 helped see the project through to completion, her daily presence certainly helps me focus on why I do what I do, for which I am truly thankful.

My most careful reader, and my most harried one, has been my husband, Tom McDonough, who has never let me put aside this project in favor of ones I thought would be easier, or quicker, or sexier. His belief in the value of what I was writing far outstripped my own, and I am ever grateful for that. He read and suggested, corrected and inspired, and it was a thankless job, for the most part. My thanks now are a small gesture, terribly insufficient to repay the love and support and advice that I have received from him along the way. I dedicate this book to him.

CÉZANNE'S BATHERS

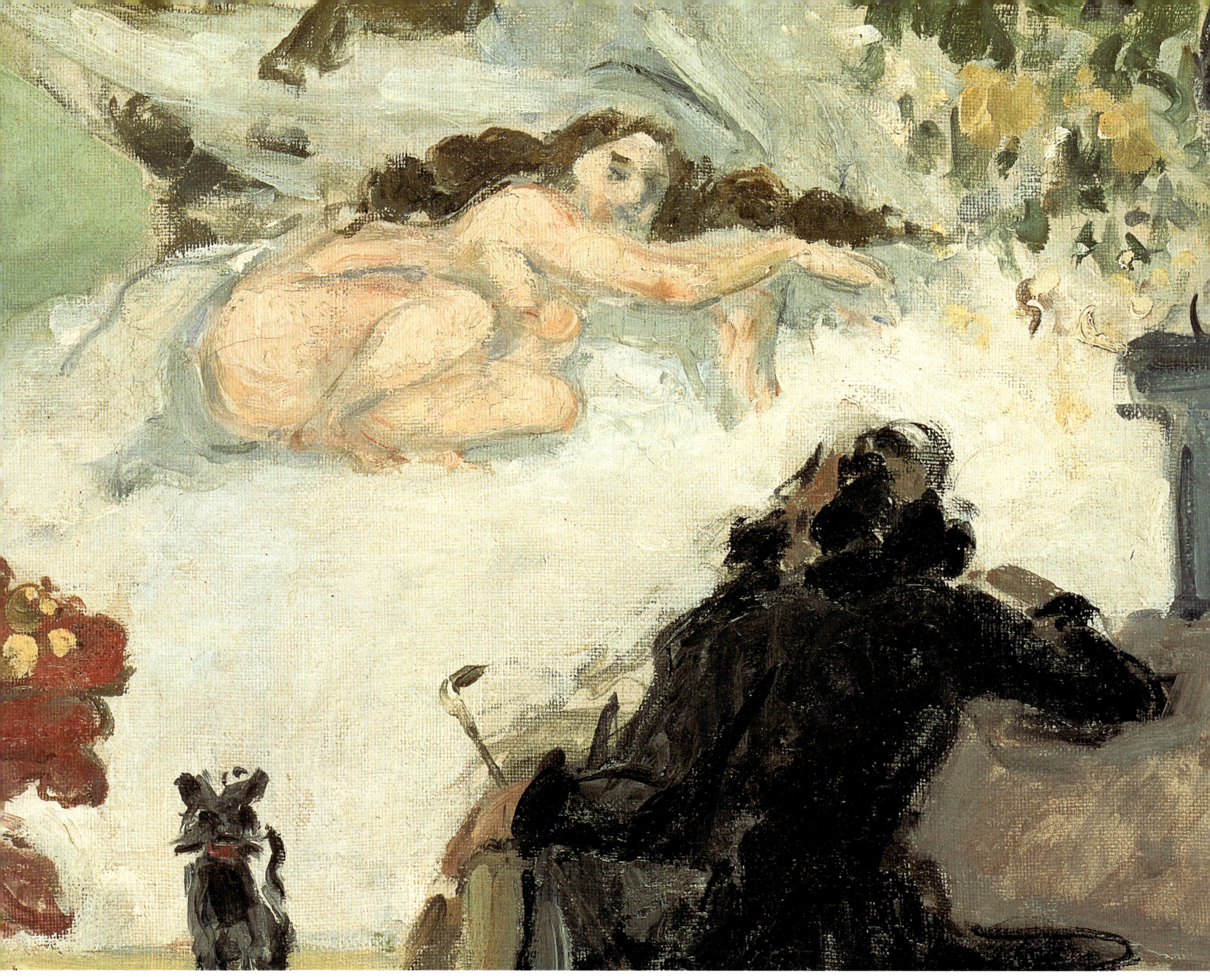

INTRODUCTION: MODERNISM'S TWO CÉZANNES

Detail of pl. VI

WE HAVE INHERITED, after over a century of commentary on his art, not one but two Cézannes: two portraits of the man that seem starkly contradictory but are, in a sense, intimately related. Witness the telling photographs taken by Cézanne's admirers near the end of his life. Ker Xavier Roussel's picture of Cézanne painting at Les Lauves in 1906 shows him spry, his brush poised, ready to make a carefully considered mark on a canvas placed perpendicular to the camera lens, its top tilted precariously forward to mitigate against the glare of the harsh Mediterranean sunlight (fig. 1). Cézanne's face is in *profil perdu,* yet we can still make out an expression of fierce concentration as he studies his motif. His body is tensed, ready for action: he is the embodiment of vital creativity. One of Émile Bernard's photos of his mentor, taken during his second trip to Aix in 1905, repeats this image of masculine power: Cézanne, though not painting, stands near the same site at Les Lauves, one of his favorite working spots (fig. 2). His figure fills the frame of the image. He looks larger than life and absolutely self-contained—even his hands are folded in front of him, bounded by the monolithic contour of his body, the pose not unlike that of Rodin's stele-like portrait of Balzac in all his virile glory. Cézanne's face is half-shadowed, but despite this his gaze seems focused, sure, as he looks directly at the photographer. His hat—that symbol of sartorial splendor and metonymic substitution for bourgeois, masculine authority—contrasts sharply with the white of the sky.

Compare these photos to Bernard's other, more famous picture of Cézanne sitting in front of his celebrated and vexing *Large Bathers*, now in the Barnes collection (fig. 3, pl. IX). The picture—or, more precisely, the man depicted therein—is no longer marked by the assuredness of those images discussed above. One can imagine the scene: Bernard having to cajole the reclusive painter to pose with his painting, then placing him seated just so in front of it. Cézanne's shy pride and discomfort registers, I think, in his stately carriage. Sitting where he is, with the painting as a backdrop, it is hard not to read him as the generative

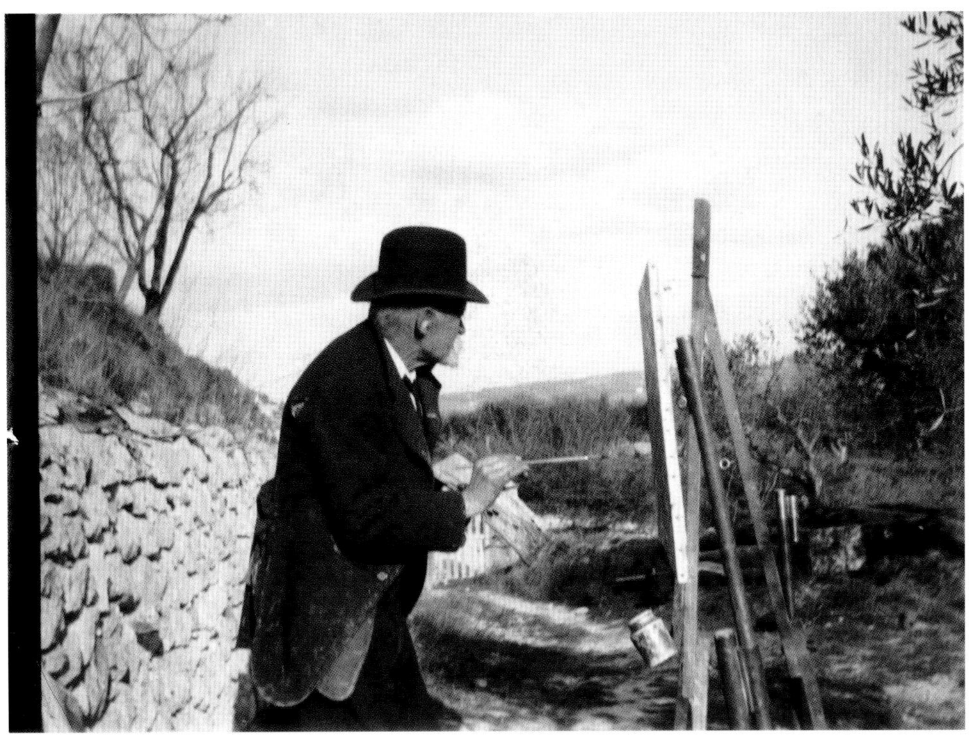

1. Ker Xavier Roussel, photograph of Cézanne at work on the hill of Les Lauves, 1906. John Rewald Papers, National Gallery of Art, Washington, D.C., Gallery Archives.

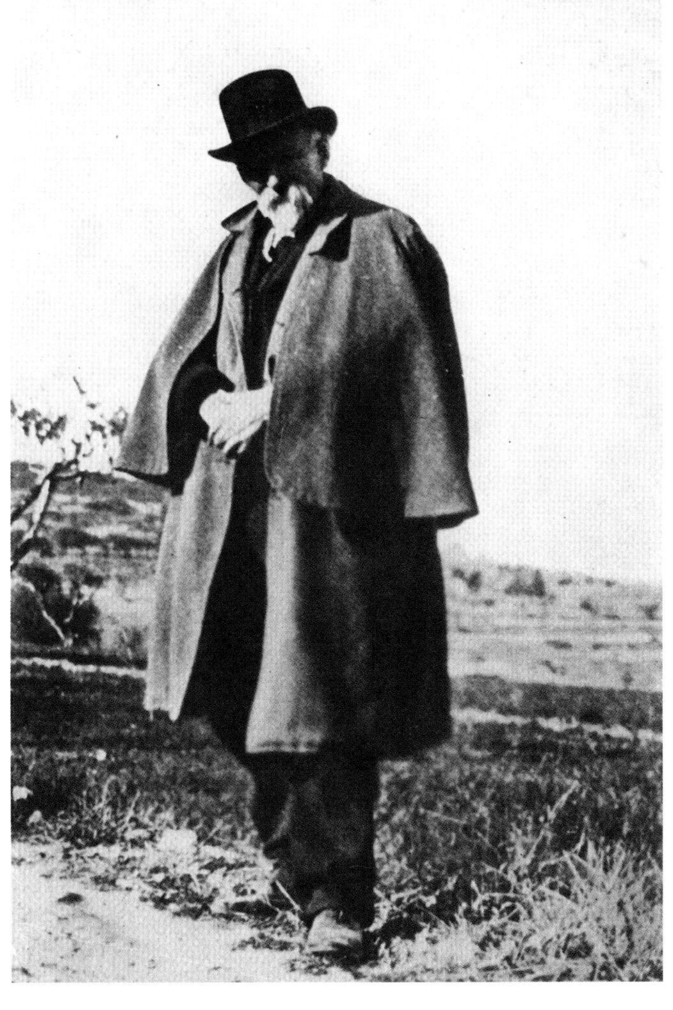

2. Émile Bernard, photograph of Cézanne on the hill of Les Lauves, ca. 1905. John Rewald Papers, National Gallery of Art, Washington, D.C., Gallery Archives. © Artists Rights Society (ARS).

source of the image behind him, as its creative font; the figures surround him, as if they are the Muses honoring his creative power.[1]

Yet just as Bernard's writings by this point in time make clear that he was becoming less and less convinced of his teacher's ability to deal with the genre of the female nude so, too, does the photograph present Cézanne not as the unequivocal master of his painting but as in some senses dominated by it, broken by its ambition, inadequate to its conception. The painting itself, in its half-finished state, has not yet achieved the full strangeness of its effects—the figures still convey some degree of anatomical truth, the surface is still thinly painted, the color still retains a relative clarity (as far as can be registered in this black-and-white photograph). And yet even this early state suggests something of what the finished canvas would possess: stylized and distorted bodies, clotted,

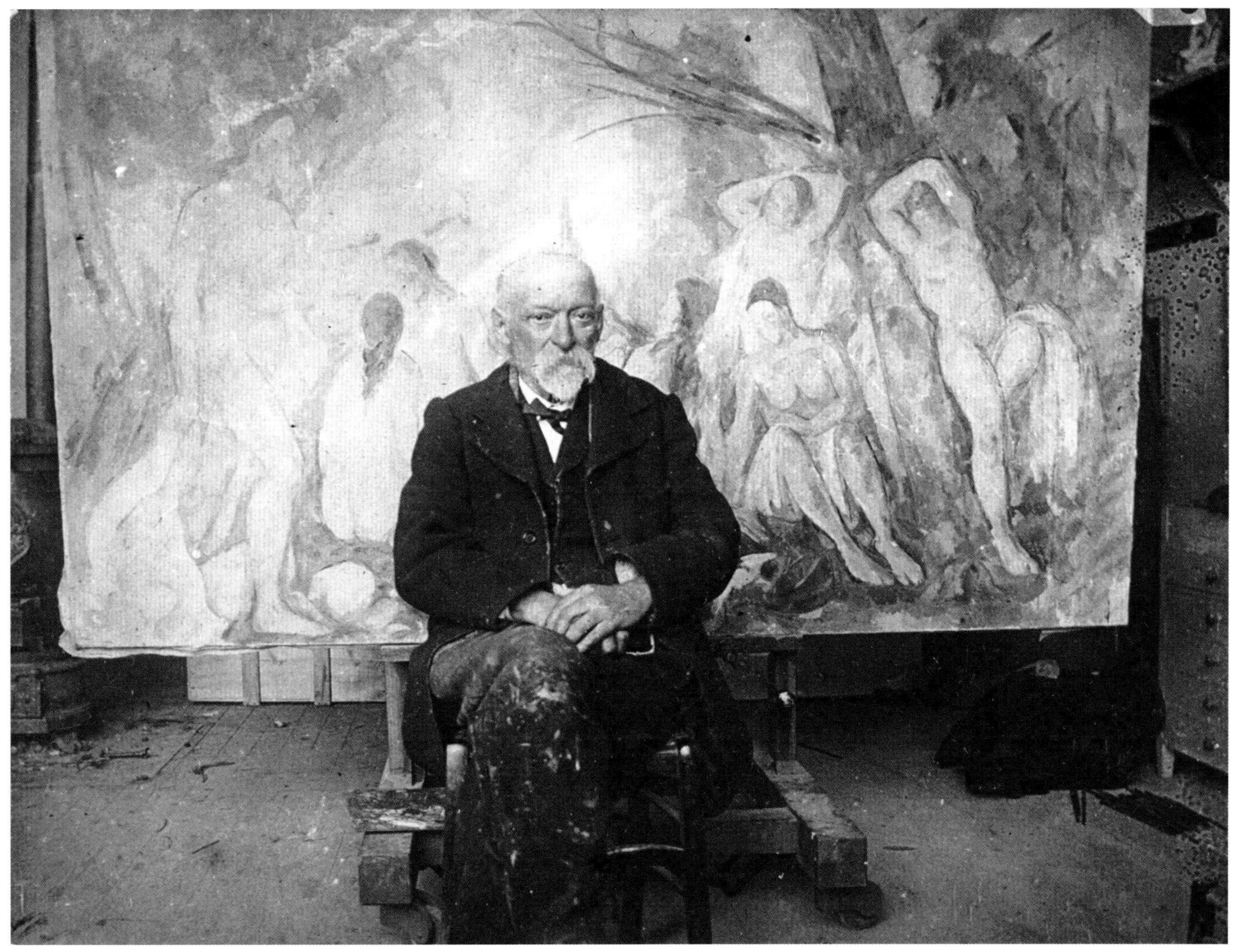

3. Émile Bernard, photograph of Cézanne in his studio at Les Lauves, seated in front of the *Large Bathers* (Barnes version), 1904. Print on silver-toned paper. © ARS. Musée d'Orsay, Paris, Vollard Archives.

scumbled skins of paint, muddied and overworked color, eccentricities of scale and composition. In other words, a thoroughly unconventional approach to painting the female form, even by avant-garde standards. In the process of reworking the painting, Cézanne would continue his reinvention of the category of the nude, a project that had engaged him since his earliest forays into the theme in the 1870s. He would recast its pleasures in a thoroughly modern way, as an erotics of paint: that is to say, he would harness the materiality of the medium to take the place of narrative fantasies of sexual possession or even of the representation of believable bodies as such in communicating fleshly pleasures. Those puzzling qualities that would characterize the final work and that marked his work on the theme of bathers—those gaucheries, as they were termed by the painter's contemporaries, the signs, in other words, of a naïve and awkward (but also sincere and authentic) hand—were in fact the terms of Cézanne's new language of the erotic, even though they were only rarely or, more precisely, only obliquely understood as such by critics who most often scratched their heads at Cézanne's strange and troubling images.

In the photograph, Cézanne is both overshadowed by the painting behind him and occludes a full view of it: as such, it stands as an appropriate metaphor for the way this artist's unconventional approach to painting has often structured his biographical portrait and, simultaneously, for the way his mythic biography has circumscribed interpretations of his painting. Bernard's difficulty in understanding Cézanne's approach to the nude determined his view of the man seated before him in the studio, not simply in his critical writings, as we will see in the coming pages, but also in this portrait. No longer the active, vigorous, virile presence seen in Roussel's photograph, no longer the solid, columnar, powerful, and strong-willed presence of the first of Bernard's pictures, Cézanne is here transformed into their opposite: now indoors, surrounded by his naked figures, his head is bare and vulnerable, his legs are crossed and his hands are clenched in his lap, his body is compacted and compressed. He no longer dominates the frame of the photograph but seems, rather, to shrink in front of the canvas that forms its backdrop. Whereas Cézanne in the landscape, in nature, was the epitome of potent masculine genius, Cézanne in his studio, in front of this painting of *baigneuses,* is the image of manhood shrunken, shriveled. At the same time, it was precisely Cézanne's strange reputation, in wide circulation at the turn of the century, as a recluse, a misanthropic hermit, an eccentric, and—most importantly—as an "impotent artist" who was inadequate (physically *and* psychically) to achieve his artistic goals, that led Bernard to understand his bathers, the most challenging paintings in his oeuvre, as something akin to failures.

It was no coincidence, I think, that the photographs of Cézanne that seem to embody a certain masterful, vigorous persona were taken outdoors, often depicting him in the process of painting the landscape, and that this other view of Cézanne—melancholic, diminished—was constructed in the studio, in relation to his bathers. Cézanne's strength as an artist and innovator was most often—even exclusively—attributed by his turn-of-the-century critics to his mastery of the genres of landscape and still life: in relation, that is, to a practice rooted in optical effects, truth to nature, and an almost monastic search for beauty. Not only were his bathers hard to reconcile to conventional expectations of the erotic nude, but they were difficult to align with this idea of visual veracity, which was understood as the most important aspect of Cézanne's artistic approach: these odd paintings of nudes in the landscape were the product of an insular studio practice, derived not from the external world but from the mind's eye. They seemed utterly incompatible with those qualities, that search for an authentic and sincere translation of the natural world, that most critics of the 1890s and early 1900s valued most about Cézanne's work.

Hence our double inheritance, the two Cézannes: both the virile "father of modern art" and an impotent genius, both the painter who was transforming the terrain of advanced painting in the twentieth century and an artist whose work was marked by inadequacies and gaucheries, both the celebrated recorder of the most subtle optical effects of the sensation of nature and the disturbing (or, as some thought, disturbed) painter of deformed female flesh. Bernard's photo at once responds to these portraits of Cézanne that were being articulated, in full contrariness, in the years around the turn of the century and plays its own part in constructing Cézanne as such a contradiction. This insistence on two Cézannes not only structures the biography of Cézanne that emerged in these years in myriad and subtle ways—Cézanne the youthful revolutionary versus Cézanne the reactionary bourgeois, Cézanne the fearless rebel versus Cézanne the fearful, fragile hermit, Cézanne the genius versus Cézanne the doubter—but also the treatment of his oeuvre, so that his landscapes, still lifes, portraits, and genre scenes have tended to be quarantined from his treatment of the nude, a subject that occupied him throughout his career, from his first brushstrokes to his last.

. . .

This book is an attempt not to reconcile the two pictures of Cézanne and his oeuvre but to understand the stakes of the distinctions between them. In one sense, this volume is an essay on Cézanne's biography—that range of writings, which took the form of fiction, art criticism, and memoirs of personal encounters with the famous (or infamous) painter, that were written just before and after his death in 1908 by figures such as Émile Bernard, Maurice Denis, Ambroise Vollard, Joachim Gasquet, Gustave Geffroy, Émile Zola, and many others, major and minor. But more crucially, this book is a reflection on his paintings of the male and female nude, his so-called bathers. For it is from Cézanne's biography, rife with images of sexual anxiety and impotence, of failure and doubt, that one may glean an interpretation of the bathers that was emerging in the 1890s and 1900s, an interpretation that could not, perhaps, be articulated *outside of* biographical terms as such. To state it plainly: my argument is that Cézanne's bather paintings radically redefined what it meant to paint the erotic nude and that his redefinition of that genre was so mystifying to his critics that they could only understand his artistic intervention as a failure of his masculinity. Hence the apparent need to write biography in the place of art analyses. The critics' recognition of the ways Cézanne reconceived the erotic nude was never stated outright in the many attempts to write about the bathers in the years around the turn of the century yet can be discerned everywhere through a careful reading of the various textual portraits of Cézanne that were written, even in the glancing form of the art critic, in the 1890s and 1900s.

Cézanne's biography—meaning his biography as a literary form, as a text—is marked by its pathos: it is a particularly unexpected narrative of artistic genius, since he is repeatedly characterized an artist who has not always lived up to the lofty goals he set for his art. Rather than overflowing with images of Cézanne as a heroic figure of avant-garde assuredness—as something like a Courbet, cutting a swath through tradition and definitively reorienting the path of nineteenth-century art—the accumulation of writings that constitute his biography as it was emerging at the turn of the century often as not picture Cézanne as a fearful, paranoid man almost paralyzed with anxiety. Needless to say, this is hardly the most obvious portrait of an artist who is central to most, if not all, accounts of European modernism. The roots of this narrative of Cézanne as an impotent genius—both in romantic and later naturalist fictions of artistic endeavor as well as in a contemporary, pseudoscientific discourse around the pathology of genius—and the stakes of this picture in an analysis of the artist's work, especially his forays into the representation of the nude, are explored in the first chapter of this volume.

In reading the early criticism of Cézanne, much of which took the form of artistic biography, it is striking the degree to which images of Cézanne's troubled masculinity were articulated in relation to a discussion of his paintings of the nude, and simultaneously by the way the bathers sat so uneasily, in the minds of his commentators, with the rest of Cézanne's oeuvre. This discomfort with the paintings—with their relation to Cézanne's "other" practice of landscape, still life painting, and portraiture and with their strangeness in relation to contemporary conventions of the genre of the nude as such—is apparent in the literature up to the present moment. The second chapter investigates the history of writings on Cézanne and his bathers and the way the various accounts of these works that emerged in the second half of the twentieth century (especially those by Meyer Schapiro, Theodore Reff, Tamar Garb, and T. J. Clark) might be harnessed to bring us closer to an understanding of Cézanne's project as one rooted in an investigation of the material qualities of paint and its potential to evoke a sensualized response. At the same time, I engage critically with these approaches to Cézanne's oeuvre, especially in relation to the deployment of a range of psychoanalytic descriptions of the operations of desire that, in their dependence on visual metaphors, remain inadequate to explain the bathers' haptic address. It was this materialized aspect of Cézanne's practice—the dislocation of the signifier of the erotic from the depicted body itself to the painted mark, the manipulation of paint on the surface of the canvas—that constituted his painterly erotics.

If the writings on Cézanne's bathers suggest something like an "erotics of paint" operating in his pictures of the nude, this is an indication that the erotic element in these works is not (as the most familiar interpretations of his oeuvre would insist) a private, traumatic, sublimated or simply repressed symbolic dimension but rather part of the paintings' public address and a sign of the painter's reaction to a number of prior interventions into the terms of the genre. That this engagement with the historical and contemporary stakes of the nude registered with the painter's contemporaries is indicated by the insistent attempts at distinguishing, and separating, one type of bather painting from another: the male and female bathers, the *baigneurs* and *baigneuses*, were understood as having entirely different geneses, the former in memory and direct observation and the latter in Cézanne's imagination, even though there was no visual justification for this belief. The implications of this segregation are entirely gendered and stem from the way Cézanne's contemporaries interpreted his gaucheries: his failures of execution were linked in the critics' imagination to Cézanne's unresolved passion for his (female) models and thus were deeply problematic when encountered in his *baigneurs* as well. Exploring this overdetermined attempt to segregate *baigneurs* from *baigneuses* is a means of recognizing the critics' understanding—inchoate as it often was—of Cézanne's interventions into the representation of eroticism.

The book ends with a reading of Cézanne's bathers that is at once thoroughly rooted in Cézanne's contemporary moment but that also suggests the implications for a later modernist practice: that of Henri Matisse, whose writings and work are filled with references to Cézanne, especially to his imagings of the nude. It is here, perhaps, that this book makes its biggest claims: Cézanne's shifting of the terms of the erotic to the material signifier of paint from the representational component of the bodies depicted was, I suggest, precisely understood by Matisse and thus set the terms for a certain strand of modernism's engagement with the sensualized body. My starting point in making this argument is Matisse's utterly stubborn *misreading* of Cézanne's bather paintings, articulated in his "Notes of a Painter" of 1908, in which he insisted on substituting for the more common description of Cézanne's bather images as lacking in bodily coherence a description that asserted their utter lack of visual or anatomical confusion. Reading *against* this text, one can come to understand Matisse's words as a self-conscious, textual dissimulation of not only the erotic effects of Cézanne's work but of Matisse's own. Like the critics who were writing on Cézanne at the same time, and who were only able to voice the strangeness of Cézanne's erotics of paint obliquely, through the form of biography, Matisse, too, was only able to address this aspect of Cézanne's practice in an indirect way: in terms of paint rather than words, in canvases in which the structural and material conditions of paintings do not sublimate or replace desire but produce it in defiance of the willfully distorted bodies on display.

If the existence of two Cézannes in criticism on the artist has proved a troubling fact for most scholars, it has also been a productive one. For that reason, this book does not set out to restore Cézanne to wholeness and unity, to reintegrate the bathers into his oeuvre, reconstructing his practice as seamless whole, or to make those pictures familiar through scholarly explication. Rather, it seeks to preserve—and, at its best moments, heighten—that radical disjuncture or discontinuity that Cézanne's first critics found so troubling and to insist on the fundamental rupture these works effected in the history of the erotic nude. The bathers could only evoke overt disavowal by even his most sensitive observers, but against the grain of this repression emerged the terms for a new conception of painting the pleasures of the body in the twentieth century.

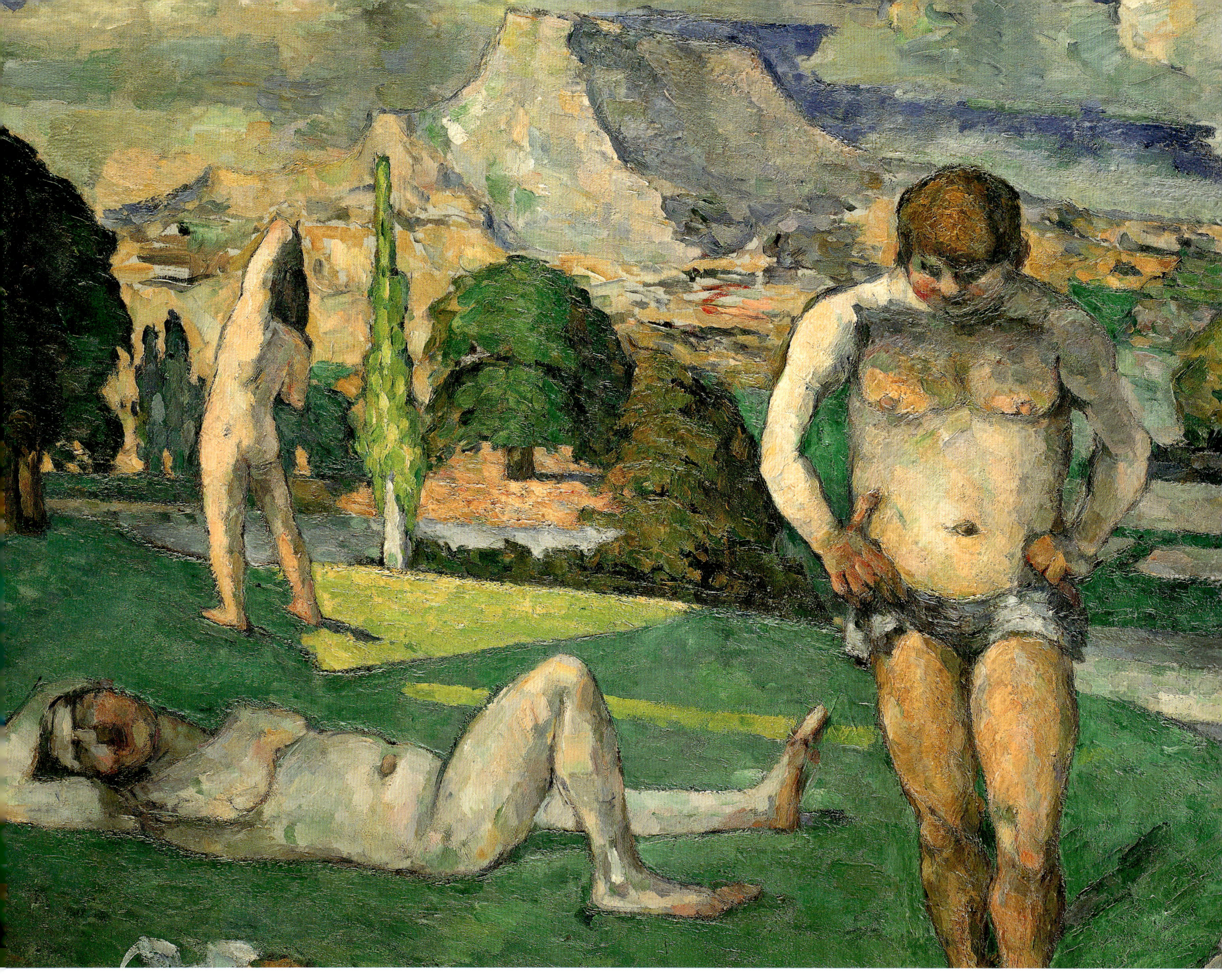

1 A BIOGRAPHY OF FAILURE

Detail of pl. II

It is not what the artist does that counts, but what he is. . . . What interests us about Cézanne is his anxiety, that is Cézanne's lesson, . . . that is to say the drama of the man. The rest is false.

PABLO PICASSO

IN 1907, ÉMILE BERNARD DESCRIBED his first encounter with Paul Cézanne, which had taken place three years earlier.[1] He writes of arriving in Aix in search of the artist, armed only with Pissarro's engraved portrait of him (fig. 4). The citizens of Aix whom Bernard approached with the print failed to recognize their neighbor in it, which left the young painter wandering around the town in what seemed like a futile search for his quarry. He finally came to what he thought was the correct house; when Cézanne opened the door, Bernard was unsure who was addressing him, so little did the real man bear resemblance to any published image: "When I was in front of him, I asked him, knowing full well that he was my old master, but uncertain of his resemblance to Pissarro's portrait: 'I'm looking for M. Paul Cézanne.'"[2] It was indeed Cézanne, and the older artist regarded his young admirer with obvious suspicion until he satisfied himself that Bernard was truly a painter and not merely a biographer—"'You write biographies, don't you? When I asked around about you, I heard that you were a man who wrote biographies. But you are a painter, aren't you?'"[3] Cézanne asks and then asks again: "'So you aren't a biographer? You are a painter!'"[4] During the course of their visit to his studio, the old man's hostility to those who would try to capture his image was manifest as Cézanne regarded a portrait bust of him done by a fellow artist from Aix (fig. 5):

"My lifelong friend Solari made that, the poor devil of a sculptor. . . . He begged me to let him do it. I said to him: 'You know that I can't stand posing. If you want, you can come to the room down there; I work up here. When you see me, watch, and do what you want.' He ended up dropping it, leaving this garbage behind; it's enough to drive

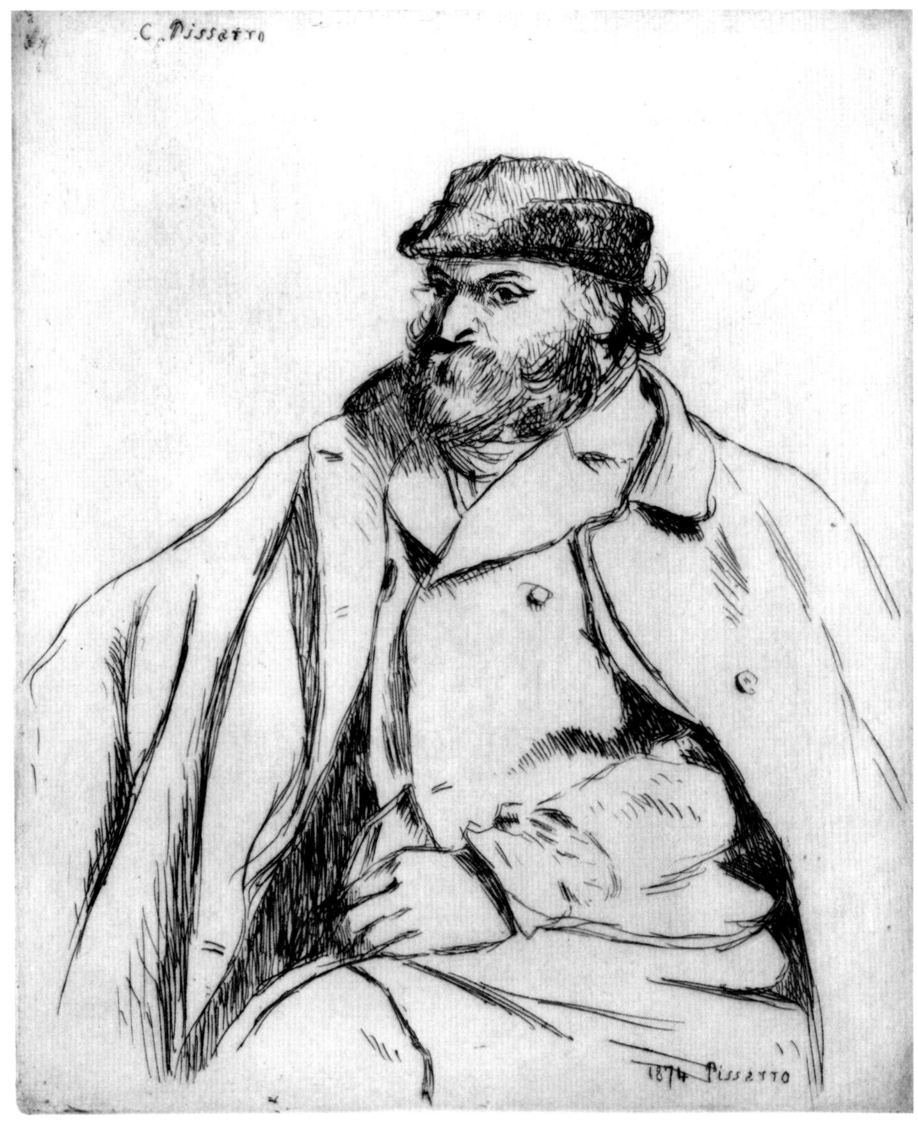

Bernard's account purports to be an objective portrait of his encounter with the artist and yet is anything but. This is not least revealed by the fact that the bust by Solari was not destroyed by Cézanne that day in 1904; on the contrary, it remained in his studio, intact, until his death. (Bernard betrays the apocryphal nature of this introduction when, later in the book, he mentions that the bust is still very much present and undamaged.) Read between the lines, however, and the lesson of this story is clear: it is meant to stand as a warning to anyone who ventures a portrait of Cézanne, whether literary or pictorial. Bernard presents Cézanne as a subject who exceeds biography, a figure of whom every attempt to capture his essence has failed—

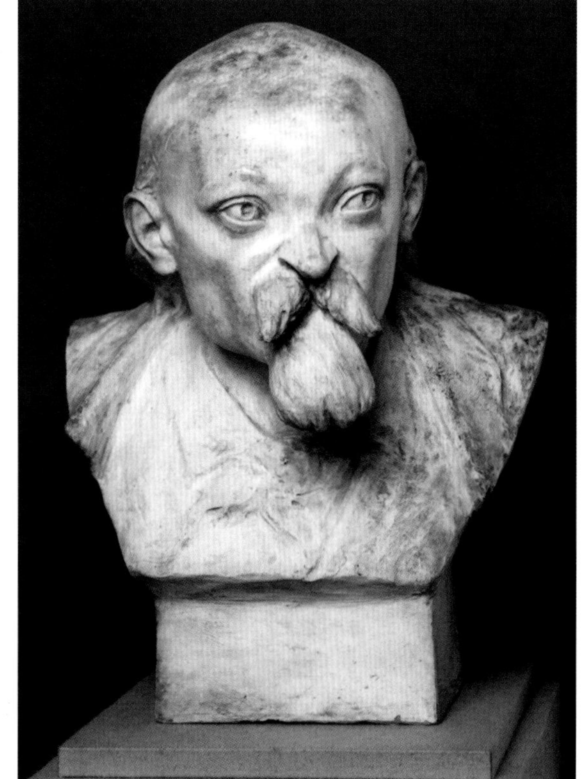

4. Camille Pissarro, *Portrait of Paul Cézanne,* 1874. Etching. Musée Bonnat, Bayonne, France.

5. Philippe Solari, *Bust of Cézanne,* 1904–5. Plaster. Musée Granet, Aix-en-Provence, France.

you to despair!" Next, Cézanne picked up the little bust and carried it into the garden; then, banging its base furiously against a paving stone, he yelled: "It's completely ridiculous!", and broke the sculpture. Separated from it's base, the aborted effigy rolled into the dirt, under the olive trees, where it remained the whole time I was in Aix, finally splitting open from the heat of the sun.[5]

Pissarro's engraved likeness was no more successful than Solari's sculptural effigy. Bernard's Cézanne is a figure who resists portrayal, who quite literally destroys it. He is a man who has not been—cannot be?—adequately described, let alone understood.

Bernard was not the only writer to level the complaint. In fact, such declarations of the insufficiencies of previous depictions of Cézanne—both visual and literary—would become a veritable trope in writings on the artist. Léo Larguier, for one, would declare in 1925 that "He has been depicted a hundred times. Some mistakenly declare that he resembles an old, churlish military man; others thought they saw a sort of hallucinating vagabond with a purplish nose and reddened eyes, coarse and always irritated. None of these portraits is accurate, and those which portray Cézanne as shaggy-haired and filthy are nasty caricatures, drawn by artists who do not know the provinces."[6] R. F. Rivière and J. F. Schnerb would characterize what they thought were the false and inadequate representations of the artist as almost comical: "Legend would have it that Cézanne is a misanthrope, a sort of unapproachable bear. Long before his death, one heard that the painter had stopped painting, that he had to dig up his past works. Those who were better informed could only refer vaguely to the residence of the master, to his lifestyle. An ironist could even have said that Cézanne was a mythic being who did not really exist."[7]

Such inadequacies in the artistic and literary record, Bernard suggests, may not be solely due to the sheer enormity of the task of representing such a complicated man—nor, as Larguier claims, simply to the cosmopolitan's failure to appreciate the provincial—but rather are rooted in a fundamental difference of approach between a biographer and a student of art.[8] As soon as he opens the door, the suspicious Cézanne asks whether Bernard is a biographer, his antenna ready to detect someone out "to get his claws" in him as was famously his greatest fear.[9] But according to Bernard, the old man was placated on learning that his visitor was a painter, not a biographer: someone who was there to hear about his work rather than his life. And lest it is imagined that such elusiveness was simply part of Cézanne's "myth," it is well to note that even the artist himself, in plaintive words written to another of his most influential biographers, Joachim Gasquet, expressed this desire to remain hidden behind his work: "All my life I have worked to be able to earn my living, but I thought that no one could do good painting without attracting attention to one's private life. Certainly, an artist wishes to raise himself intellectually as much as possible, but the man must remain obscure. The pleasure must be found in the work."[10] If Bernard succeeds in his own account, he suggests, it is because he heeds Cézanne's warning and precisely does *not* approach his subject as one who would try to contain him in word or image but as a student, as an artist.

This is not to say that Bernard himself shied away from the task of writing biographically about Cézanne—far from it. For while the young artist's attention was directed more than most toward the elusive Provençal painter's methods and theories of painting, Bernard's various accounts of Cézanne's work were at least as involved in discovering the essence of the man as those of his contemporaries. Bernard's, like almost all of the early texts on Cézanne by artists like Maurice Denis or dealers like Ambroise Vollard or critics like Gustave Geffroy or poets and nationalists like Joachim Gasquet—in a sense, the "primary sources" of Cézanne studies—was written as biography or at least argued for a profound link between this man's art and his life and character. And yet, as important, all of these documents argued for their authors' almost exclusive authority to speak for Cézanne's work. This was especially true of Bernard, who "discovered" the artist in Père Tanguy's color shop in Paris on the rue Clauzel and was one of the earliest writers to bring these paintings into public view and who was subsequently alienated by Cézanne's own equivocal feelings toward his young acolyte, crowded out of his position as privileged interpreter of Cézanne's work by a noisy field of new enthusiasts and increasingly disillusioned by Cézanne's radicality in the face of his own rigidifying conservatism. For Bernard, writing accounts of Cézanne's life and art was a way of making an argument about the stakes of painting and his relationship to it; this fact becomes most visible when one attends to the subtle and not-so-subtle shifts in his writings as his hostility toward Cézanne and his work deepened over the years.[11] So when in 1907, the year after Cézanne's death, we read Bernard describing the inadequacy of Pissarro's etching or Solari's bust, we are not simply meant to recognize the inadequacy of these particular portraits or merely to acknowledge in some sense the false claims of realism in naturalist art—whether academic, like Solari's, or avant-garde, like Pissarro's—in the face of an artist who lays waste to traditional notions of *vraisemblance,* but we are asked, too, to concede the illegitimacy of past representations generally in the face of Bernard's claim for the authority of his own.

In light of such motivations that subtend not just Bernard's but almost all contemporary writing on Cézanne, writing that was to a great extent driven by a desire to cast him as the authoritative predecessor to a range of artistic practices in the early twentieth century and that was, to a surprising degree, written in biographical terms, the modern-day scholar is left with an important question: how to use these texts, which comprise to a great extent the body of primary source material on the artist? If one is going to write about Cézanne, in other words, the methodological issue of how to treat biography and biographical interpretation must be addressed from the start. At the very least, one has to determine which biographies to believe, given the biases of the writers in question: it is a curious, but perhaps not wholly surprising, fact that modern scholars choose their biographers wisely, those interested in a relatively formalist take depending more on Émile Bernard, for example, and those pursuing psychoanalytically driven interpretive strategies relying more on Joachim Gasquet.[12]

Given this problematic partiality, one might be tempted to exclude such texts outright from consideration—especially in light of the theoretical suspicions cast on the biographical method as a whole by post-structuralist literary critics like Roland Barthes, and subsequently by art historians like Rosalind Krauss, both of whom argued that recourse to the authority of the artist in determining a work's meaning unduly closed off the play of possible significations within a given text.[13] But in the case of Cézanne, to treat these documents either as wholly tainted or as having only a limited use because of their biographical form would be untenable, for one would be left very little else to go on. As unsatisfying would be an approach that merely analyzes such narratives as repeated attempts to create a "myth of the artist," a familiar tack that reveals nothing but the paucity of the scrutinized text, leaving an absence in the place of the artist who is revealed only as a negative condition.

The questions posed here, then, are these: how to take Cézanne's biography, the accumulation of texts written during his life and immediately after his death, seriously? How to use them as historical documents in a way that neither relies on their interpretive assumptions nor dismisses them as purely mythical constructions? This book is, in part, an attempt to answer these methodological questions. Biography will be read as an extension, or even a working through, of other critical languages, and the images of Cézanne-the-man that contemporary accounts provide are equally, or more importantly, arguments about the stakes of Cézanne-the-artist. As a form of art criticism, biography became a way of writing about the elements of Cézanne's painting in terms that were as yet unavailable at that moment in modernism's early history. Left without adequate language to deal with the radicality of Cézanne's practice, critics turned to the narrative of the artist's personal history as a means of articulating the meaning of his paintings.

Whatever Cézanne's biography tells us about his life, in other words, it tells us more about his painting, if only we would take the trouble to read it.[14] One might say that this is the other lesson of Bernard's parable. He chose to start his book on Cézanne, a book through which he hoped to define the critical terms in which his mentor would be understood by a younger generation of artists, with a critique of previous portrayals, and he took pains to point out his status as a painter and not a biographer: Bernard did not intend to refute the value of biography per se, but to argue for the authority of his own description of the man. Bernard's text claims to be the "right" one: he is staking out the legacy of Cézanne's art by writing his biography. As such, we the readers must recognize that Bernard's *Souvenirs sur Paul Cézanne*—any biography of a painter for that matter—is not simply the narrative of a life but rather is essentially about painting.

CÉZANNE, ZOLA, AND ARTISTIC IMPOTENCE

The sign of impotence and the sign of genius, these are the two extremes that we must reconcile if we want to appreciate Cézanne fairly and productively. Is it such a rarity, or is it not the case for almost all of the great inventors?

CHARLES MORICE, "PAUL CÉZANNE"

And what does it mean that Cézanne's biography, as it was elaborated by his most ardent supporters, was so strange, so unlike the more familiar, heroic mythologies of virile genius that litter the pages of art history? Despite the fact that Cézanne was being positioned as the father of a new art, the recurring tropes that made their way into the now-canonical biography of the man might lead one to question whether he had the capacity to conceive anything, let alone the terms that would define modern painting. The clichés are familiar: first, that Cézanne was an artist plagued by doubt, by a fear of failure, by an almost paralyzing anxiety about making his painting adequate to the representation of nature; and second, that he was a man deeply troubled in his relation to women and perhaps even to his own masculinity.

Cézanne's artistic paralysis is suggested in Zola's shocking pronouncement that Cézanne was "a great aborted genius"; in Bernard's overly emphatic denial of Cézanne's resemblance to Claude Lantier (the protagonist of *L'Oeuvre,* Zola's panorama of artistic failure and decrepitude) and his simultaneous description of Cézanne in terms of failure and impotence; in Vollard's tale of the excruciating experience of sitting for a portrait for this artist whose innate "inability to complete" required endless reworkings of the canvas and ultimately resulted in that famous spot left bare on his knuckle; in Merleau-Ponty's important analysis of "Cézanne's doubt"; and in countless other stories and judgments more often than not recounted by his greatest admirers and supporters.[15] It is no coincidence that many of these articulations of Cézanne's doubt use language that seems to connect his artistic uncertainties with more troubling, sexual anxieties. In fact, as we will see throughout this book, Cézanne is consistently presented, in the literature that emerged after the great Vollard exhibition of 1895, as a man whose fears and uneasiness about women not only impacted his real relationships with flesh-and-blood females but also appeared in every brushstroke that he laid on canvas. Such was his reputation that Élie Faure, for example, could claim that "this great sensualist feared women more than anything else," while Georges Rivière, alarmingly, could interpret Cézanne's self-imposed distance from women as the result of a "ferocious misogyny," borne of the fact that "Cézanne saw woman as the traditional enemy of man," possessing a "satanic beauty."[16]

Through these texts emerges an image of Cézanne as a painter plagued by "artistic impotence," a charge repeatedly leveled at him in the early years of writing on his work, the opposite term of the heroic masculinity and creative fecundity that was ascribed to figures like Gauguin and Renoir in the later nineteenth century and that was most famously and libidinally embodied by Picasso in the twentieth century.[17] Instead, Cézanne, along with his contemporaries Degas, Van Gogh, and Toulouse-Lautrec, was an artist whose legend was structured by an uneasy relation to his masculinity and by an uneasy relation to his own representations of femininity.[18] For Cézanne, artistic impotence incorporates both scholarly "givens" that I have elaborated: his post-romantic doubt or anguished frustrations over "realizing" his sensations and his desire to reach that near-impossible goal of transcribing nature. Both of these are somehow intrinsically linked to the artist's other, sexual inadequacy. Cézanne's doubt, then, seems less existential than physical, and one is led to wonder at the motivation of this particular formulation of Cézanne's artistic genius by his supporters. "*How did we believe that this man who was frightened of other men and who hid himself from women was virile enough to leave a fruitful legacy [féconder le future]?*"[19] These words of Élie Faure, in their plaintive tone, capture the oddness of Cézanne's biography, given the claims that were being made for his work. And in order to understand this strange narrative of a life, one must interrogate its sources—in this case, Émile Zola's novel *L'Oeuvre*, and its protagonist, Claude Lantier, the personification of anguished creativity and thwarted genius.[20]

Often read as a condemnation—whether of impressionism in general or of specific painters in particular—the protagonist of Zola's story has come, over the years, to be closely identified with Paul Cézanne.[21] Zola's novel was widely held to be a roman à clef ever since Paul Alexis, writing in anticipation of the book's publication, said that Zola "will be obliged to use his friends" to formulate his characters.[22] Despite this, none of Cézanne's artist-contemporaries who commented on *L'Oeuvre* immediately upon its publication in 1886 recognized Cézanne in it at all; Monet, in a letter to Zola, goes as far as to say that he was at the very least thankful that the novelist took pains to make his characters utterly *unlike* any of the impressionists.[23] Even John Rewald, whose biography of Cézanne relies in great part on the "evidence" contained in Zola's novel, acknowledged that the public, in searching for the model for Zola's portrait of an impotent impressionist on the verge of madness, thought first, and perhaps exclusively, of Manet, for Cézanne was at that time still little known.[24]

In fact, identifications between Cézanne and Lantier only came years after the book's publication. By the mid-1890s, possibly because of the new visibility of Cézanne's paintings in Paris, or because of Zola's by now outspoken contempt for his childhood companion's art, or because of new market pressures to create an interesting "back story" for an artist's work in order to bolster sales, writers seeking to introduce Cézanne—a legend of isolated genius, an "artist's artist"—to the Parisian art public started to draw connections between the real artist and the fictional one.[25] In 1895, Arsène Alexandre wrote an article about Cézanne that was actually titled "Claude Lantier"; Georges Lecomte, writing in 1900, made the connection between the fictional character and the real artist as did Louis Vauxcelles in 1904.[26] Almost all of the published biographical information on Cézanne emerged from this period on, well after the publication of *L'Oeuvre,* and like Alexandre, Lecomte, and Vauxcelles—though perhaps not as explicitly—most writers on Cézanne from this period relied to some degree on Zola's novel for their information.[27]

In other words, if there is a compelling similarity between Cézanne and Lantier, it may be because Cézanne's early commentators used Zola's novel as the source for their own writings. Émile Bernard's telegraphic description of Cézanne's youth, to cite but one example, is culled almost directly from Zola's novel: "In Provence. A romantic youth, with poems, with poetic promenades with Zola, his schoolmate, by his side; Hugo, Musset, scattered in the leaves of the trees on the banks of the Arc; an excited arrival in Paris, late-night conversations in front of the great city—under the stars. Then a little misery from his surly but rich family; a marriage; public failures, failures next to impotent artists; the paroxysm of theories (his best period thanks to his solitude and search for the absolute)."[28] Joachim Gasquet's influential biography of the artist borrows freely from *L'Oeuvre,* not merely for biographical detail but, often, for dialogue as well, in some cases taking Cézanne's words directly out of Lantier's mouth.[29] Maurice Denis's journal entry, recounting his meeting with the Provençal artist, epitomizes this borrowing. He describes Aix, the Jas de Bouffan, the paintings he sees on the wall, and then goes on to describe his encounter like this: "My mind is filled with visions of Claude in *L'Oeuvre* (by Zola). *Cézanne. At the door. . . .*"[30] Just as Denis's first meeting with Cézanne was prefaced by thoughts of Claude Lantier, we, too, have very little picture of Cézanne outside of *L'Oeuvre* because most of what was written on him during his life was inevitably marked by Zola's novel.

What is particularly curious about this phenomenon of writers borrowing from Zola's description of Claude Lantier in their own descriptions of Cézanne is that, while most of the commentators quoted here were the latter's most devoted apologists, Zola's Lantier is, on the surface, hardly the most likely figure on whom to model their idol. How to account for the willingness of commentators to accept Zola's portrayal of artistic impotence in their view of Cézanne? In order to address this question, one must first understand that Zola's novel is far from a morality tale. It is not a condemnation of the failed genius but rather reveals an empathy toward him. Second, one must recognize Zola's text as participating in a larger discourse on the nature of creativity and genius that developed in the nineteenth century, a discourse that hinged on the idea of degeneration and the pathologization of genius.[31]

For Zola as for others in the later nineteenth century, failure was not the result of moral weakness in spite of the male artist's genius but was an inevitable outcome of it, perhaps even a sign of artistic authenticity.

Zola wrote *L'Oeuvre* between 1885 and 1886, and he took exactly nine months to do so—an apocryphal detail, perhaps, considering the novel's theme explicitly links artistic creation with the procreative act. *L'Oeuvre* provides a panorama of artistic genius or rather of the failure of artistic genius, since not one of its characters manages to be an authentic artist and a well-adjusted individual at the same time. Claude Lantier, with his "lesion of the eye," is the most dramatic of these *artistes manqués;* he is plagued by an ultimately fatal "inability to complete" his paintings. Lantier's hereditary deficiency means that he is an incomplete genius, condemned to creative and physical impotence: we see Lantier "slumped on a chair, tortured by his own impotence, his inability to decide where to place his own brushstroke, and at the same time trying to make bold resolutions" (121) or "[refusing] to acknowledge his impotence, burning with the desire to do something, to create something in spite of it" (56). This creative impotence has decidedly sexual overtones, for Lantier, "chaste as he was, . . . had a passion for the physical beauty of women, and insane love for nudity desired but never possessed, but was powerless to satisfy himself or to create enough of the beauty he dreamed of enfolding in an ecstatic embrace" (49). He falls in love with Christine, a young woman who for a time seems to calm his restlessness, for she is both an outlet for his repressed sexual desires as well as a facilitator of his painting—she is at once lover, wife, mother, and model. The two conceive a child on the day Claude's painting, *Plein-Air,* is mocked mercilessly by the crowds at the Salon des Refusés. This child, "the child of suffering and pity, scorned from conception by the brainless mockery of the crowd" (168), a sign of Claude's creative potential, is born a cretin, whose head grows larger and larger in inverse proportion to his declining intelligence and who eventually withers and dies. The young boy is a living testimony to Claude's degeneracy. After a period of frustrated artistic inactivity due to the stability of domestic life, Lantier returns to painting with all of his thwarted passion, and there occurs a horrible struggle between Claude's monumental canvas, his living and breathing wife, and Claude himself—a struggle that ends in Claude's suicide.

Zola completely collapses physical insufficiency with artistic insufficiency, such that the one is not simply a metaphor for the other but is its cause and simultaneous effect: Claude struggles valiantly against his own artistic impotence in the creation of *Plein-Air,* a work that is ultimately marred by his endless reworking and doubt; Claude's son is conceived in the depressed aftermath of the failure of that painting at the Salon des Refusés and is thus evidence of Claude's degeneracy (or hereditary lack) as well as the product of his artistic sterility (vis-à-vis the occasion of his conception); the child eventually dies, whereupon Claude paints him and submits this painting to the Salon, where it is accepted as someone's "charity." Claude's painting, *Dead Child,* the only work he ever exhibited at the Salon, is thus doubly sterile—it is a painting that represents his physical failings as well as gives evidence of his artistic ones. It is, needless to say, another failure. The impotent artist will then spend the rest of his life working and reworking a painting of nudes along the banks of the Seine, the inadequacies of which will eventually kill him.

However, while Lantier's story may be the focus of the novel, all the authentic artists in the novel experience the same paralysis as Lantier and describe it in the same terms of sterility, impotence, and deformed procreation. In fact, for Zola, the *lack* of such artistic paralysis was precisely the sign of artistic *inauthenticity*. The three most authentic artists in Zola's *inferno,* Lantier, Pierre Sandoz (Lantier's friend since childhood, a novelist who acts as Zola's *porte-parole* in the narrative), and Bongrand (a painter of the generation of 1848, who is modeled on Zola's close friend and mentor, Flaubert), all suffer from artistic paralysis and describe it in a similar manner. Impotence haunts them in other ways too—for Lantier, in the deformed child he fathers, for Sandoz, in his childless marriage, for Bongrand, in his bachelorhood, and for all three, in the failure to leave behind (in the sense of the French *féconder)* an artistic following or school. In contrast, Chambouvard, a self-satisfied sculptor based on Courbet and Hugo, in his lack of self-consciousness or self-examination before the creative task, and thus his lack of doubt or feelings of failure and inadequacy, is the epitome of the inauthentic artist.

Even Pierre Sandoz, the author's alter ego and the most "well-adjusted" of the novel's characters—the one interpreted by most readers of *L'Oeuvre* as representing Zola's idea of the "correct" path of genius distinguished by sexual and creative moderation—is an artist for whom failure, and indeed impotence, is a constant presence in the creative process. His complaint, though not fraught with as much tortured passion, mirrors Lantier's own struggles: "When I bring forth I need forceps, and even then the child always looks to me like a monster. Is it possible for anyone to be so devoid of doubt as to have absolute faith in himself?" (304). At Lantier's funeral, Bongrand gives voice to the same notion, claiming Claude is "lucky to be away from it all, instead of wearing himself out, as we do, producing offspring who are either headless or limbless and never really alive" (425). Sandoz's last words to us—uttered in response to Bongrand's frustration—are thus filled with bitter irony: "And now, back to work!" he says, as if there was any possibility of productive work in the bleak universe that Zola presents.

Claude Lantier's failure, Zola tells us, is not *solely* the result of his hereditary lack but is also a function of the time in which he lives: in a sort of backhanded eulogy at Lantier's funeral, Sandoz claims that "his trouble was not all personal by any means; he was the victim of his period. The generation we belong to was brought up on Romanticism; it is soaked into us and we can do nothing about it. It is all very well our plunging head first into violent reality, the stain remains and all the scrubbing in the world will never remove it" (419). And indeed, Zola might well be talking about his own struggles with his literary legacy, for his fictional creation of the *artiste manqué* has for his ancestors a host of romantic forefathers who themselves struggled before the creative task—think, for example, of Delacroix's description of the young Michelangelo paralyzed in his studio or Balzac's Frenhofer, descending into the madness of self-deception as he progressively obliterates the near-perfect image of his Belle-Noiseuse in an attempt to bring her to life.[32] However, whatever the romantic heritage of Zola's conception of artistic genius, it is precisely in rooting the creative struggle in the physical body of the artist that Zola declares his contemporaneity. Lantier no longer struggles exclusively with the psychic tortures of creativity, but also with the physical effects of degeneracy; his artistic impotence is not just a psychological despair but is also an actual physical deficiency, marked by sterility and impotence.

Throughout the novel, Zola describes failure and frustration as the inevitable by-product of sincere artistic engagement. The inevitability of artistic failure for Zola has two roots. The first is physical, relating to the medicalization of genius in the later nineteenth century: in a period when doctors and scientists were identifying any deviation from the norm as evidence of pathology, creative talent came under scrutiny as a sign of disease or perversion. The crucial treatises on degeneration that appeared in the second half of the nineteenth century—including works by Jacques Joseph Moreau de Tours, Benedicte Augustine Morel, Césare Lombroso, and Max Nordau, among others with which Zola was familiar—identified the excessive intellect of the genius, and specifically of the artistic genius, as the sign and source of their potential degeneracy, a degeneracy that included as its possible symptoms sexual irritability, sterility, precocity, one-sided talents, eccentricity, and impotence.[33] In Césare Lombroso's formulation, articulated in his 1897 book *Genio e degenerazione,* "Like men, nature abominates and sterilizes . . . those animals who dare to think a little more than their fellow members of the species." An excessive development of one part of the body—the mind—must necessarily be accompanied by the diminishment or decay of another—the reproductive organs; this excessive development might lead to sterility or impotence but could equally result in other forms of sexual "perversions," including "unrestrained and irregular development."[34] Lombroso's follower, the physician Max Nordau, was more shrill in his assessment of the literary and artistic figures of his time; his portrait of Verlaine, for example, is terrifying in its description of genius-induced degeneracy:

> We see a repulsive degenerate subject with asymmetric skull and Mongolian face, an impulsive vagabond and dipsomaniac, who, under the most disgraceful circumstances, was placed in jail; an emotional dreamer of feeble intellect, who painfully fights against his bad impulses . . . , and a dotard who manifests the absence of any definite thought in his mind by incoherent speech, meaningless expressions, and motley images. In lunatic asylums there are many patients whose disease is less deep-seated and incurable than is that of this irresponsible *circulaire* at large, whom only ignorant judges would have condemned for his epileptoid crimes.[35]

Nordau did not limit the physical symptoms of disease to facial and cranial abnormalities, as Lombroso did; he in fact identified the impressionist painters' "nystagmus, or trembling of the eyeball," as the source of their unique style of painting.[36]

Zola's *Rougon-Macquart* novels join these texts in presenting a panorama of deviancy, and Lantier in *L'Oeuvre* possesses the salient traits of the degenerate genius that were being elaborated in the medical discourse. Lantier's son, Jacques, representing the end of the degenerate line, almost caricatures the predicted outcome of the degenerate genius: his overdeveloped brain (in his case, overdeveloped only in terms of size, not intelligence) necessitates a compensatory lack of physical capabilities, resulting in fatal weakness and loss of vital energy.

But there was also an artistic, as opposed to scientific (or, more properly, pseudoscientific), basis of this construction of artistic genius. For Zola, the second root of inevitable artistic impotence is the ultimate impossibility of achieving the idealistic goal that any authentic avant-garde sets for itself: to represent nature. It is the ultimate task and one doomed to failure—and it is here we see most clearly Zola's romantic heritage, for this is a common theme in writings of that period.[37] That the novel was to explore the theme of the excessive ambition of progressive artists was elucidated by Zola in his preparatory notes for the book: "It is a question of knowing what rendered [Lantier] incapable of satisfying his aims: him more than anyone, his psychology, his heritage, the lesion of his eye; but I would also like to see our modern art in this, our fever to want everything, our *disequilibrium* in a word."[38]

If Sandoz escapes Lantier's fate in *L'Oeuvre,* it is not because he always lacked this prideful ambition—a drive that proves the sincerity of the authentic artist—but because he has by the end of the novel given up any hope of realizing it. Sandoz had, from his youth, wanted to compose a series of novels whose conception was not unlike Zola's original vision of the *Rougon-Macquart* series. That he finally renounces his quest for the absolute in art is the very act that marks his failure at the same time as it saves him from an end as horrible as Lantier's.[39] Sandoz's capitulation to pragmatism is itself a retreat from artistic authenticity and success; he, too, makes manifest Zola's belief that there is failure inherent in the authentic artist's impossible goal of artistic perfection. This results, according to Zola, in artists who are only able to point out the way, without ever arriving there.

Zola did not pass judgment on this issue only in the realm of fiction; thus he could be found avowing in 1882 that "This is why the Impressionists' struggle is not yet over: they remain unequal to the work which they attempt, they stutter without being able to find the word. But their influence is no less profound, because they follow the only possible course, they march towards the future."[40] Zola's disappointment at the failure of impressionism to realize its potential is tempered by a belief, still, in its goals. The impressionists remain the most important artists on the scene for Zola; it is the worthiness—and unattainability—of their goal that proves the depth of their talent. Their failure, then, is the mark of their genius.

It is in the conjunction of these two roots of the inevitability of artistic failure—the medical and the romantic—that one can begin to understand the link Zola makes between degeneration and genius, between artistic impotence and cultural regeneration. Like *Plein-Air*, his doubly sterile painting *Dead Child* makes Lantier the laughingstock of the Salon, but he has fully transformed the practice of painting, nonetheless: "'The Salon's *your* victory this year,' says Sandoz. 'Fagerolles isn't the only one to plagiarize you, far from it! They're all doing it. They all got a good laugh out of *Plein-Air,* but it nevertheless caused a revolution! Look around you. Look, there's another *Plein-Air,* and there's another, and another, the whole Salon's *Plein-Air!*' . . . He was right; broad daylight, after gradually filtering into contemporary painting, had at last come into its own" (344). Lantier's artistic impotence begets a Salon full of mongrel creations, hybrids of avant-garde and academic ideas, but it is an ultimately productive legacy in Zola's mind. Claude's aborted genius is posited, in the end, as a source of cultural regeneration.[41]

This is the context in which I would like to place Zola's construction of Claude Lantier and his assessment of Paul Cézanne, both of which have slowly penetrated our contemporary view of the artist. Zola's assessment of Cézanne not as a great *but* aborted genius as some would have it but rather as a great aborted genius, the two terms linked as if mutually dependent and not mutually contradictory, is tied to Zola's conception of artistic authenticity. There is artistic impotence, a failure rooted in the body of the artist itself, inherent in creation at the end of the nineteenth century. Huysmans cites it when he praises

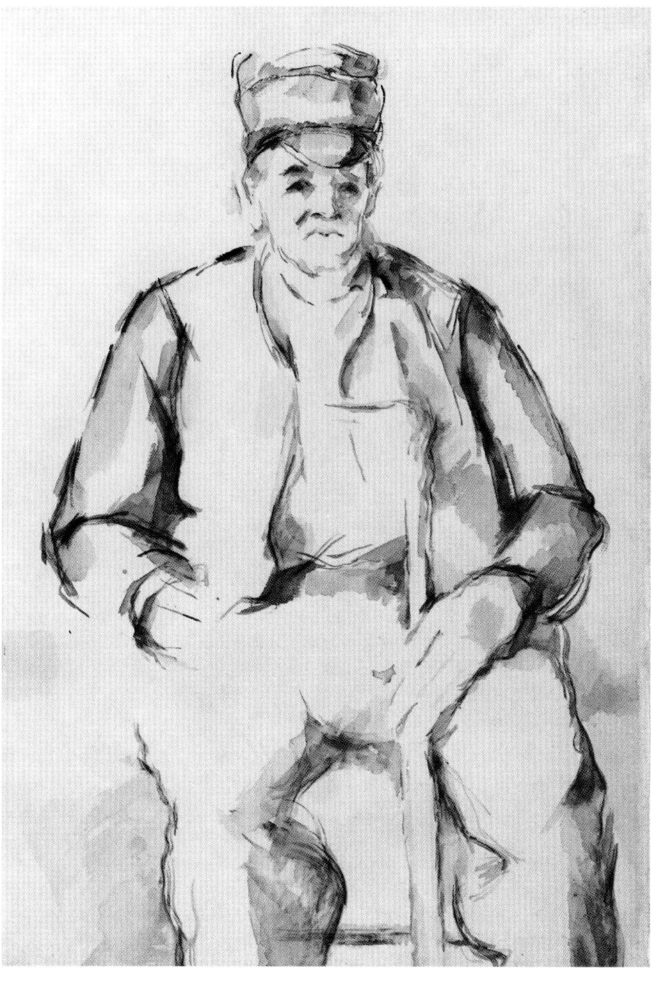

6. Cézanne, *Seated Peasant*, ca. 1900–1904. Watercolor, 45.8 x 31 cm. Kunsthaus Zurich.

Cézanne as "an artist with diseased retinas who . . . discovered the premonitory symptoms of a new art"; Arsène Alexandre acknowledges it when he describes the artist as the "discoverer who doesn't profit from what he discovers [,] . . . an artist without issue but not without utility"; Bernard feels it when he writes his *Souvenirs de Paul Cézanne* in which he was "unable to break free of Zola's Cézanne, or rather of the figure of Claude Lantier, . . . consistently [picturing] Cézanne as an artist bordering on failure, although in pursuit of the highest goal"; Rilke's early observations on the painter suggest it in his description of Cézanne's masochistic relationship with the creative task.[42]

For Zola, and indeed for subsequent commentators, this artistic impotence was perfectly embodied by Cézanne. And no wonder, given that Cézanne himself recalled his earlier, essentially romantic identification with Frenhofer very late in his life, in the famous questionnaire and in reported comments to Bernard ("Frenhofer, c'est moi!"), and that he lamented not being able to achieve his goal of making his painting adequate to nature.[43] No wonder, too, when disciples primed by *L'Oeuvre* met their hero and saw an old man whose body was in a state of decay owing to the ravages of diabetes and whose eyesight was failing him in his attempts to penetrate nature (a sexualized operation thwarted, needless to say). By the time commentators like Arsène Alexandre, Émile Bernard, and Ambroise Vollard were making their own judgments about Cézanne, testing the validity of Zola's alleged portrait of the artist as Claude Lantier, Cézanne himself was interrogating old age and impotence, as Linda Nochlin has pointed out, in his pictures of elderly peasants, in "the contrast between the sheer energy of the peasant's bloated bottom as opposed to the implications of impotence of the material referent—actual sagging balls" (fig. 6).[44]

If the persona of Cézanne seemed to invite his biographers to portray him as an artist plagued by both artistic doubt and sexual anxiety, as incomplete or as *impuissant,* in the varied senses of those words, it was also because a new notion of artistic genius was developing at the end of the nineteenth century for which these notions were crucial. By virtue of being incomplete, Cézanne joins a pantheon of troubled masculinity, an illustrious group of fin-de-siècle geniuses that includes the likes of Edgar Degas and Vincent Van

Gogh, and perhaps even Émile Zola himself. What I would like to suggest, then, is that if there has been a *failure of biography* to deal adequately with Cézanne's oeuvre, it is because we have not sufficiently recognized that Cézanne's is one of many *biographies of failure*—stories suffused with notions of degeneration and cultural evolution—to have been written in the later part of the nineteenth century.

THE STORY OF A LIFE AS THE STORY OF PAINTING

While it is useful to disinter the various tropes that determined the construction of Zola's portrait of Claude Lantier, and consequently the construction of the canonical portrait of Paul Cézanne, I do not mean to present *L'Oeuvre* as a mere cautionary tale of the dangers of biographical criticism as such. Rather, I am interested here and throughout this book in the artistic implications of such constructions, implications that go beyond their mere myth-making functions. In other words, whatever role romantic notions of artistic genius or fin-de-siècle notions of cultural degeneration and regeneration played in Zola's elaboration of Lantier's character—and whatever the ways the romantic and pseudoscientific discourses mutually fed and reinforced each other—*L'Oeuvre* is, it seems to me, above all a work of art criticism. And it is precisely those critical stakes—and the way that this fictionalized biography defines those stakes—that are important here.

Two major themes concerning the goals of modern painting run through *L'Oeuvre.* The first concerns Zola's belief that the artist's task was to create a definitive statement of his artistic beliefs—in other words, to create a masterpiece. The second concerns the role of the nude in advanced painting. Both issues are crucial to any discussion of Cézanne's pictures of bathers, but they are even more crucial to understanding the ways that biographical narrative was deployed to articulate the aims of contemporary painting.

As for the first of these themes: it is no coincidence that English-language translators of Zola's *L'Oeuvre* have chosen the title *The Masterpiece.*[45] Zola considered calling his novel "Le chef-d'oeuvre," though he ended up using a slightly more neutral term (and one that did not echo as directly one of his important literary precedents, Balzac's *Le chef-d'oeuvre inconnu* [*The Unknown Masterpiece*]). Even so, Zola's whole narrative was structured around the idea that the goal of painting was to create a masterpiece—a finished, complete work (as opposed to sketches or studies) that embodies all of the avant-garde beliefs that went into its production. It is precisely the fact that Claude Lantier creates marvelous patches of painting without ever managing to sustain such genius over a whole canvas that is the mark of his degeneracy; his oeuvre is presented as nothing more than an accumulation of sketches, "those little girl's legs, that woman's body, . . . that little landscape, a bit of Plassans country" (54), all bits and pieces rather than complete paintings. Zola's description of Lantier's painful realization at the Salon des Refusés that his painting was a failure because it was unfinished—a realization prompted by the roaring laughter of the mocking crowd (139)—is not simply a depiction of the artist shunned or misunderstood by an ignorant public. Rather, Zola presents this "unfinishedness" of Lantier's work as an objective reality that the artist, because of his degeneracy, cannot see clearly himself.

After Lantier and his model and lover Christine move out of Paris, his incapacity to complete a painting comes to the fore: "He started a score of pictures of [Christine]. . . . As he was never satisfied he scraped his canvases after two or three sittings and set to work again at once on the same subject. A handful of studies, unfinished but full of engaging vigor, were saved from the palette knife and hung on the dining-room walls" (171). The unfinished studies to which Zola refers serve two functions in his narrative: their "engaging vigor" is the evidence of Claude's potential for genius, the sign that this artist has the capacity to create a masterpiece; at the same time, their lack of finish is the sign of what is keeping him from realizing this potential—it is the sign of his degeneracy. Upon Claude's return to Paris, after yet another failed attempt to have a canvas accepted by the Salon, he spends a whole year "paint[ing] by the force of habit, but never finish[ing] anything" (270). Even his last, monumental painting, the one that will eventually kill him, starts out as "a masterly sketch, one of those sketches in which genius comes flashing through the otherwise indeterminate mass of color" (268). Lantier's fatal flaw, then, is that he cannot transform these sketches, these brilliant starts, into anything more.

At Lantier's funeral, his remaining loyal friends ponder the meaning of his horrible suicide: he has hanged himself before his monstrous painting of a nude woman bathing in the Seine. Sandoz and Bongrand lament Claude's fate: "He'd a hero's capacity for work; he was a brilliant observer with a brain packed with knowledge and the temperament of a great and gifted artist . . . and yet he has nothing to show," says Sandoz. "Nothing at all," Bongrand affirms, "not a single canvas; nothing, so far as I know, but a few notes and sketches that every artist turns out and are not meant for the public. No doubt about it, the man we're burying today is a dead man; dead in the fullest sense of the word!" (417). Claude's "incompleteness," then, is characterized by his failure to leave an artistic legacy, and this legacy is defined by the masterpiece. By using the term *féconder* in this context, Zola links artistic creation and procreation, implying that producing an artistic legacy in the form of a finished masterpiece is akin to begetting a son; in other words, it is a proof of virility. Because he failed to leave behind these masterworks, Claude is sure to be forgotten. He is dead to history.[46]

In the end, however, it is not solely Claude's own insufficiencies—"that kink in his genius, those three grams more or less that would have made all the difference," as Sandoz puts it (419)—that account for his failure. Lantier's situation was consistent with the time in which he lived, in which a taste for the impression, the incomplete work, was dominant. In Sandoz's words, we hear Zola's indictment not simply of Lantier's inadequacy but of the failure of a current generation of artists to bring to fruition the lessons learned from Lantier's art:

> His trouble was that he was not man enough for his own artistic formula. By that I mean he hadn't quite the genius necessary to establish it on a firm foundation and impose it on the world *in the form of some definitive work*. . . . And now what is there to see for all he's done? Nothing; nothing but effort being frittered away on all sides; nobody producing anything more than sketches or hasty impressions; nobody capable of being the master everyone's looking for. (421, my emphasis)

Zola, through his spokesman Sandoz, returns repeatedly to the idea of hard work and effort, both as an argument against the Academy's belief that the modern method was the result of laziness, of a failure to learn how to draw and paint properly, as well as a kind of plea to modern painters, who had abandoned the goal of creating finished, masterly paintings in favor of devoting their energies to creating impressionistic sketches that did not amount to much.

This should come as no surprise: it was a theme repeated in his art criticism of the 1880s, which increasingly imposed a realist, or even at times academic standard of formal completion in painting.[47] In addressing the work of the impressionists in his 1880 review, "Le Naturalisme au Salon," for example, Zola equated their loose and open brushwork with a lack of diligence, writing that "To my mind, one must capture nature in a momentary impression; only, one must fix this moment on the canvas forever, by a largely studied facture. Without question, outside of work there is no possible solidity."[48] The impressionists' failure to achieve that solidity drove Zola to harsh judgment:

> The greatest disappointment is that no artist in this group has powerfully and definitively realized the new formula that they all employ, scattered in their works. The formula is there, divided into infinite parts; but nowhere, in any of their work, does one find it expressed in a masterly way. They are all precursors; the man of genius has not yet been born. We can clearly see what they want to achieve, and we grant that they are right; but we search in vain for the masterpiece [*le chef-d'oeuvre*] which must impose the formula and force all heads to bow before it. This is why the Impressionists' struggle is not yet won: they remain inferior to the work that they attempt, they stammer without being able to find the word.[49]

For Zola, the very fact that none of the impressionist painters have achieved the masterpiece of which he speaks is evidence of their impotence, an impotence as painful as Lantier's, because, like him, the impressionists have the potential to make brilliant paintings. They are the best that contemporary painting has to offer: "They are full of holes," he writes, "they too often let their brushwork slip, they are too easily satisfied, they prove themselves to be incomplete, illogical, exaggerated, impotent; never mind, it suffices that they work toward a contemporary naturalism to place themselves at the head of a movement and to play a considerable role in our school of painting."[50]

By the turn of the century, it was assumed by many of Cézanne's champions (or at least by those who believed the character of Claude Lantier to be a cruel portrait of Cézanne) that the cooling of the relationship between Cézanne and Zola was the result of the publication of *L'Oeuvre*.[51] Ambroise Vollard, who interviewed both the novelist and the painter shortly after the publication of the book, provides an interesting insight on the decline of the famous friendship in his monograph on Cézanne, published in 1914.[52] The words of the two comrades, as recorded by Vollard, indicate that if there was indeed a rift that could be blamed on *L'Oeuvre,* it was not at all over the biographical portrait of Lantier. For in *L'Oeuvre,* Zola had constructed his narrative around Claude Lantier, a character who embodied the idea of artistic impotence, in order to articulate the stakes of avant-garde painting and argue for the achievement of the definitive artistic statement—the masterpiece—as its gold standard. And, as Vollard's testimony makes clear, if it is likely that Cézanne recognized little of his actual life in the biographical account of that *artiste maudit,* it is certain that he emphatically rejected the artistic argument that was being made by his friend, the critic. Such is the lesson of the only sustained account of Cézanne's reaction to *L'Oeuvre:* Cézanne, at least, understood the text as an argument about the path for contemporary art and took issue with it on those terms.

In Vollard's text, Zola is clear about his disappointment with Cézanne and in fact places the blame for his own poor opinion of the artist on Cézanne's shoulders, treating it as the result of his failure to live up to the promise of genius that Zola had recognized in him.[53] He states quite directly that Cézanne's failure provided the inspiration for *L'Oeuvre.* Even the act of writing the novel was an attempt to return Cézanne to a moderate and successful path of creation: "'I did everything to bring dear old Cézanne back to his senses. . . . It was he who inspired *L'Oeuvre,*'" says Zola. "'The public went mad over the book, but Cézanne was indifferent. After that nothing could bring him out of the clouds; he withdrew more and more from the work-a-day world.'"[54]

Vollard subsequently reported Zola's comments to Cézanne and records the painter's response. The artist does not mention Zola's misunderstanding of or lack of sympathy toward his painting and instead explains the deterioration of the friendship as a slow process of two figures, so alike in their youthful ideals, growing apart as a result of the vicissitudes of success; Cézanne, it seems, was unable to accept Zola, his comrade-in-arms in their radical youths, as a "dirty *bourgeois.*"[55] When Cézanne finally does mention *L'Oeuvre*—and Vollard has taken pains to make it clear that the novel was *not* the cause of the rift—it is clear the artist feels that Zola is profoundly ignorant about art. Vollard recalls his words: "'You can't ask a man to talk sensibly about the art of painting if he simply doesn't know anything about it. But by God!'—and here Cézanne began to tap on the table like a deaf man—'how can he dare to say that a painter is done for because he has painted one bad picture? When a picture isn't realized [*réalisé*], you pitch it in the fire and start another one!'"[56]

This passage is telling: Cézanne does not object to Zola's descriptions of artistic impotence or sexual degeneracy, he does not take offense at the characterization of Claude's cruel insensitivity toward his wife and child, he does not vent his rage at Zola's ultimate judgment that the painting of the new school, while sincere, had lost its way from virile naturalism to a feminized and flawed symbolism, nor does he express his anger at Zola's harsh judgment of his capabilities. To none of these biographical details of Claude's character—details that would cleave onto Cézanne's own biography soon enough—did Cézanne object. Rather, what Cézanne cites as Zola's greatest offense is his idea that a single failed painting could lead an artist to his demise, his belief that any artist could invest so much—his life—in a single image, the way Lantier does, obsessing over a single canvas until, recognizing it as a failure, he hangs himself in front of it. In the face of this melodramatic and romantic notion, Cézanne's is the voice of the pragmatist: "When a picture isn't realized, you pitch it in the fire and start another one!"

And no wonder Cézanne would object, for, according to the proof of Cézanne's practice, "finish" was no longer the criterion by which one could judge an artist a success. If Zola failed to recognize this aspect of Cézanne's approach, other critics did, eventually. In an essay of 1906, Théodore Duret urged that Cézanne's work should not be held to an anachronistic standard:

> Cézanne is, above all, a *painter* in the proper sense of the word; he investigates first and foremost the material quality of paint and the power of color. However, to those who can only understand drawing which exhibits precise and limited lines, he did not draw; for those who expect a painting to offer historical or anecdotal motifs, his, offering nothing like that, might as well not have existed; for those

who want the surfaces to be covered equally, his, because of their roughened spots and the fact that he sometimes goes as far as to leave parts of his canvas bare, appeared to be done by an impotent man [*impuissant*]; his touch, because he juxtaposes equally colored tones, or sometimes superimposes them, resulting in a thick density, seemed coarse, barbarous, monstrous.[57]

Cézanne's paintings, with their imprecise and reworked line, surfaces that were not completely covered with pigment, and coarsened skins of paint, did not appear to be masterpieces to his contemporaries, Duret says, nor were they conceived as such.[58] Rather, they were attempts to realize his sensations on canvas, more *impression* than *chef-d'oeuvre*.[59]

It was, one might say, the *nonlinearity* of Cézanne's work that mitigated against its being read according to the criteria of "finish" or of the masterpiece, the sense that there was neither a clear origin nor a clear goal in Cézanne's practice. One might locate that nonlinearity in the development of Cézanne's motifs, in the way that his painting method refused the drive from sketch to masterpiece: he did not work from *croquis* to *esquisse* to *étude* to *ébauche* to finished painting but rather visited and revisited themes and motifs in many different forms, in all mediums, often creating pencil studies and watercolor sketches after completing major paintings.[60] One might call this the logic of the series, and indeed it is the seriality of Cézanne's continual engagement with motifs such as the Mont Sainte-Victoire, for example, or the bathers, that seems to undermine the drive to the masterpiece. One could never say that Cézanne's oil paintings have primacy over his watercolors or drawings, any more than one would say that one of Monet's paintings of haystacks has primacy over any of the others. They are each, rather, instances of a potentially limitless process of realizing *sensations*, a term that connotes the meeting of self and nature, neither of which is a constant, and thus implies an endlessly fluctuating series of encounters rather than a stable image that can be recorded once and for all.[61] As Geffroy wrote in 1901, "Art does not proceed without a certain level of incompletion, since the life it reproduces is in perpetual transformation."[62]

One might also locate this nonlinearity, as Yve-Alain Bois does, in the actual application of paint on the canvas, "a molecular process which is not simply additive, but multiplying . . . geologically constructed of layers, or rather of levels, of skeins of molecules more or less loose, each skein responding both to the one that precedes it and to the whiteness of the support."[63] The block-like, "molecular" brushstrokes used by Cézanne correspond, it seems, not to the clear needs of the motif but to the need of the painter in representing sensation. As such, there was no point at which the process of making a painting came definitively to an end; thus "Cézanne's characteristic dabs of paint and rectilinear patches of color . . . seemed incomplete by their very nature, because the suggestion is that more can always be added."[64] His habit of laying down the first strokes of paint on a canvas not to define contours or establish broad outlines of his motif but to delineate the meeting of planes, the overlappings of edges and objects, his working from the outside of an object inward, and of moving from place to place on his support, filling in details in one area without having even sketched in a plan in others, spoke to this nonlinearity.[65] It is a practice especially apparent in graphite and watercolor works such as *The Château Noir* (1887–90), and it results, in a sense, in the breakdown of the narrative logic of composing a painting—at least according to the terms insisted upon by Zola (fig. 7).

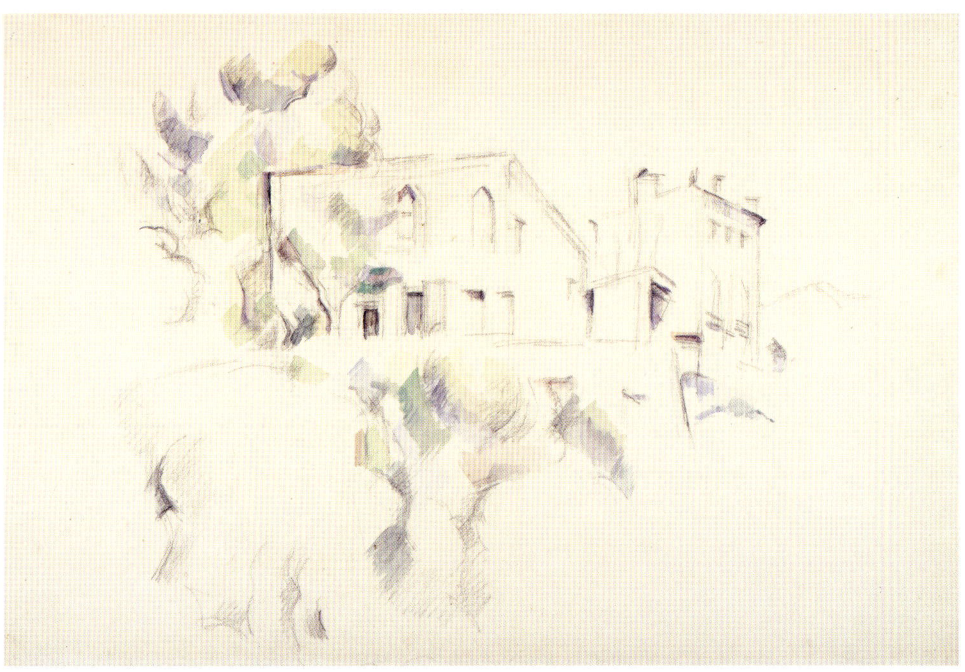

7. Cézanne, *The Château Noir,* 1887–90. Watercolor over pencil, 36 x 52.6 cm. Museum Boijmans-van Beuningen, Rotterdam, Netherlands.

Not only is Vollard's account scattered with images (surely painful for the art dealer) of Cézanne setting on whatever painting was nearest and attacking it with the full force of his rage, but he also describes Cézanne's insistent return to canvases that had been abandoned—literally abandoned, some of them even left in the bushes—in order to rework and reconceive, in order to start again or recover the sensations that had, for whatever reason, failed to live up to his expectations.[66] The very application of paint to the canvas, the multiple contours and reworked lines, the layers of painted strokes, the visibility of the changes of mind and direction that went into the creation of a single image all seem to indicate that Cézanne constantly returned to his images, moments later, days later, sometimes months or years later, and his technique records that process of revision in a material way on the canvas.

The circularity of Cézanne's practice, the constant return to the same set of resonant images, poses, and sites, the search for the realization of his *sensation*—all of these things suggest a potentially limitless repetition without a clear and fixed result. If Cézanne's work could be described in terms of artistic impotence, it would be on the basis of this repetitive, obsessive method.[67] To explain this quality of his work, the constant search for form that never seemed to yield definitive results, Zola employed a metaphor of impotence, its pointless and desperate persistence described by Bongrand as being "like old men [who] persist in trying to make love" (206).

While Cézanne's response to Zola's indictment is illuminating in and of itself—demonstrating as it does the way Cézanne seemed to be substituting a more modern notion of a process-driven painterly practice for Zola's traditional (even academic) nineteenth-century notion of the punctual masterpiece—it is equally instructive as a matter of methodology. Cézanne's reaction to *L'Oeuvre* and to his erstwhile friend's entrenched notions of artistic achievement indicates the way such biographical accounts (explicitly fictionalized or not) must be read: as a form of art criticism and not necessarily as the more or less successful narrative of a life. And in this insistence on reading *L'Oeuvre* not in terms of how well it portrayed him as a man but in how well it portrayed the act and imperative of painting at that moment in history, Cézanne seems only to be responding to Zola's intentions for the book: one recalls the novelist's words to Vollard, and his claim that *L'Oeuvre* was in fact written in order to point out the errors of Cézanne's aesthetic ways, in order to set him on the right track. Lantier was not so much a portrait but an object lesson; Cézanne was right not to take it personally.

With this lesson in mind, one might turn to the second theme that runs through *L'Oeuvre,* one more directly relevant to a discussion of Cézanne's bathers: that of the avant-garde artist's mastery of the nude. For if Zola creates a resonant portrait of an *artiste manqué* in Lantier, it is through his depiction of Lantier's inability to paint the naked female model. More importantly, this failure is not merely narrated as a failure of virility—as a matter of the artist's fear of women, or excess passion toward them, or physical impotence—but rather as a failure of representation. For it is the inability of Lantier to successfully *represent* Woman on the canvas, to contain her power on the picture plane, that is the object of Zola's most pitiless critique.

This struggle between Lantier and the task of painting the nude is equally a struggle between Lantier and Christine, the young woman he meets on a dark and stormy night in Paris and who eventually becomes his model and lover. Claude's feelings toward her from the start are a mixture of passionate obsession and suspicion, and he is constantly plagued by doubts about her past and her purity as well as the threat she poses to his career. Over the course of their relationship, Christine eventually comes to sense Claude's erotic investment in the act of painting and thus sets out to conquer it—and him. For a while, she seems to triumph in her battle against Claude's art. In the early days of their passion, Lantier turns away from his task almost entirely, retiring from Paris to the village of Bennecourt where he is loathe even to pick up a brush. Instead of turning to his painting to sate his desires, he abandons his work, for Christine "appeared so desirable that he continually left his painting to lie down beside her and let the sweetness of the earth lull them both into oblivion" (162). It is as if, by satisfying his passions, Lantier has nothing left for his art, since "Christine was all that mattered to him now. It was she who enveloped him in a searing flame that caused his artistic ambitions to shrivel up to nothing" (163).

Christine is portrayed as a threat to Lantier's artistic drive, in the tradition of the femme fatale: she causes his ambitions to shrivel up to nothing. But she does not consciously thwart his work and gently extracts promises from her lover that he will do more work tomorrow; when those promises go unfulfilled, she is both uneasy and thrilled "at the thought of the power she had over him, . . . by the perpetual sacrifice he was making for her" (162). Eventually Christine urges Lantier to resume his work, "as yet unaware of the terrible rival she was creating for herself" (171). Willing to sacrifice the home that she loved and the well-being of the cretinous child they bore together, she insists the new family move back to Paris so that Claude can return to the art world he misses so much.

Only when Lantier starts to work on a large, ambitious canvas must his young lover acknowledge the power of her competitor. In his obsession with his work, Christine's husband "had forgotten all about her, as if she meant nothing to him[;] . . . she had felt him moving farther and farther away from her, into a world to which she could never hope to aspire" (250). As their relationship deteriorates, Christine realizes the enormity of her situation:

> She had one rival, and one rival only: painting. That was what was stealing her lover. She was ready to strip herself to the last stitch and give herself to him naked for days or weeks on end; she was ready to live naked if that meant she would win him back and be able to claim him for her own when he sank once again into her arms! What more had she to offer but herself? It was fair enough, surely, for

her to risk her own body in this one last struggle, knowing that to lose would be to admit that she was a woman with no more power to charm. (276)

This battle between Christine and painting is pitched on the field of Lantier himself: the only way she can declare her victory in the struggle against art is by exercising power over her lover and husband, by forcing him to forget painting in favor of her. At the same time Lantier's only defense against Christine's power is through painting. In the face of the physical presence of his wife, a naked presence that threatens to cut off his access to the realm of art by diverting him toward the pleasures of the flesh, Lantier turns to the image of the nude on the banks of the Seine, the final, monumental, terrible canvas before which Claude's body will eventually hang. As Christine realizes the difficulty of her task, Claude is completely won over by his art, body and soul; even his "carnal desire had transferred itself to his work and the painted lovers he created for himself. They were the only women now who could send his blood pulsing through his body, the women whose every limb was the product of his own efforts" (280).

This shift of affection from wife to painting is the result of a profound disappointment or even trauma: the painted nude becomes, in Zola's narrative, a kind of obsession by which Claude can stave off his ambivalent feelings regarding Christine and the (imagined) secrets of her past.[68] Where she is mystery, the painted nude is utterly known to Claude because it is the product of his own creation. We are privy to Lantier's musings:

Back there in the country, when his passion was at its height, he thought happiness was achieved when he possessed a real woman and held her in his arms. He knew now that that had been nothing more than the old, old illusion, since they were still strangers to each other; so he preferred the illusion he found in his art, the everlasting pursuit of unattainable beauty, the mad desire which could never be satisfied. He wanted all women, but he wanted them created according to his dreams. . . . He wanted to love them only for the beauty of their coloring; he wanted to feel them perpetually beyond his grasp! (280)

Zola's description of Claude's longing is especially resonant, for he describes the artist as longing for the possession of a woman made ideal through the process of representation, a woman whom he could know fully because he controlled her very existence on the surface of the canvas, a woman who was "created according to his dreams" and who could not threaten his being or his creative task because she was, by virtue of her status as mere image, "perpetually beyond his grasp" rather than always troublingly *there* in flesh and blood, unknowable, mysterious, uncontrollable, like his wife was. It is not too much to suggest that what Zola was proposing—what Claude was attempting to achieve—was the creation of the image of the nude according to the terms of the psychoanalytic concept of the fetish.[69] Through this lens, the image of woman is rendered in a way invisible her biological lack, so as to displace the sight of woman's imaginary castration and thus assuage "man's narcissistic fear of losing his own phallus, his most precious possession."[70] The painted nude, in these terms, should satisfy the demands of the devouring gaze, "which seeks reassurance in the polished surfaces and sealed orifices of the idealized body."[71] To the extent that he, too, seemed to valorize such comforting and pleasure-producing images of female seduction, Zola's thinking was hardly out of line with his contemporary moment, for even the most advanced painting

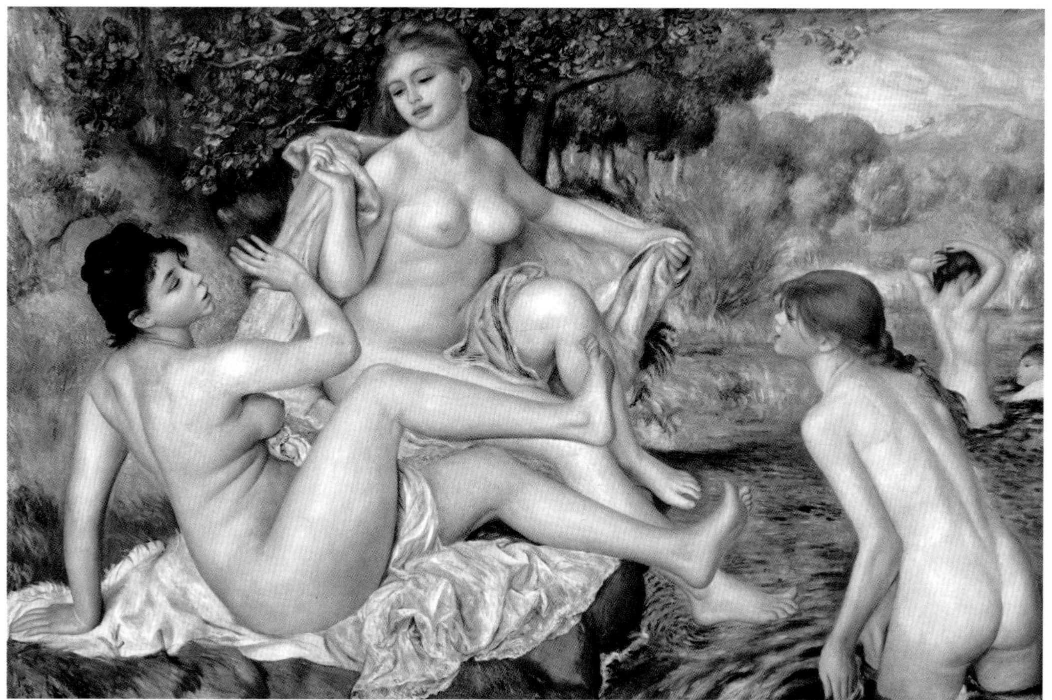

8. Auguste Renoir, *Large Bathers,* 1884–87. Oil on canvas, 117.8 x 170.8 cm. Mr. and Mrs. Carroll S. Tyson Jr. Collection, 1963. Philadelphia Museum of Art.

practice of the day was filled with pictures of the most reassuring and unthreatening feminine allure: think of Renoir's frolicking bathers, tumescent, balanced on juicy, smooth haunches, skin hairless and totally without blemish, pink and luminous, as the most obvious example (fig. 8).[72]

It is in the distance of his painting from this ideal of feminine plenitude that we witness the depths of Lantier's failure. Zola indicates the painter's decline by modeling his final, monumental canvas after the paintings of the Symbolist artists whom the author despised, such as Gustave Moreau, whose images of Salomés and Sphinxes and Bathshebas inevitably come to mind in Zola's descriptions of Lantier's jewel-encrusted bodies and gilded figures (fig. 9). And even in this decrepit task, the emulation of a style of painting that was far removed from Zola's preferred naturalist or realist mode, Lantier falls short, for no matter how hard he tries to create his nude figure as a fetish, compulsively adorning her loins with Byzantine decorations, returning over and over again to the space between her gilded thighs, the sign of her sex—and thus the reminder of the threat she represents—resurfaces relentlessly. Claude's incapacity to achieve a depiction of sexual plenitude reaches its apogee in a scene that is both wrenching and violent: he continually reworks the figure over the course of many years until one day, "blind with rage, with one despairing gesture [Lantier] thrust his fist through the canvas" (284). This is not just an iconoclastic gesture but also a murderous one, as seen through Christine's eyes: "His fist had smashed clean through her rival's breast, ripped it open and left a

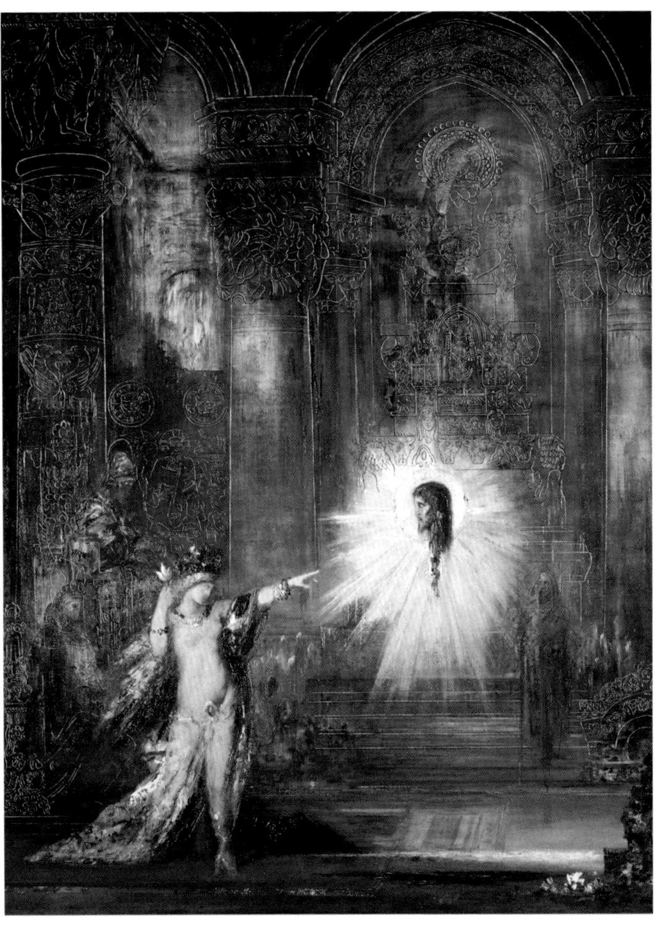

9. Gustave Moreau, *The Apparition*, 1874. Oil on canvas, 142 x 103 cm. Musée Gustave Moreau, Paris.

great gaping wound. She was killed at last!" (284). Thus the sign of the woman's sex to which Claude has returned continually in his depiction, hiding and thus highlighting it behind a veil of blossoms and rubies, rips through the canvas as a literal tear, brought back into view as "a great gaping wound" by the violence of Claude's impotent rage.

Christine feels the effects of Claude's carnal struggle with his painting as a betrayal, as if the painted nude had been a real woman: she is driven to rage and despair, "impelled by the irrepressible fury of a wife affronted under her own roof, deceived while she lay asleep in her own room" (401). In the final confrontation between Christine, Claude, and the painted nude, the scales fall from Claude's eyes as he sees the monstrosity he has produced, the woman with bright gold thighs whose sex is encrusted with flowers and jewels. "Could he himself have unconsciously produced this symbol of insatiable desire, this extrahuman image of the flesh turned to gold and jewels in his hands as he strove in vain to bring his work to life?" (407). With this moment of clarity, Christine hopes she has triumphed. As the unhappy couple makes love, she exclaims: "'You're mine at last! Now I know I'm the only one! *She's* dead, now and forever!'" (410). Christine's triumph, however, is short-lived, for early in the morning, as she sleeps, Claude is compelled to take one last look at his aborted masterpiece. Christine finds his abject body hanging before the hateful picture, ever in the thrall of the nude depicted in it: "His face was turned towards the picture and quite close to the Woman whose sex blossomed as a mystic rose, as if his soul had passed into her with his last dying breath and he was still gazing on her with his fixed and lifeless eyes" (413).

Ultimately, Zola's novel proposes that the goal of painting the erotic nude is to create an image in which the threat posed to the male psyche by woman's sexuality is managed and diffused, an image that provides pleasurable and safe looking for the male viewer. In this, he profoundly misrecognized the conditions of the genre after the intervention, in the 1860s, of Manet with his brazen *Olympia* and coolly defiant *Déjeuner sur l'herbe.* And if Cézanne articulated outright his rejection of Zola's insistence on completion and finish as the standard by which modern painting should be judged successful, the following chapters will argue that Cézanne's own paintings of the nude, the series of bathers, evidence his refusal of Zola's contention that the nude should be understood only in terms of an outmoded notion of eroticized pleasure. Cézanne's bathers propose quite another definition of eroticism, one not managed, contained, or bounded by the idealized and sanitized figure but one set loose over the play of the surface, produced through the process of painting itself, one in which the eccentricities of the artist's touch over the surface of the body—the obsessive quality of which was, for Zola, the sign of impotence—would substitute for the pleasures of the flesh, would challenge the pleasures of the eye, and would create a pleasure of *matière*.

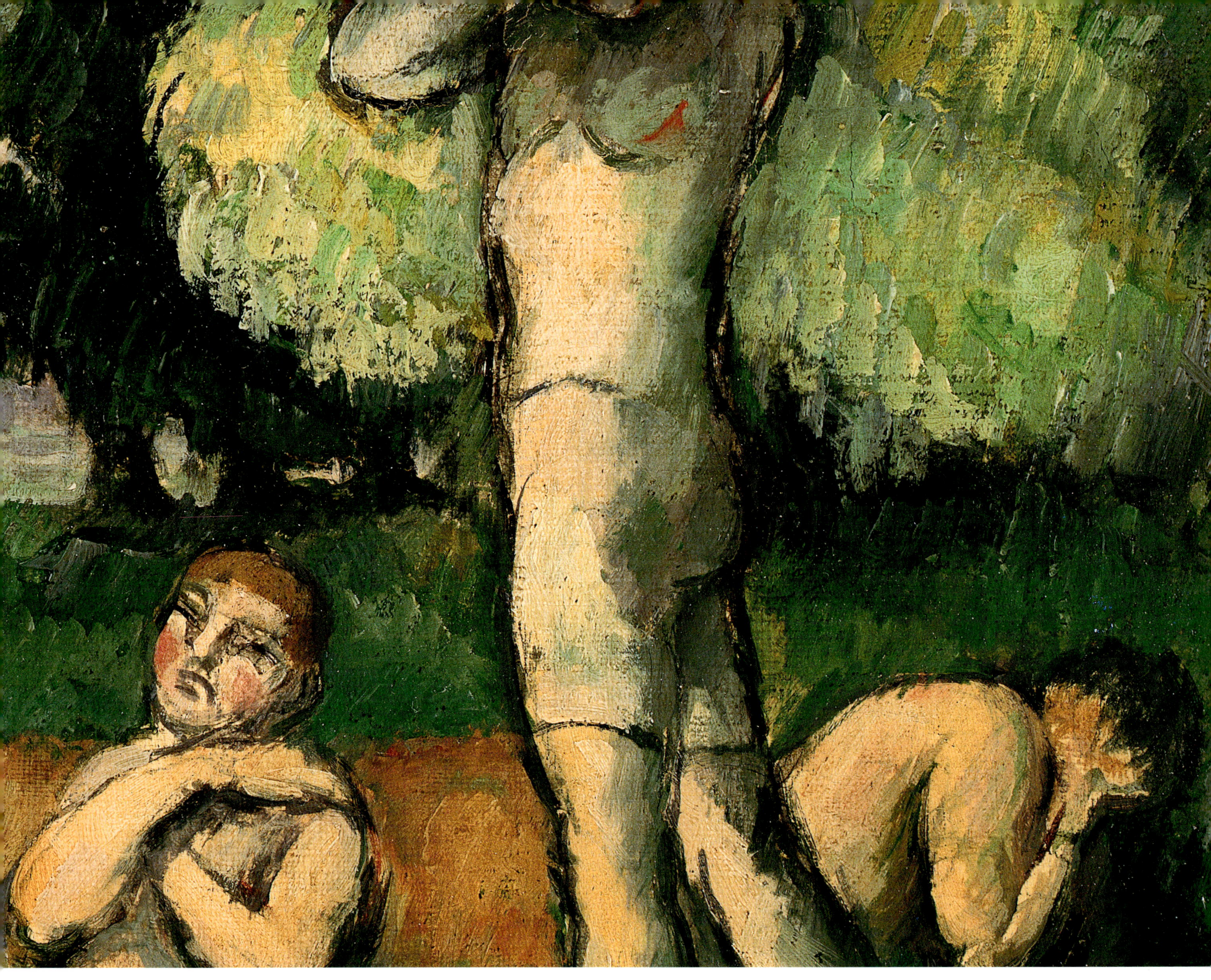

2 CÉZANNE'S BATHERS AND THE EROTICS OF PAINT

Detail of fig. 52

LET US START WITH THE CÉZANNE PAINTING that Matisse once owned, the *Three Bathers* of 1876–77 (pl. I). Three women are arranged around a swimming hole, one seated, one bathing, the third frozen in mid-stride, her back toward us. It is not a large canvas, measuring about 20 by 21 inches, but it has a certain monumentality, derived at least in part from the heaviness and solidity of the figures—a solidity that verges on massiveness and that as such is certainly at odds with most depictions of the female nude at this point in the nineteenth century—and in part from the stylized geometry of the canted trees, which form a sort of tent over the heads of the women. Despite these features—the weightiness of the women, the stability of the pyramidal composition, the rootedness of every element depicted—the image is hardly static. On the contrary, everything about this painting seems activated by the painter's restless brush: the parallel, diagonal strokes of yellow, green, purple, ochre, and blue in the foliage register as the flick of the artist's wrist, a nervous, quick, repetitive action; the delicate, lacy tree branches near the top evidence an almost sketch-like willingness to rework and reposition, and, most importantly, to allow the evidence of that revision to remain visible; the thickened skin of paint on the bodies of the bathers, especially on the torso and flattened breasts of the bathing woman at the center of the canvas and around their exterior contours shows us, quite materially, the areas on which Cézanne focused most of his painterly energy. If this almost compulsive movement over the surface of the canvas has implications for the actual buildup of pigment, it also has consequences as regards color: look at the way that the greens and yellows of the foliage contaminate the bodies in the foreground, as if the painter could not distract himself from their flesh for more than a moment, or the way the blues of the sky infect the trees; look at how the painter has to introduce a dark green patch at the very center of the canvas, a dull void needed to keep the bathing woman anchored to the painting, to balance the weightiness of her heavily worked form.

Despite Matisse's fervent admiration for the painting—he wrote that it had "sustained [him] morally in the critical moments of [his] venture as an artist"—and his belief that the work, like all of Cézanne's canvases, was a picture of order and clarity in which "all confusion had disappeared," to most of Cézanne's contemporaries, paintings like this one were deeply problematic.[1] Faced with the unconventional or even naïve articulation of figures, the visible traces of endlessly reworked contours, the clotted buildup of paint in some areas and the utter insufficiency of pigment in others—given these gaucheries, in other words—even Émile Bernard, Cézanne's most avid interlocutor, could not decide if the bathers were as elegant as sixteenth-century Dianas, as he once wrote, or whether they were utter failures. Order and clarity were, for Bernard, in short supply in Cézanne's bathers; on the contrary, for him they were marked by illogic and disorder and confusion.[2]

Bernard was hardly alone in his ambivalence. If Cézanne's contemporaries found these paintings strange, even inexplicable—and at the very least the relative *lack* of writings on the works would suggest that this was indeed the case—it was due, perhaps, to two things: first, to the fact that the paintings were difficult to reconcile with what was becoming understood to be Cézanne's artistic project, and second, to the fact that they were difficult to reconcile with the genres of historical landscape and the nude, both traditions with which Cézanne's work seemed to engage rhetorically. But the most formidable challenge posed by these pictures—the challenge that faced writers on Cézanne as soon as the paintings appeared in Paris in the 1880s and 1890s and continues to structure the discourse on them today—is that the bathers seem at once indifferent to erotic concerns and riven by them. The question, then and now, is: how to reconcile this contradiction? How to read the eroticism of Cézanne's bathers?

THE PROBLEM OF THE BATHERS

In terms of sheer numbers, the paintings of *baigneurs* and *baigneuses* were hardly the most visible element of Cézanne's oeuvre; he made only 80 or so oil paintings or painted sketches on the theme, out of almost one thousand canvases. (By contrast, he painted over 150 portraits, almost two hundred still lifes, and around 375 landscapes over the course of his career.)[3] Of the exhibitions of his paintings that occurred before his death in 1906, few included images from this series, and in all only thirteen were shown during his lifetime, including *Les baigneurs: Étude, projet de tableau* known as *Bathers at Rest III* (1876–77) (pl. II), at the third impressionist exhibition of 1877; two versions of his *Bather with Outstretched Arms,* along with four other bather canvases, at the Vollard exhibition of 1895; and five or six paintings at the 1904 Salon d'Automne.[4] After his death, a retrospective exhibition was held at the Grand Palais in conjunction with the 1907 Salon d'Automne. Here, none of the smaller paintings of bathers were displayed; however, two of the three great *machines*—the London and Philadelphia *Large Bathers* that he toiled upon during the last years of his life—were given a central place among his canvases.[5]

But while the bathers may be outnumbered by the landscapes or still lifes or portraits, and while they may not have been extensively displayed in Cézanne's lifetime or shortly after his death, they were hardly a footnote to the oeuvre: the *Bathers at Rest III* was exhibited repeatedly by Cézanne in the 1890s and 1900s, and when it became notorious for being rejected by the French museums as part of the Caillebotte bequest in 1893 Cézanne turned it into a lithographic print; moreover, the three *Large Bathers* were the only monumental canvases Cézanne painted. The bathers, then, were an insistent, even nagging presence within the body of work of an artist who was increasingly being presented by his interlocutors as a detached, disinterested, even misanthropic man concerned only with issues of color, formal arrangement, and the task of capturing visual *sensations* in pictorial form.[6]

The bather images presented any number of problems for critics in relation to this emerging interpretation of Cézanne's work. They were *not* painted from life—Cézanne relied instead on studies that he had made in the 1860s when he studied at the Atelier Suisse and on printed sources such as Armand Silvestre's *Le nu au Salon*—therefore their status as transcription of optical truth was untenable (fig. 10). And they were deeply, unrelentingly *strange*, too: their figures unconventional, even deformed, their surfaces veering from barely worked to heavily impacted, their stylized compositions belying any attempt to read them as plein air exercises. Even the fact that Cézanne chose to address both female *and* male nudes—and, given the number of times he exhibited *Bathers at Rest III* before 1907, one might say that he particularly insisted on this aspect of his work—made these paintings eccentric, in need of explanation and even justification by his critics, for the male nude had largely gone out of fashion by the second decade of the nineteenth century.[7] But, despite the fact that they seemed to conform to no normative or even avant-garde notion of beauty or erotic pleasure, most troubling was the artist's almost obsessive return to the theme and the very unexpected way that he undertook it, suggesting that the paintings were hardly dispassionate formal exercises.

If the bathers were difficult to reconcile with Cézanne's larger project as a painter, they were equally difficult to understand vis-à-vis the genres of historical landscape or of the erotic nude as they existed in the late nineteenth century in France. In advanced painting practice since the 1860s, the long-venerated theme of the figure in the landscape had been a particularly important site of a range of avant-garde gestures. These interventions into the tradition seemed to veer from modernizing it via its overt eroticization in defiance of academic calls to idealize the nude, to reviving it via an aestheticized classicism that recalled the genre's origins in the Arcadian works of Poussin. To understand the first of these interventions, one might turn to Courbet's oeuvre, which does not simply place the eroticized nude in the landscape but equates her forms and dark, unex-

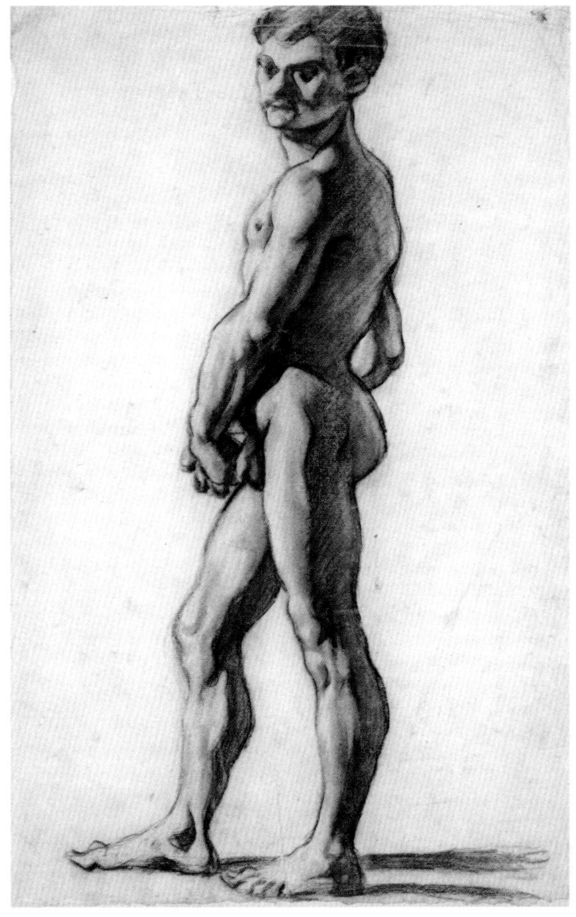

10. Cézanne, *Academic Nude*, ca. 1865. Black chalk on paper, 49 x 31 cm. Fitzwilliam Museum, Cambridge, U.K.

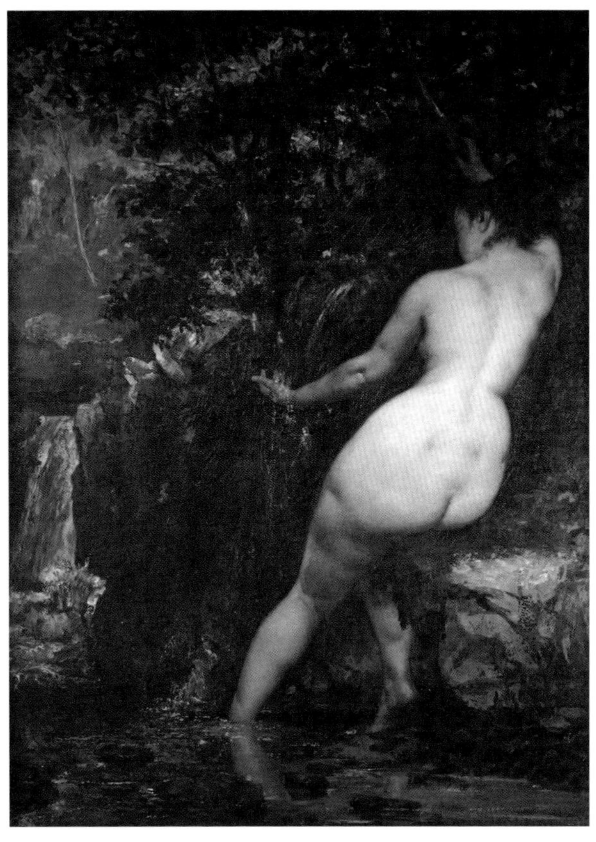

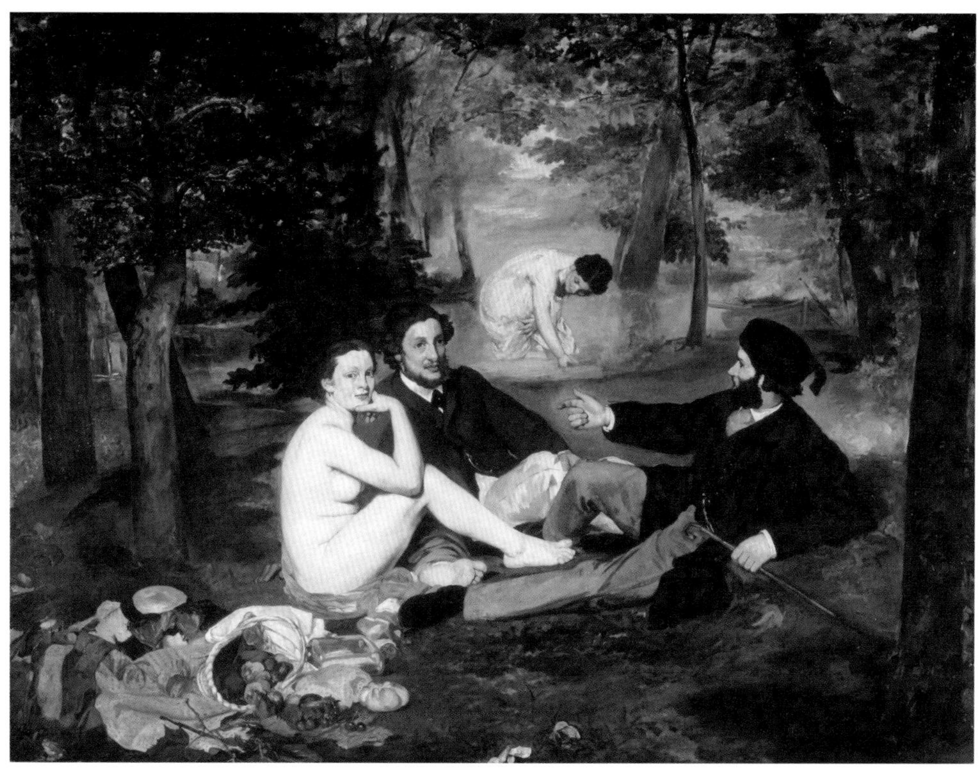

11. Gustave Courbet, *The Source*, 1868. Oil on canvas, 128 x 97 cm. Musée d'Orsay, Paris.

12. Édouard Manet, *Le Déjeuner sur l'herbe*, 1863. Oil on canvas, 208 x 264.5 cm. Musée d'Orsay, Paris.

plored crevices with those of the landscape to which she is intimately connected.[8] The theme is brought to its apogee in the uncanny repetition of the composition and aspect of *The Source of the Loue* (1864) in the scandalous *Origin of the World* (1866), with its deep, penetrable voids, but is present more directly and explicitly in paintings such as *The Source* (1868) (fig. 11) and *The Bathers* (1853). Or one might look to Manet's *Déjeuner sur l'herbe* (1863), a painting that deploys art historical visions of Arcadia as a setting for its utterly contemporary clothed men and naked women (fig. 12). Yet for all its urban, disinterested sophistication it was no less invested in this spectacularization of sex, transforming an erstwhile image of idyllic pleasure into a satire of modern sexual mores.[9]

But whatever the extent to which Cézanne learned the lessons of those painters, his bathers were neither of these things: neither an attempt to shock contemporary sensibilities nor a satire of them, neither a representation steeped in sensual and painterly excess nor a demonstration of blasé, mocking restraint. They lacked—for want of a better term—the anecdotalism of the paintings of his avant-garde forbears: the rhetoric of *real* bodies, contemporary bodies, bodies that did not live up to academic demands for the ideal and for the transcendence of base desire and that precisely derived their erotic charge from that fact. Cézanne's bodies were too abstract, too much a product of his hesitant line and excessive brush, too much ideas than women (or men) for that.

And yet they did not conform to the other major approach to the genre—the one that might seem to explain this ideational quality—either: the revived classicism of the Poussinesque idyll, as epitomized by the paintings of Puvis de Chavannes (fig. 13) and also, to a degree, by a range of Symbolist practices including those of Maurice Denis and Émile Bernard. Whatever the extent of Puvis's disruptions of classical traditions of the nude—whatever the various ways he made their bodies strange, whatever the insufficiencies (by academic standards) with which he rendered his figures, whatever the extent to which he "proposed a completely different relation between the body and painting from the one entrenched in the academic paradigm of idealization"—works such as *Young Girls by the Seashore* are almost ascetic in their purity and their lack of erotic address: in their sense of transcendence, in other words.[10] Cézanne's nudes are, I think, quite different. Though borrowing from art historical sources and possessing a sense of timeless, even Arcadian, pleasure, something in his paintings always seems to interrupt the serenity of their compositions. Even in Cézanne's most classicizing images, such as the Paris *Bathers* (ca. 1890) (pl. III), which quotes freely from the art historical canon, unexpected elements remind us of bodies in all of their fleshy sensuality: think of the vitality of the hastily painted young man in the back waving his arms over his head in a strange gesture of savage sport or the impacted form of the towel held by the central figure, seen from the back, a form that begs to be read as a dislocated body part, an orifice, a sign of sex.[11] Think, moreover, of the way in which the insistent presence of the painted mark interrupts our absorption in those very figures, the way the artist's touch overrides the illusionistic transparency on which a transcendent idealism would seem to depend.[12] Such paintings were emphatically *not* Poussin remade after nature, no matter what anyone—Cézanne or his critics—would otherwise have us believe. Despite the subordination of figures to compositional necessities, despite the suggestions of Virgilian nostalgia, despite any nod toward classicism, Cézanne's paintings are too *carnal*, it seems to me, still too invested in bodies and their strangeness, to be properly Poussinesque (fig. 14).[13]

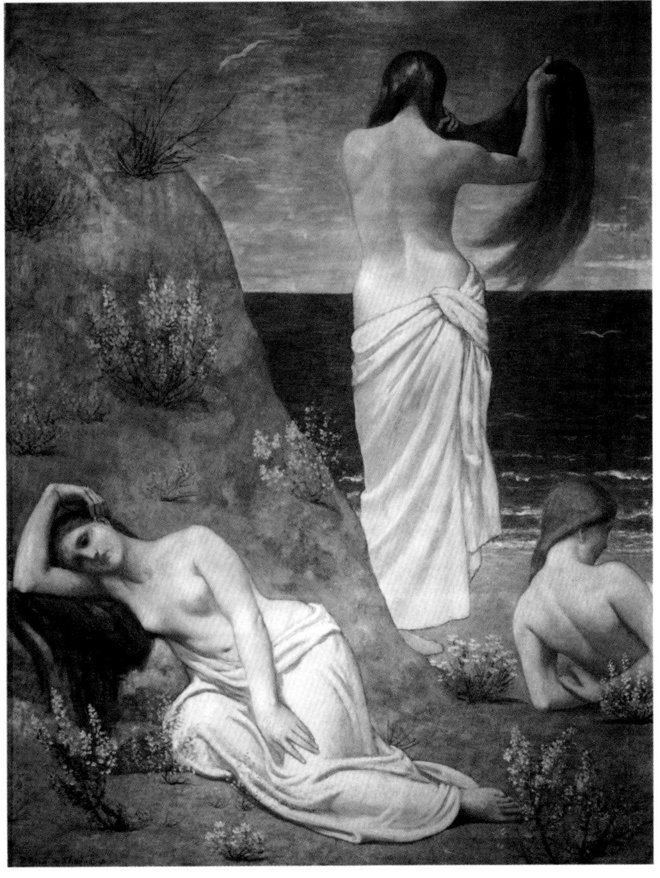

13. Pierre Puvis de Chavannes, *Young Girls by the Seaside* (small version), 1887. Oil on canvas, 61 x 47 cm. Musée d'Orsay, Paris.

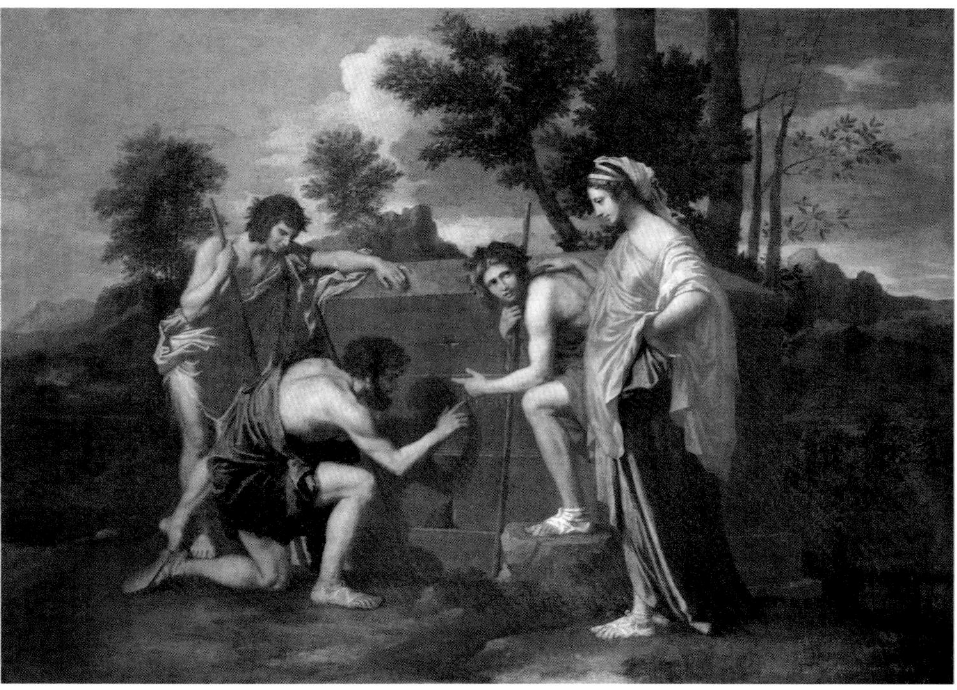

14. Nicolas Poussin, *Arcadian Shepherds,* ca. 1650. Oil on canvas, 85 x 121 cm. Musée du Louvre, Paris.

This is the paradox of Cézanne's bathers: the way that they hover between the modernity of Courbet and Manet and the countermodernity of Puvis, the way they seem to reject an eroticism produced by the fantasy of encounter with a real(ist) body and yet do not reject that eroticism outright in favor of an ascetic classicism.[14] If the modernity of Cézanne's practice generally is to be found in his technique—in his distinctive fusion of color and drawing, in his unique brushstroke, which seems to carry with it the suggestion of a bodily sense of the visual encounter with nature, in his willingness to deform and exaggerate in service of compositional structure, in his unconventional notions of finish and unfinish—then his bathers are no less modern than his landscapes or still lifes or portraits, since they, too, are marked by these qualities. And if the modernity of the bathers is to be found in his technique so, too, is their eroticism. It is to the materiality of the bathers—the way these odd canvases are constituted *as paintings*—that we must turn to discover Cézanne's argument about the way one must go about painting the nude at the end of the nineteenth century.

ANXIOUS MODERNISMS

There have been few attempts to relate Cézanne's bathers to the larger history of the genre of the nude other than as a matter of iconographical source searching; this is perhaps unsurprising given the extent to which Cézanne's physical isolation from Paris and his intensely private and withdrawn nature have been an excuse to treat his project as removed from contemporary historical and art historical concerns generally.[15] Instead, most scholarship has focused on the question of how these images relate to the rest of his oeuvre. Do they, for example, form a crucial link—an explanation, even—for the artist's early work, the erotic, often violent scenes primarily done the 1860s and 70s (although occasionally appearing later as well), paintings such as *A Modern Olympia* (1873–74) (pl. VI) or *The Eternal Feminine* (ca. 1877) or the even stranger *Abduction* (1867) or *The Temptation of St. Anthony* (ca. 1870)? Or is the lack of narrative impulse and restrained technique evidenced by the bathers a sign that Cézanne had abandoned the theatricality of the early scenes and their underlying romantic drama in favor of the cool formalism of his later still lifes, portraits, and landscapes? The answers to these questions are not so simple, for the disparity between these two moments, early and late, is acute: between, on the one hand, the hothouse quality of *A Modern Olympia (The Pasha)* (fig. 15), with its sticky whorls of brackish paint, or the violent excess, thematic and painterly, of *The Murder,* or

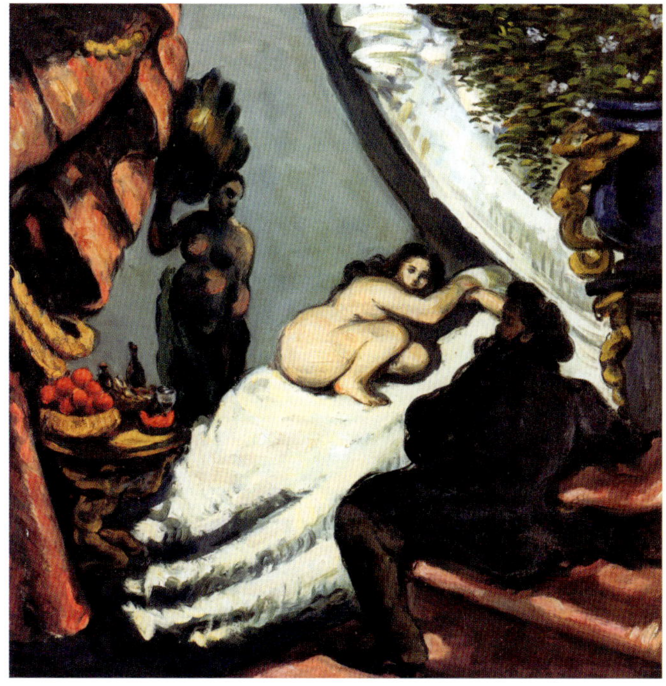

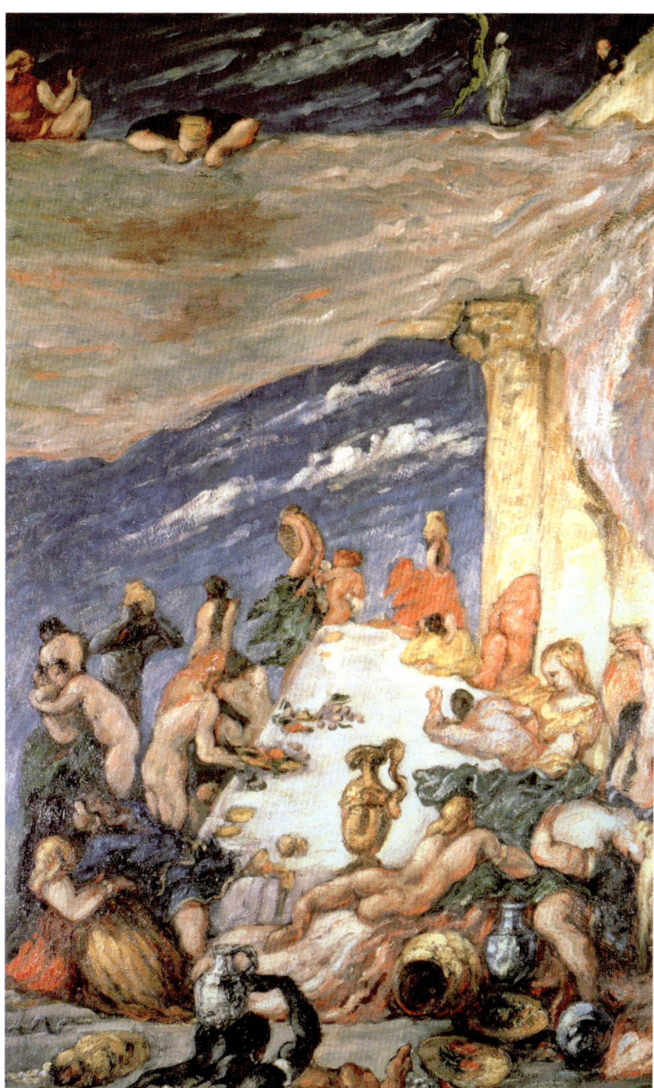

15. Cézanne, *A Modern Olympia (The Pasha),* ca. 1870. Oil on canvas, 56 x 55 cm. Private collection.

16. Cézanne, *The Feast (The Orgy)* (also known as *The Banquet of Nebuchadnezzar*), ca. 1867 (possibly later). Oil on canvas, 130 x 82 cm. Private collection.

the baroque energy of writhing bodies and clotted pigment in *The Orgy* (fig. 16), say, and, on the other, the cool classicism of the Paris *Bathers,* where each figure seems to take a structural role in the vertically punctuated play across the surface of the canvas, or the Art Institute of Chicago's *Bathers* (pl. VIII), in which the artist's so-called constructive strokes, those lozenges of color dabbed on the surface, create a structural integrity that the barely delineated bodies cannot sustain on their own.[16]

For later scholars, there have been a number of strategies for reconciling the bathers with the rest of Cézanne's oeuvre. Many of Cézanne's most influential critics have tended to emphasize the formal qualities of the works, interpreting the stylized compositions and deformed figures as having been subjected by the painter to a strict science of arrangement in order to achieve pictorial harmony. In this way, they can be seen as manifestations of Cézanne's plastic impulses. Kurt Badt, for example, writes:

Cézanne's bathers—sitting, standing, or lying—exist solely for the sake of their being together, for the compositional relationships between them. All personal or temporal features about them, such as their faces, are absorbed into a superior entity. Their gestures reveal nothing about them; they have been transcended into something universal, distant, impersonal, almost faceless and they stand for the idea and the unity of the picture in which they feature, which are what is permanent about it.[17]

In this account of Cézanne's bathers, figures have been transformed into something like still life objects, content is relegated to a mere afterthought of pictorial experimentation, bodies are reduced to mere conceptual pretexts, and the work's relation to a genre that had become, in Cézanne's lifetime, more and more invested in erotic address is rendered irrelevant. To achieve such a reading, much interpretive work must be done, and that work consists largely of reading Cézanne's biography. A formalist account, in other words, relies on the idea that whatever the passionate excesses of Cézanne's early work, whatever the violence and sexual frankness of those paintings, whatever the whiffs of drama and poetry, whatever the gross distortions of form and naïve application of paint, such qualities were successfully repressed by the painter at some point in the 1870s and thus have nothing to do with the later paintings, including the bathers. And this narrative of repression is supported by a biographical narrative: that of a young artist, a rebel in a red sash out to conquer the capital, coming under the calming influence of his mentor Camille Pissarro, encountering the discipline of impressionist painting, meeting his lover Hortense Fiquet (a woman who would at first sate his passions, then extinguish them), settling into a regular family life, and eventually ascending to the status of *bon bourgeois* through the inheritance of his father's estate.[18] The transformation of Cézanne from bohemian to gentleman in biographical terms is read into his work: in rejecting his youthful excess and revolutionary dreams, he was also imagined to be rejecting his eccentric early paintings.[19] And such a rejection is understood as complete—Badt refers to this sea change in Cézanne's work as a "conversion" and goes so far as to suggest that "it meant a true renunciation of his former ego" and not merely a "change of technique or a new style."[20]

The other major tendency in scholarship on the bathers—most brilliantly demonstrated in the work of Meyer Schapiro—has been a psychobiographical one, which seeks to understand the relationship between Cézanne's nudes and the rest of his oeuvre according to the psychoanalytic model of sublimation.[21] This interpretive mode positions the early work not as an insurmountable problem in relation to the artist's later practice—a problem that must be swept, as it were, under the scholarly rug—but rather sees in those eccentric and melodramatic pictures the key to unlocking the meanings of his later nudes.[22] Obviously, the reliance of the sublimation model on Cézanne's biography is overt and extensive, though the biography it constructs for the artist is somewhat different from that of the formalists. Though reading the same events—the influence of his friendship with Pissarro and his encounter with impressionism, a stabilized family life, his retreat from the capital and consequent *embourgeoisement*—the sublimation model emphasizes a specifically sexual narrative. Cézanne's sentimental education—his move from sexual excess to an equally unhealthy sexual asceticism—replaces the story of his transformation from bohemian to bourgeois. Tales of Cézanne's sexual traumas and anxieties, his fears of women, his unsatisfying relationship with his unloving wife, his fear of being touched: all these biographical details are brought to bear on a reading of the works.

More importantly, instead of imagining that the motivations that drove the disturbing early works were completely set aside in his later career, this interpretive mode imagines them constantly threatening to reemerge, diverted and transmuted into pictures of laudable idealism but never far from the surface. Rather than a narrative of the transformation from sensibility to sense, we have a narrative of passion displaced—put to aesthetically reified aims but never entirely dissipated.

Meyer Schapiro's famous description of the Philadelphia *Bathers* (pl. XI) was written in defiance of critics for whom the theme was understood simply as a pretext for the painter's investigations into compositional structure, perspectival construction, and the play of color and light. Schapiro, by contrast, found all these elements profoundly meaningful, not just formally but in a psychosexual sense as well. He writes:

> It is the largest of Cézanne's pictures and because it is also the most formal in aspect, it has been cited often as an example of his ideal of composition and his restoration of classic monumentality after its lapse during the nineteenth century. It is exceptional among his work, however, in the marked symmetry and the adaptation of the nude forms to the triangular pattern of the trees and river. There is here, I believe, a search for constraining forms, an over-determined order which has to do with Cézanne's anxiety about women. Beautiful as it is, the composition is not the typical Renaissance pyramid. . . . The triangle here is a form of constraint, with another expression than the older solemn design. . . .
>
> In freeing himself from his troubled fantasy, Cézanne transposed the early erotic themes into less disturbing "classic" objects, nudes whose set postures and un-erotic surface, taken from the frozen world of art school and museum, make them seem purely instruments of his art. But something of the original anxiety is reflected in the arbitrariness and intensity of the means of control.[23]

The formalism of the bathers, then, their seeming indifference to eroticized visual pleasure, their strict structures, are *not* the sign of Cézanne's abandonment or normalization of a troubled sexual life but rather are precisely the measure of the sexual anxieties out of which they were born. They are not the sign that the perturbations of the early work have been set aside in his later career but the signs of precisely how hard Cézanne must work to keep them from being visible on the picture surface.

Sublimation also structures Theodore Reff's reading of the formal workings of the bather series: he sees a redirection of libidinal investment not simply in the transition from early to late period in Cézanne's oeuvre but also in Cézanne's ongoing reconception of the theme of bathers up until the end of his career. Tracing the stylistic development of the series of *Large Bathers* from the Barnes version (pl. IX) through the London version (pl. X) and finally to the Philadelphia version, Reff notes a progressive refinement of conception—an increase in the number of figures, a reduction of size of bathers in relation to landscape, a greater distinction among the groups of figures, a movement from a frieze-like arrangement to a division into pyramidal clusters, etc. More than mere tinkerings,

> [t]hese slight compositional changes ultimately have a far-reaching effect, *as the corporeality of the first version is gradually transformed into the spirituality of the third.* The larger, more expansive figures of the first, some of them overtly sensual in posture, give way to the smaller, emotionally neutral figures of the third, whose poses are calmer and clearly constrained by the pyramidal groupings. In the

same way, the congested, agitated landscape of the first, with its dramatic contrasts of trees, clouds, and sky, is replaced by the serenely spacious setting of the third, whose soaring trees form an arch reminiscent of Gothic vaulting. Even in execution the opaque, heavily encrusted texture of the first seems coarse in contrast to the half-transparent, thinly painted surface of the third, whose untouched areas and incisive lines create a flickering, delicate effect. But it is above all in its coloring that the latter achieves its dreamlike otherworldliness: the same pale tones of tan, gray, green and blue, above all of blue, pervade the sky, water, and foliage, suffusing them with a common cool atmosphere, without the dramatic tension of the earlier versions.[24] (my emphasis)

In arguing that the evolution of Cézanne's bather paintings is marked by a shift from corporeality to spirituality, from sensuality to neutrality, from agitation to calm, from opacity to transparency, from warm colors to cool, Reff echoes Schapiro, for he finds in these formal and technical choices the painter's insistent, even desperate, attempt to bring under control his messy and passionate impulses vis-à-vis his early subject matter, resulting in works with an "air of tense, repressed sensuality."[25]

Both interpretive models—the ones that privilege the purely visual address of the paintings and the ones that organize themselves around the model of sublimation—result in a reading of the works as unerotic in their final state: for the formalists, this is the result of a successful repression of youthful passions and melodramatic literary themes, while for Schapiro, it is the sign of Cézanne's attempts to sublimate his desire and fear of women. (However, as I suggest below, the success of this repression is less certain for Reff.) But in neither case does the reading sit easily: in neither case, in other words, does this claim of the bathers' lack of eroticism ring true. Note, for example, the language that Fritz Novotny uses to assert the superiority of Cézanne's landscapes over his bathers: "Whatever significance these pictures [of bathers] have in the history of painting, they are not the works that represent the consummation of Cézanne's career. For that we must turn to the turbulent, ecstatic last view of Mont Saint-Victoire in the distance—the stirring climax of Cézanne's art, together with the late forest landscapes of timeless peace and breathless quiet."[26] By isolating the works from the rest of Cézanne's practice, Novotny attempts to limit their significance, to make their strangeness less important in our view of the artist. However, his text is haunted by that strangeness. Novotny's choice of words suggests the persistence of an erotic element in Cézanne's bathers, a suggestion that seems simultaneously to provoke an anxious denial: one might say, in fact, that the author's repression of the eroticism of the bathers erupts into the language used to describe the mountains and landscapes of Cézanne's last years, which he characterizes as "turbulent," "climactic," "ecstatic," etc. For Schapiro, too, the eroticism of the bathers is an ambiguous, always-present element, despite his reading of the Philadelphia *Bathers* as finally having transmuted those impulses. This is due, in large part, to the instability of the concept of sublimation as such: the paradox is that, according to Freud's writings on the topic, it would seem that in the case of sublimation the drive can either be satisfied or successfully repressed. But in other places, Freud suggests such satisfaction or repression is not possible.[27] Perhaps it is not surprising, then, that the erotic element seems constantly to reemerge in Schapiro's sublimatory reading as a thing that must be accounted for.

The most sustained analysis of the bather paintings to date—Mary Louise Krumrine's *Paul Cézanne:*

The Bathers, a study done in conjunction with a 1989 exhibition that brought together over 130 paintings, watercolors, drawings, and prints on the theme—depends heavily on the type of psychosexual narratives that Schapiro and Reff employed to such great effect. In her contribution, Krumrine traces what she refers to as Cézanne's syntax of figures, read through their poses, body types, and arrangements in groups, starting with the artist's earliest figural compositions.[28] Through this taxonomic study of poses, she finds a recurrence of types over the course of Cézanne's career, leading her to read into the later, enigmatic bathers the more overt eroticism and violence of the earlier images, the temptations of Saint Anthony, the modern Olympias, the Bathshebas, etc. She argues that "Cézanne returned time and again to the bathers as a way of confronting, expressing, and finally controlling his changing attitude toward women and resolving his other psychological complexities, particularly his doubts about his own sexual identity."[29] Raising the specter of Cézanne's strange biography, filled with tales of his fears of women and sexual anxieties, Krumrine explains in this case not the formal structures of the pictures—as Reff and Schapiro do—but the logic of their content: the repetitions and returns of characters take on the qualities of unconscious operations, rooted in libidinal investments and past traumas. Krumrine's account, like Reff's and Schapiro's before hers, serves another important function as well: by grounding the later bather images in the early work—by seeing the late, transcendent style as the overdetermined outcome of the erotics and violence of his early narrative paintings—all three scholars make Cézanne's oeuvre a logical whole that is marked by a conceptual continuity rather than merely a stylistic one. In other words, whatever the visual or formal differences—whatever the sense of radical break—between Cézanne's work of the 1870s and the 1890s, there is, they argue, an ideational unity that allows us to imagine Cézanne's project as a singular one, one emphatically *not* marked by shifts and redirections. However, where for the formalist writers, biography existed as a parallel and reinforcing text to an overriding visual analysis of the works, and where for Schapiro a psychobiographical reading of the works was always subtended by an insistence on seeing these subjective, psychological impulses as expressed through a historically-bounded range of possible visual languages, for Krumrine (as for the majority of writers on the bathers) the relation between biography and image is both transparent and circular: the content of the images is used to prove Cézanne's anxieties, fears, and violent passions toward women, and those same stories of his psychosexual traumas are then used to explain the pictures.[30] Moreover, nothing intervenes to structure this relation between image and unconscious.

If the formalist scholars and those scholars such as Schapiro and Reff who depended on the notion of sublimation to structure their readings provided models for understanding the effects of Cézanne's technical and compositional decisions in his paintings of *baigneuses* and *baigneurs,* they did so only by refusing to see the bathers as erotic in their final aspect. Conversely, if Krumrine's study freely admits the erotic quality of the works, she does so only through the analysis of the content—iconographic and taxonomic accountings of bodies—rather than through an argument based on form, technique, and composition. But it seems to me that the eroticism of the bathers is *both* overt *and* an effect of his formal play: the question, then, is whether there is a way of reading Cézanne's bathers that combines a formal accounting of his technique with an

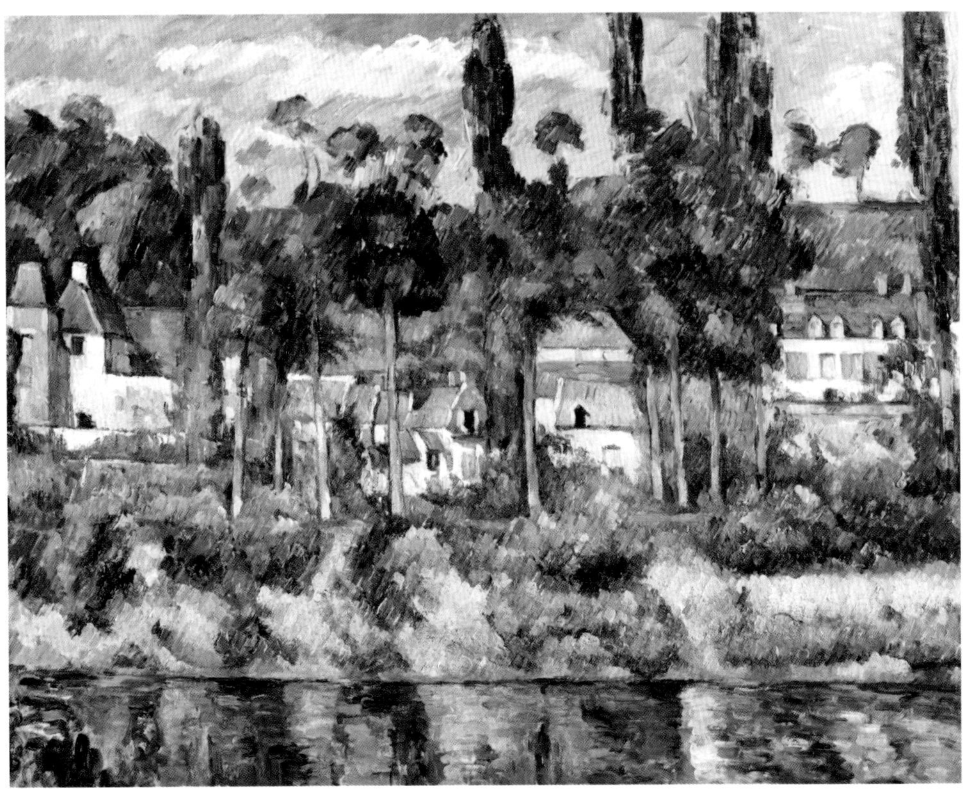

17. Cézanne, *The Château at Médan*, ca. 1880. Oil on canvas, 59 x 72 cm. Burrell Collection, Glasgow, Scotland.

acknowledgement that the bathers are, in the end, meant to communicate the erotic. Three writers have suggested an answer to that question: Theodore Reff, Tamar Garb, and T. J. Clark.

THE MATTER OF BODIES

Theodore Reff first proposed that Cézanne's brush marks—the material traces of his encounter with the canvas—should be understood as the vehicle for the communication of the erotic in his painting in a 1962 article on Cézanne's "constructive stroke." There, he argued that Cézanne's method of building up his canvases out of a web of fine, parallel strokes such as we see in *The Château at Médan* (ca. 1880)—a process that had previously been understood by critics as one of gradual refinement, under the influence of Pissarro, of his early, quasi-baroque style to the later, cool formalism of his characteristic landscapes and still lifes—should in fact be interpreted quite differently (fig. 17).[31] The constructive stroke, argues Reff, did *not* appear, as might be expected, in these more neutral paintings of mountains and apples; rather, it was first put into use in a consistent manner in a set of pictures that included *The Temptation of Saint Anthony, The Eternal Feminine,* and *The Battle of Love I* (figs. 18–20). As such, argues Reff, "rather than an analytic device adapted to the observation of natural phenomena, as it is usually interpreted, [the constructive stroke] would appear a pure invention originating in works done entirely from imagination."[32] Reff goes on to claim that the constructive stroke should be understood as a sign of Cézanne's desire to sublimate the messy (and often violent) eroticism of his earlier work:

> By systematizing even the size and direction of the brushstroke, normally the most spontaneous element in painting, he affirms a desire for complete consciousness of all that enters the work, leaving nothing to accident or whim. And this in turn reflects an effort to master within himself the turbulent impulses that had led him to choose such themes of struggle, temptation and ironic adoration in the first place. It is as if he strove to incorporate these hidden feelings into the domain of constructive professional activity, submitting them to strict aesthetic requirements through which he might ultimately neutralize them.[33]

For the formalist scholars, the constructive stroke was understood as a means by which Cézanne banished romantic and baroque expressions in favor of a cool classicism that would obtain for the rest of his

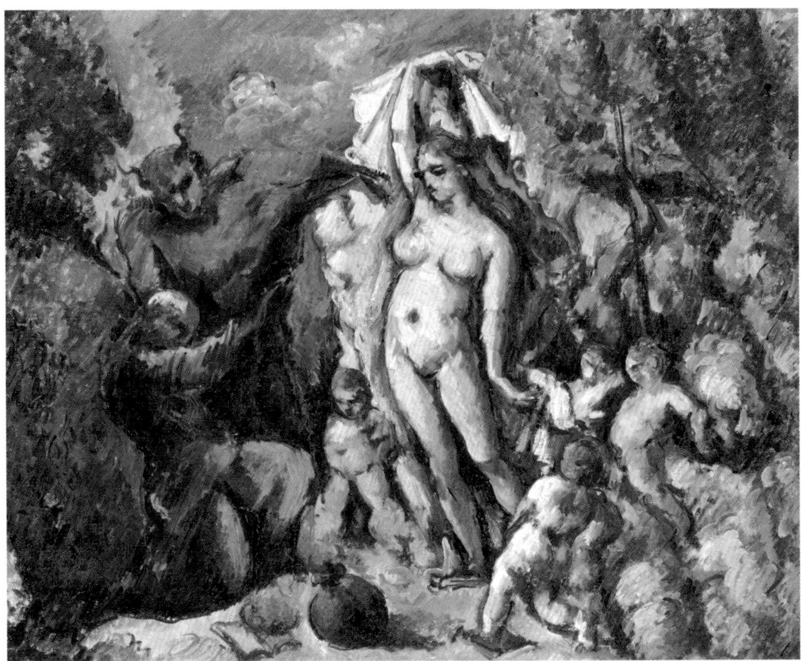

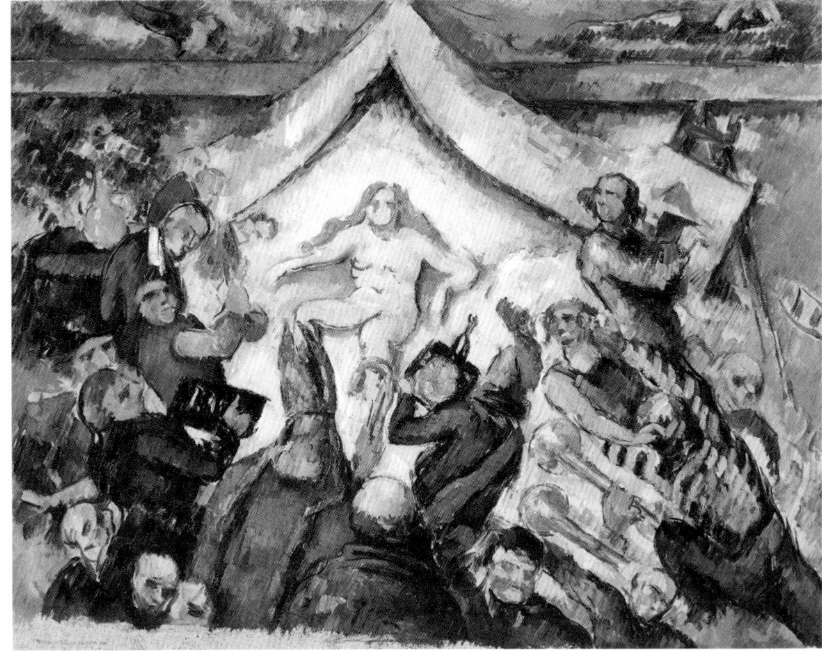

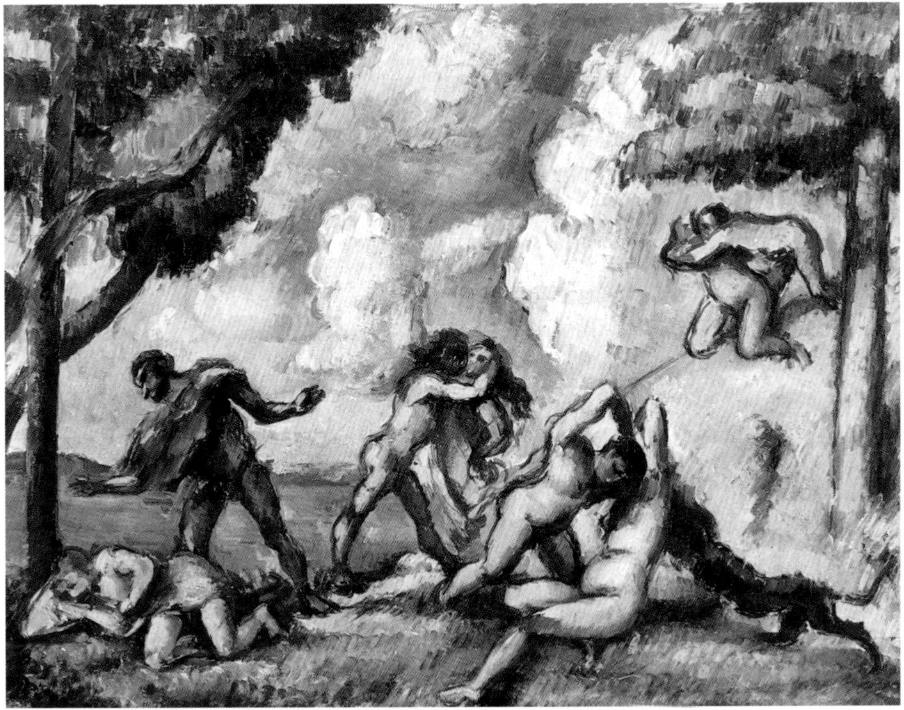

18. (*above left*) Cézanne, *Temptation of St. Anthony,* ca. 1877. Oil on canvas, 47 x 56 cm. Musée d'Orsay, Paris.

19. (*above right*) Cézanne, *The Eternal Feminine,* ca. 1877. Oil on canvas, 43 x 53 cm. J. Paul Getty Museum, Malibu, Calif.

20. (*left*) Cézanne, *The Battle of Love I,* 1879–80. Oil on canvas, 42 x 55 cm. Private collection.

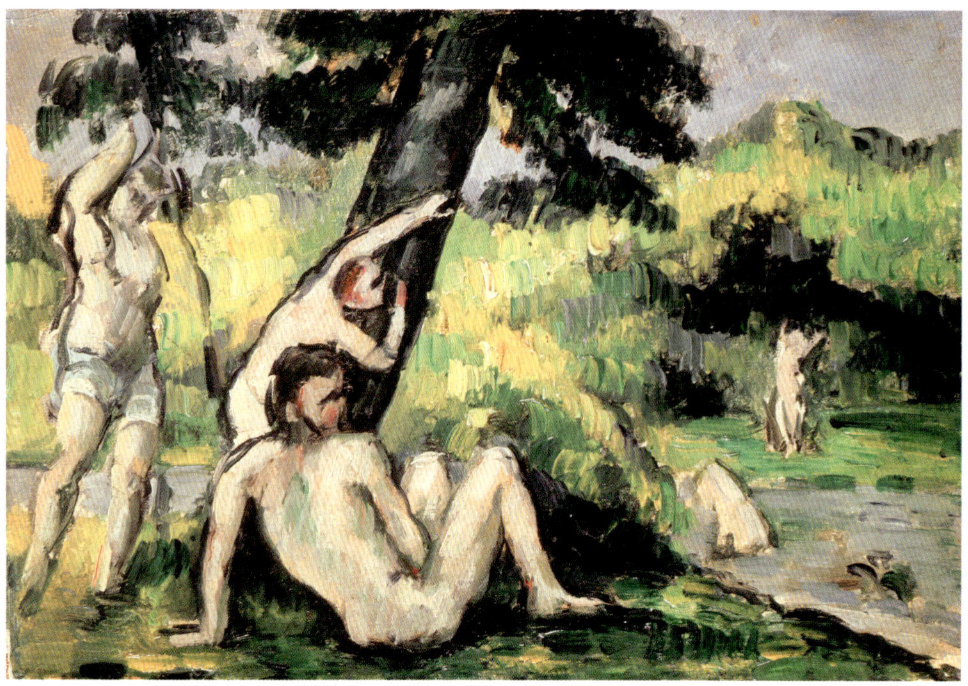

21. Cézanne, *La Baignade*, 1875–77. Oil on canvas, 19 x 27 cm. Private collection.

career and, for Reff, it was understood as the sign of Cézanne's struggle to master his desires, a struggle in which he would ultimately triumph in his late work but that was rooted, crucially, in the early, vehemently unclassical, paintings.[34] But, in fact, neither of these narratives is precisely correct. Subsequent scholarship on the period—as well as the publication of John Rewald's catalogue raisonné in 1996—would suggest that it is neither in the later landscapes and still lifes *nor* in the "fantasy compositions" like *The Battle of Love, Temptation of Saint Anthony,* and *Eternal Feminine* that the so-called constructive stroke first appears. Rather, it is in the bathers.[35] The technique is worked out in pictures such as *La Baignade* of 1875–77 (especially in the background foliage and the figure of the seated male nude in the foreground) and in the activated surface of the Matisse *Three Bathers* of circa 1876–77, and Cézanne only begins to use this characteristic "touch" in his landscapes and still lifes, and in imaginary compositions like *Eternal Feminine,* starting in 1877 or so (fig. 21). The constructive stroke, then, was not a way of leaving something behind, of sublimating a desire, but of mobilizing something in the positive sense: in other words, this eroticized touch first appears *not* in relation to a set of paintings with subject matter that Cézanne, in his artistic evolution and encounter with impressionism, was in the process of setting aside or even disavowing—these "literary" themes of sexuality and threat—but in relation to a motif that would occupy him until the final years of his life. The constructive stroke represents the complexities of his most mature work.

With this matter of chronology in mind, I would argue that if Cézanne's characteristic brushwork signified the erotic, it was not, as Reff proposes, a sublimated desire that was at stake. On the contrary, and in the context of a critical field that, in the late nineteenth century, was fully invested in the idea of the artist's subjective encounter with the world as the "content" of his materialized mark on the surface of the canvas, Cézanne's brushstroke was an overt sign of the erotic, a very public proposal for how the erotic nude might be reconceived after Manet's *Olympia,* which had laid bare the paucity of the genre.[36] Not a sign of private and fully interiorized psychic struggle, but a declaration of what might constitute visual pleasure in the painting of the erotic nude. And, frankly, it may have been the *only* sign of the erotic that obtained in these paintings, paintings in which bodies are lumpy and fat and flattened and "bruised," their skin infected with blues and greens and yellows instead of healthy pink, round, smooth, voluptuous, and available to the hungry gaze.

. . .

Tamar Garb writes that her decision to tackle the bather paintings was a way of leaving aside both the formalist and psychobiographical approaches that have up to now dominated the interpretive terrain in the hope of providing a feminist reading of the works.[37] Or rather one might say that Garb's is an attempt to reintegrate visuality and sexuality in a reading of the bathers, those two terms having been separated in previous scholarship. "Neither of these readings of Cézanne's work [the formalist or the psychobiographical] is grounded in an assertion of painting as a bodily function, a supremely physical act," she writes. "For all its concentration on form, the formalist account is idealist and abstracted, discounting the physicality of the process of painting and the sensory and erotic dimensions of viewing. The iconographers and psychobiographers on the other hand are concerned with imagery and with the drives and repressed desires that produce that imagery."[38]

Thus, Garb sets out to answer Maurice Merleau-Ponty's call for a corporeal account of painting.[39] In his 1945 essay "Cézanne's Doubt," Merleau-Ponty elaborated his understanding of perception as being a function of our lived, bodily experience of the world, a bodily experience that includes spatial relationships, touch and movement, sense of time and color, and other kinaesthetic sensation.[40] His account forged a path between that of the formalists and that of the psychobiographers—the meaning of Cézanne's work, he contends, can neither be determined from his life nor from art history (i.e., considerations of influences, technique, even the artist's own claims for it)—by emphasizing the embodied nature of vision.[41] It is not sufficient, however, to simply extend the philosopher's phenomenological account of Cézanne's search for sensation to the bather images because, first, Merleau-Ponty's account hinges, rhetorically, on a plein-air encounter between painter and landscape, and the *baigneurs* did not arise out of such a confrontation, and second (and more importantly) because if painting is a corporeal activity for Merleau-Ponty, the body in which it is grounded is not a gendered body. Rather, the philosopher speaks of a universal condition of subjectivity that remains, implicitly, masculine.[42]

Garb's own, feminist analysis focuses on the fraught relationship between the artist's touch—his flurry of brushstrokes that constitute each image—and the bodies that seem barely to emerge from the primordial substrate of pigment. In contrast to, for example, Renoir's *Large Bathers* from 1887, with its familiar juxtaposition of Arcadian natural setting and idealized female body, smoothly painted, voluptuous, unblemished, and above all sexy, Cézanne's female figures, such as those in the Philadelphia *Bathers* (pls. XII and XIII), are much more cursory and awkward, with little indication of their features and bodily aspect. Even more alarming is the way these bodies seep into each other, so that two figures can share buttocks and shoulders, others can share hand and hair, and all seem to fade out at the extremities, with hands and feet often left incomplete. Such eccentricities of depiction are no less apparent, Garb argues, in the Art Institute of Chicago male bathers; they are the result, she argues, of Cézanne's overriding formal or conceptual impetus, namely the capturing of visual sensations in pictorial form: "As with the female bathers, the bodies of the male figures have been subjected to a field of sensation which obliterates, obscures, and smudges their bodily presence, at times collapsing the difference between figure and ground and subsuming the body into a profusion of paint which creates an equivalence between flesh and foliage, solid structure and surrounding space."[43]

In the face of a formal method that obliterated sexual difference in its search for a system of mark-making that could adequately represent the immediacy of visual sensation, "reducing the signs of sexuality to a schematic and cursory form of notation," Cézanne was forced to find other ways of inscribing that lost sexuality within his bather images.[44] In short, "in Cézanne's bather paintings, the bodies alone are not an adequate guarantor of difference. If sexual difference is to be secured in his pictures, then it needs to be established elsewhere than in its inscription on the body."[45] That "elsewhere," Garb says, was in the pictorial structure of the image: in the arrangements of the male bathers in horizontal, frieze-like patterns that heighten the phallic nature of the figures and of the female bathers within pyramidal schemes that purportedly evoke the female sex.

Garb's account allows us to understand the way in which the formal tensions of Cézanne's paintings of the nude—the resistance that the artificial, overdetermined compositional structures provide against the threat of total painterly dissolution imposed by Cézanne's nervous brushstroke—could produce a meaning that exceeded the limits of the visual. Where Roger Fry, speaking of the Philadelphia and London *Large Bathers,* identifies the rigidity of their compositional schema—too obtrusive, too determinative of the bodies' forms—as the source of the paintings' dry and willful aspect, and where Meyer Schapiro identifies those same compositional formulae as significant only in terms of the repressed desires for which they compensate, Garb points out how such formal choices actually contributed to the meaning of these works in a positive sense, as the reassertion of sexual difference in the face of painting that seemed to put the very terms of painting the nude in the nineteenth century at risk.[46] Not simply source of failure or an index of repression, the compositions play a constitutive role in the production of meaning in these paintings, a meaning moreover not limited to a personal or psychic need on the part of the artist but readable and comprehensible in the visual culture of Cézanne's time.

What is curious about Garb's elegant and convincing argument, however, is the way her thesis echoes some of the earliest modernist criticism of Cézanne's work. In explaining how this radical practice came into being—how this utterly conventional and thoroughly nineteenth-century man managed to make paintings that almost upended the Western tradition of the nude by creating images no longer invested in the coherence of the body as a vessel for painterly and erotic pleasure—Garb writes:

> The pictorial demands of a modernist practice with its assault on conventional modes of representation (its rationalist scaffolding, traditional perspective and rigid separation between figure and ground) has indeed brought with it a disruption at the level of the sexual. As the figure and the landscape are subsumed into a new mode of looking—one which stems from a psychic and bodily encounter with the world of physical sensations, a visceral witnessing of a world in which time, space and matter can be represented in paint and translated into color—the body and the landscape are irreparably altered. *The fluidity of the paint constructs a fluid sexuality, the imaginative projection of a screen of sensations destroys difference and the assault on definition produces, inadvertently, a sexuality which seeps outside of its conventional margins, its narrow normative structures.*[47]

For Garb, this dissolution of sexual difference, effected through the notational brushwork, the wedding of figure and ground, and the anatomical insufficiencies of the male and female form is both inevitable and inadvertent: "They [Cézanne's gaucheries] are not necessarily intentional or deliberate," she contends. "It was the intensity of engagement at the level of the visual which produced the ambiguities at the level of the sexual."[48]

How far is this formulation from those of turn-of-the-century critics who claimed that Cézanne's technical insufficiencies were simply the result of his excessive sincerity, that is to say his commitment to the visual, his drive to realize his sensations? Maurice Denis, for example, speaking of Cézanne's attempt to synthesize empirical observation with "sensibility," observes that Cézanne, "constrained already by his need for synthesis to adopt disconcerting simplifications, . . . deforms his design still further by the necessity for expression and by his scrupulous sincerity. It is herein that we find the motives for the gaucheries for which Cézanne is so often reproached, and herein lies the explanation of that practice of naïveté and ungainliness common to his disciples and imitators."[49] R. F. Rivière and J. F. Schnerb reiterated the idea when they wrote: "It is not that he defended the superficial mistakes in his drawing, mistakes which were neither negligence nor inability, but which were evidence of an excessive sincerity . . . [,] of an excessive defiance of purely manual address, a distaste of all movement where the eye directs the hand without the intervention of thought."[50] By taking for granted the truth value of the modernist account of Cézanne's search for a visual equivalent of his *petit sensation*—especially ironic given that she sets out to explain a group of paintings not conceived as transcriptions of objective reality—Garb's argument replicates the ideological stakes of that narrative. For in her argument, the function of Cézanne's brushwork—of the liquidity of paint that seems to melt bodies into their surroundings, of the harmonization of color over the pictorial skin so that flesh, foliage, and sky are made of the same chromatic stuff, all these issues that contribute to the erotic signification of these works—is simply understood as an incidental outcome of Cézanne's larger project.[51] That is, of Cézanne's project as adumbrated from Maurice Denis onward, a project that privileges the visual to the exclusion—except as inadvertent trace—of gender or sexuality. Although Garb's reading performs the important task of introducing the issue of gender, sexual difference, and erotic pleasure into our discussion of Cézanne's paintings—in a way that is not restricted to private, psychical investments—it is limited by the fundamental misrecognition of Cézanne's project by modernist accounts. Eroticism, and the discourse of the erotic nude, is not a tangential concern or accidental outcome of Cézanne's method of painting: it is that project's central concern.

. . .

If Garb's argument proposes a way of reading Cézanne's bathers that is not dependent on the concept of sublimation—by insisting that the articulation of sexual difference and thus the conditions for erotic pleasure in representation are utterly apparent in the very structure of the paintings rather than displaced or repressed—T. J. Clark's reading bypasses the concept by arguing that the images spring from a theoretical moment invested in the ability of representation to be equal to the operations of desire.[52]

Clark's essay on Cézanne's large bather paintings (the *Grandes baigneuses*) is, he says, an attempt to provide a "materialist" interpretation of the works, one that proposes an underlying sympathy between aesthetic modernism and philosophic materialism as systems of thought. It is titled "Freud's Cézanne," signaling the author's interest in the historical coincidence of Cézanne's pictorial investigations and Freud's early theorization of the unconscious, in which the psychoanalyst sought to understand the unconscious in wholly anatomical or physical terms. By focusing his own analysis on this early, materialist Freud—a figure for whom sublimation was unthinkable because the effect of desire would be readable in the very substance of the body, not transmuted or reified or idealized in any way—Clark wants to avoid the more typical Freudian readings of Cézanne. Rather, tracing Cézanne's own interest in positivist and materialist thought, Clark wants "to see Cézanne as belonging to the world of Helmholtz, Charcot, and the *Revue encyclopédique.* As positivist and materialist in the strong senses of those words. Freudian in the way of Freud in 1895."[53]

What this means, for Clark, is that the *Large Bathers* are Cézanne's attempt to represent the drama of sexual differentiation—of the gendering of the subject—not as an imaginary, abstract process of thought but as a set of physical effects, as a matter of bodily constitution and dissolution. The Barnes painting is for him a translation of "that moment in the dissolution of the Oedipus complex at which the threat of castration is so intense and overwhelming that the male child is unable to take the exit into repression—and instead remains frozen in a world where, in spite of everything, the Father is absent and the phallic mother's return is awaited."[54] The Philadelphia *Bathers,* on the other hand, characterized by the generalization of its figures, their rhyming and repetition, the "strict but obscure choreography" that seems to govern their arrangement and its air of tension, of constraint, translates, in material terms, the end result of this ascension to sexual difference, "the tragic positing of sexuality as fate."[55]

If Clark wants to avoid a "typical" Freudian reading of Cézanne—one that reads the artist's paintings and biography as evidence of the artist's sexual traumas and fear of human contact—it is only because he takes such an interpretation as given. In other words, he does not hesitate to identify the figure leaning against the tree in the Barnes painting as a surrogate for Cézanne himself, dreaming of the return of the phallic mother, of the erasure, in melancholic retrospect, of sexual difference. "You will gather," Clark writes at one point, "that if I saw it necessary or possible to psychoanalyze Cézanne, I would hazard the guess that in his case . . . the late *Bathers* were his effort to reconstitute a world of sexuality which, at some level, he had never left."[56] It is not, then, that Clark finds no purchase in this almost canonical reading of Cézanne's psyche. It is, rather, that he conceives the interest of these paintings to lie not in their psychic content as such but in the way the imagining of that psychic content takes place: as a materialist argument, in which the strange duplication of bodies, the melting of flesh into flesh—shared buttocks and shoulders, hands and hair—are evidence of Cézanne's attempt to "show us the body's interminable shifting and reconstruction in the space of desire," even as the artist insists on showing us that space literally, so that those moments of corporeal coalescence are visible at every stage.[57]

The prominence of theatrical metaphors in Clark's descriptions is striking: he continually refers to the Oedipal scenario, to the dramatis personae that populate the paintings, to scenes and stagings. For what Clark ultimately argues is that Cézanne's images represent tableaux of sexuality, of the Oedipal drama and its (ir)resolution.[58] For Clark, the stages of Freudian psychic development are set on their own stage, with different bodies acting out the different needs, desires, and fantasies of the artist, with the bubbling of paint signifying only metaphorically, as the *acheronta movebo*—the release from the powers of hell—of the artist's repressions.[59] The materialist arguments in these paintings, in other words, are solely a matter of form: of phallic mothers with penis heads, of bodies that share buttocks and shoulders, of dreaming figures and caring ones. Condensation and displacement have exact visual cognates in Cézanne's paintings. If fantasy is materialized in these paintings, it is in terms of the shape of the body, its distance from or proximity to other depicted bodies.

Clark's materialist account, though it never says so out loud, is to some extent invested in the language of phenomenology in arguing that the bathers are an extended meditation on the experience of being-in-the-world.[60] Yet Merleau-Ponty never imagined that this sort of imagining could simply go on "out there"—fully exteriorized from the imagining subject. Whatever the degree of Clark's agreement or disagreement with Merleau-Ponty on the specifics, it seems curious that in an argument that hinges on the idea of bodily empathy, of fantasies of contact and separation, there is no mention of the body doing the fantasizing: Cézanne's body, his adult body, not that of some fantasized childhood, in other words. What I mean to say is that the idea of Cézanne's touch, of his physical engagement with the picture surface, is left out of Clark's account. And Clark's failure to account for this—his insistence that Cézanne's own meditations about the sensual and sensory experiences of bodily interactions occur only on the level of form, not in terms of touch—means that his account also avoids the issue of *matière,* of the physical substance of paint, both as a formal effect as well as a trace of the artist's process. Clark's is a materialism without *matière.*

But Cézanne's bathers, I would argue, are not simply another *scene,* primal or otherwise, from the Western tradition of the nude—they are not, as Clark wants to claim, genealogically linked to Titian's dramaturgy in *Diana and Acteon* or *Diana and Callisto.*[61] On the contrary. If we can be sure of nothing else about Cézanne's work, we can be confident that he had already said his piece when it came to the idea of conceiving of the erotic in theatrical terms—in terms of actors and tableaux, of bodies and their shapes, in other words: that was the lesson of *A Modern Olympia,* done in 1873–74, just two years before *Bathers at Rest III* and *Three Bathers.*

STAGING THE EROTIC

In 1874, Cézanne took part in the first impressionist exhibition. He showed three works, according to the exhibition catalogue: *The House of the Hanged Man* (fig. 22), a landscape study, also from the area around Auvers (likely *The House of Père Lacroix, Auvers-sur-Oise,* 1873) (fig. 23), and *A Modern Olympia.*[62] None of these choices was accidental, by any means. All three contributions served to declare Cézanne's artistic allegiances as well as to announce his adversarial position in relation to the emerging avant-garde in Paris. The two landscapes—*The House of Père Lacroix* and *House of the Hanged Man*—were souvenirs of his time spent in Auvers and Pontoise painting alongside Pissarro, whom he would consider a mentor and teacher until the end of his career and who was instrumental in bringing him into the impressionist circle in the first place. (The association between the two artists was reinforced by the fact that Pissarro himself also showed a number of Auvers-period landscapes during the exhibition.) But the paintings, with their opposing

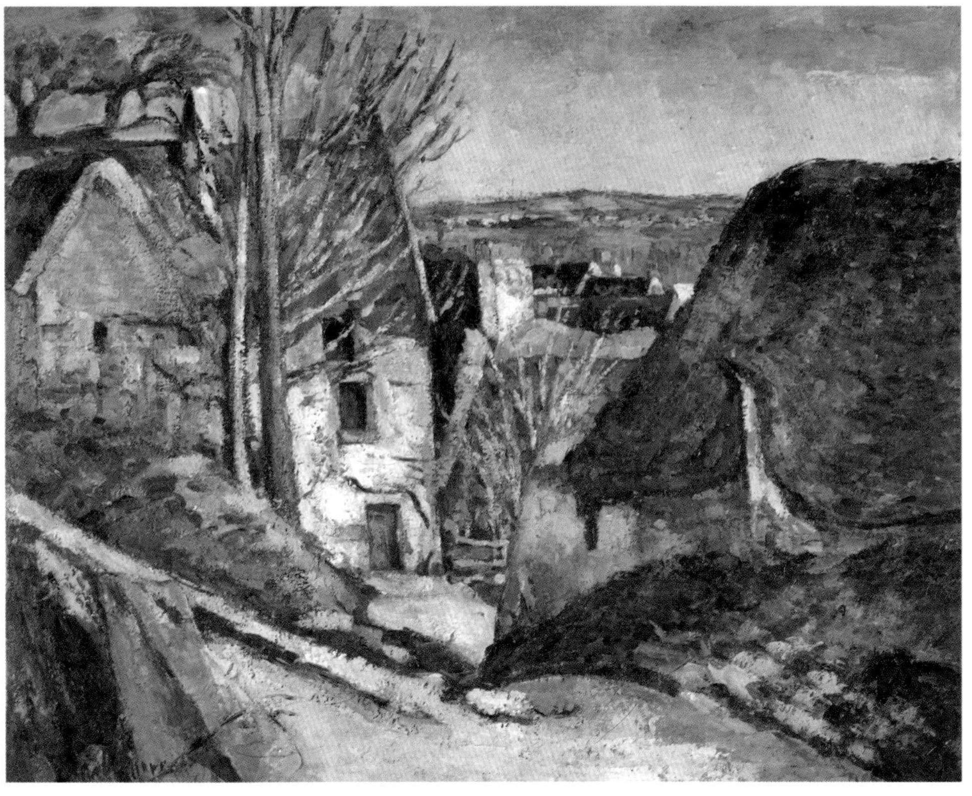

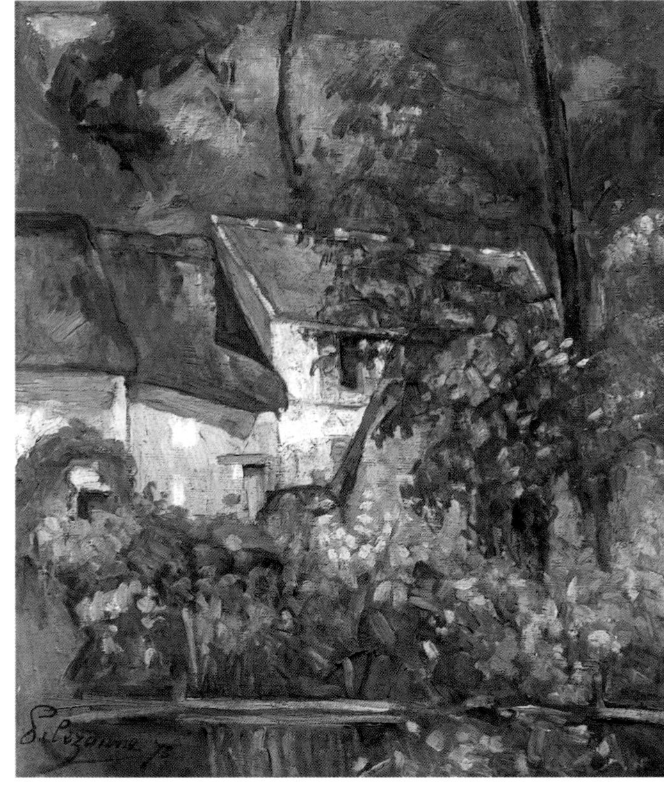

22. Cézanne, *The House of the Hanged Man*, ca. 1873. Oil on canvas 55 x 66 cm. Musée d'Orsay, Paris.

23. Cézanne, *The House of Père Lacroix, Auvers-sur-Oise*, 1873. Oil on canvas, 61.5 x 51 cm. Chester Dale Collection, National Gallery of Art, Washington, D.C.

styles, allowed Cézanne to declare both his competence in the techniques of impressionist brushwork as well as his desire to stand apart or even distance himself from the movement. Note the demotion of architecture in favor of the play of brushwork in the foliage and the water's reflection in the foreground of *The House of Père Lacroix* in contrast to the solid stoniness, the muddy and sandy dryness of the built-up, earth-toned pigment in *House of the Hanged Man:* where one exemplifies the flickering virtuosity of the impressionist hand, and its lack of concern for structural scaffoldings, the other emphasizes a ponderous materiality that is emphatically unimpressionist.

A Modern Olympia was, if anything, even more declarative a submission: it was a painting in which Cézanne wrote his own artistic biography, positioning himself in relation to the artists who had set the terms for avant-garde practice in the 1870s and specifically as the inheritor of a radical realist project.[63] The painting's title and subject matter—involving a triangulation of naked woman, black maid, and bourgeois man—obviously referenced Manet's *Olympia,* a painting so important to Cézanne that, late in his life, he declared that "One must always have this before one's eyes. . . . It's a new order of painting. Our renaissance dates from it" (fig. 24).[64] Manet was hardly the only touchstone here, however. The composition of *A Modern Olympia* derives from Delacroix's *Death of Sardanapalus:* baroque interior, white expanse of bedclothing, figure of sensual indulgence elevated in

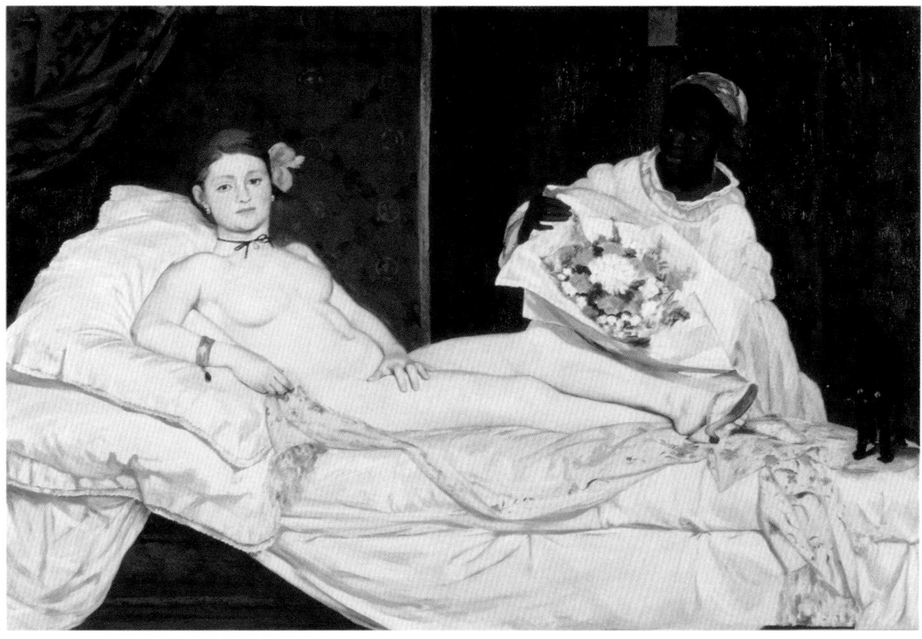

24. Édouard Manet, *Olympia,* 1863. Oil on canvas, 130.5 x 190.0 cm. Musée d'Orsay, Paris.

25. Eugène Delacroix, *Death of Sardanapalus,* 1827. Oil on canvas, 392 x 496 cm. Musée du Louvre, Paris.

the background (fig. 25).[65] But where Delacroix's exoticized depiction of the Assyrian king positions him on the bed stretched out like an idol, passively viewing, with sadistic pleasure, the writhing nude bodies at his feet, Cézanne comically reverses the scenario. His male figure is buttoned up and ordinary (it is, perhaps, a self-portrait), and he sits in the foreground, tense with anticipation, looking at the nude female who now takes the venerated place on the frothy white marshmallow of a bed.[66] The virility of Sardanapalus, his sexual power, is replaced by the banality—and even impotence—of Cézanne's male protagonist, who seems more shy voyeur than Casanova. Finally, the painting declares Cézanne's allegiance to Courbet: in an earlier version entitled *A Modern Olympia (The Pasha)* (ca. 1870), the male figure is not a self-portrait, as in *A Modern Olympia,* but rather is likely a portrait of Courbet, with his powerful, slightly portly, build, full head of hair, and curly, even "Assyrian" beard

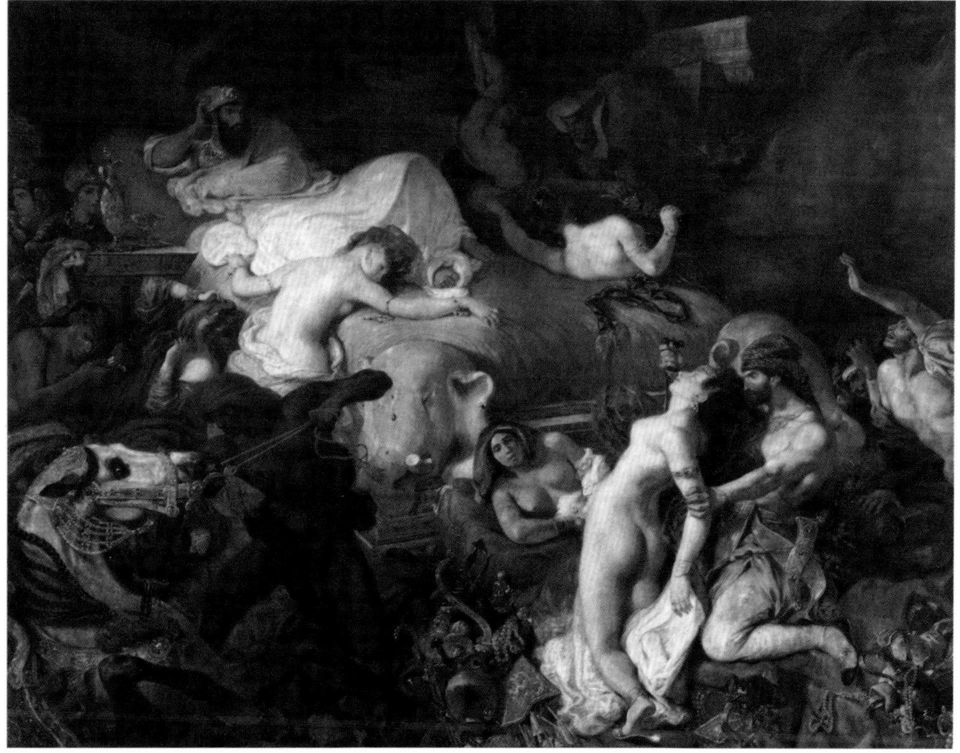

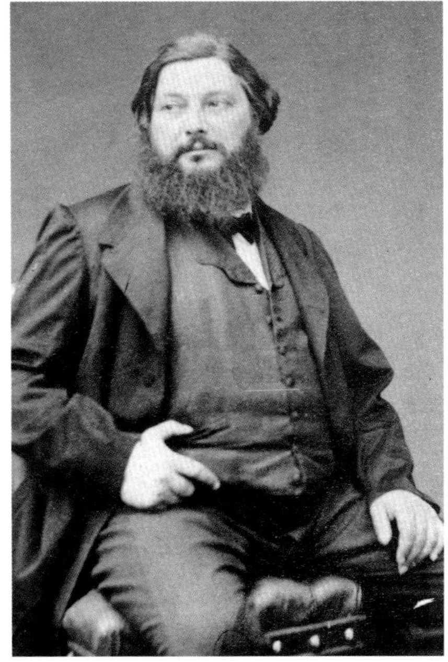

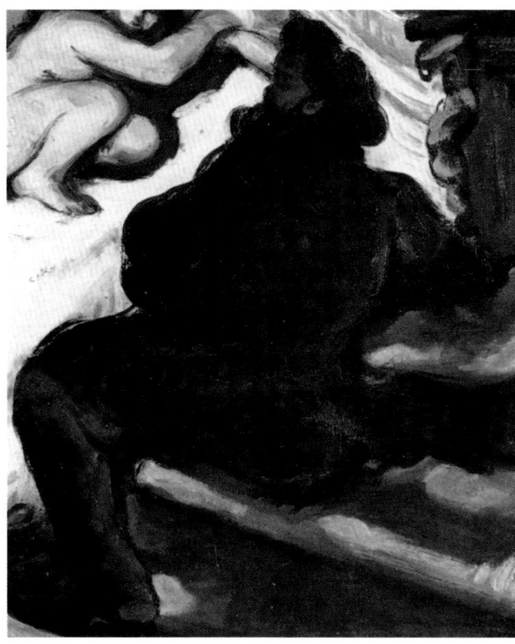

26. Pierre Petit, *Courbet,* n.d. Photograph. Bibliothèque nationale de France, Paris.

27. Detail of Cézanne, *A Modern Olympia (The Pasha),* ca. 1870.

(figs. 26 and 27). Moreover, in replacing the cool detachment of Manet's *Olympia*—in which the relationship between nude (prostitute) and viewer (male client) is scandalously implied but never stated—with a much more frank assertion of male desire in the face of female flesh, Cézanne seems to recall Courbet's own critique of *Olympia.* Describing its excessive flatness and lack of modeling as "the Queen of Spades stepped out of her bath," Courbet railed, too, against its lack of overt eroticism, and "corrected" this deficiency in his own painting, *Woman with a Parrot* of 1866, with its hothouse sexiness and lascivious gaze (fig. 28).[67] (Manet, of course, shot back in this battle of artistic conception with his own *Woman with a Parrot,* the *Young Lady in 1866* [fig. 29]. In the face of Courbet's frank fleshiness, Manet's painting presents a woman dressed from chin to ankle in an elegant dressing gown; the only hint of erotic escapade is the cool, enigmatic look in her eye and the man's monocle hanging around her neck.[68])

Cézanne, then, brought together the most relevant artistic personalities of an earlier generation—Delacroix, Courbet, and Manet—in his *Modern Olympia;* thus, whatever comedy is contained in the work, whatever caricatural aspects, whatever the stories of its origins as a dinner-party *blague,* the painting takes on the character of a manifesto.[69] But if these three figures were deemed most relevant by a young Cézanne, it was not simply in terms of their position within a newly emerging lineage of modern painting—and Cézanne's *Modern Olympia* was thus not merely imaging the younger artist's professional self-construction within the Parisian art scene. Rather, these were the three painters who had in many ways defined the stakes of the genre of the nude in the years leading up to 1874. (If a fourth figure—Ingres—seems conspicuously absent in this pantheon, it is perhaps not surprising, given the somewhat overdetermined place he occupied in Cézanne's thinking; the younger artist declared his hatred for Ingres's art more than once in his long career and made fun of it at every turn, despite relying, as I observe in chapter 4, on the older classicist in his notion of bodily deformation and eroticized pleasure.)

In other words, if *A Modern Olympia* is a manifesto—and specifically, a manifesto about the painting of the nude—it is one that was intent on defying the traditions of that genre, a genre that depended on imaginary encounters between viewers and depicted figures, a genre conditioned (in the eyes of late-nineteenth-century observers) by the theatricalization of sexual encounters in the form of the brothels and *maisons de luxe* of Paris, a genre that had always depended on the proximity of bodies to communicate its eroticism.[70] This farcical take on Manet's notorious

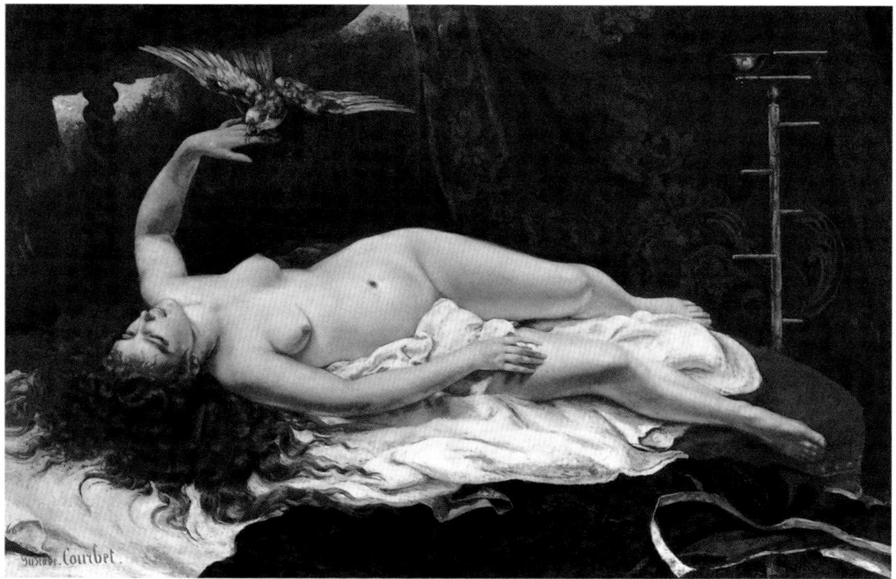

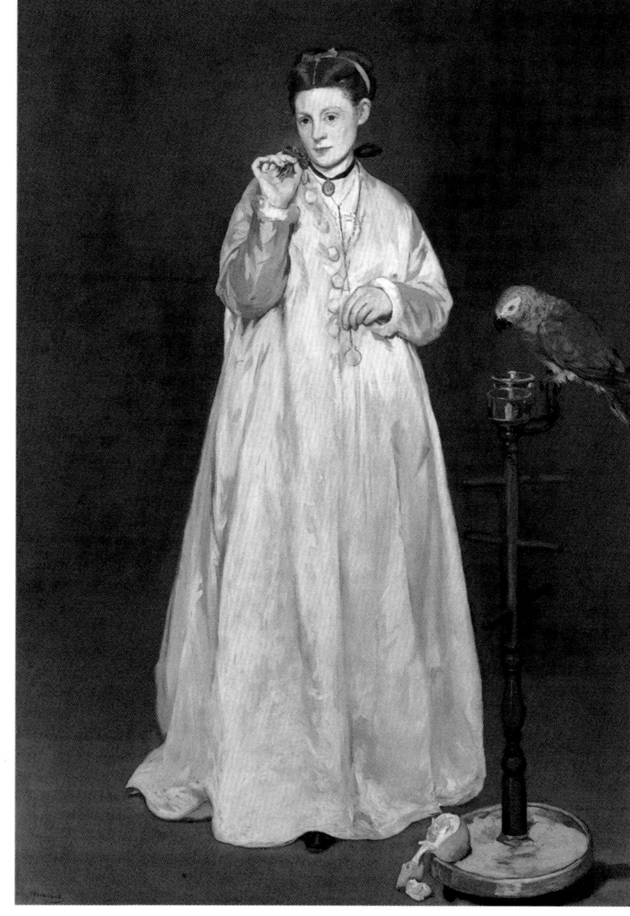

prostitute made plain what Cézanne thought of the erotic encounter conceived only in theatrical terms, in terms of corporeal drama.[71] He effectively announces his intentions in the way he organizes the picture as a sort of proscenium space, with heavy curtains and raised, frothy bed separating the object of desire from her suitor, who sits on the couch below looking, only looking. The flourish with which the black servant unveils this modern Olympia's body enhances the theatrical effect. And it is Olympia's body itself—or rather, I should say, the utter insufficiency of her body as an object of erotic contemplation—that signals to the viewer the gimlet eye that Cézanne is casting on this spectacle: folded almost in half, legs hiding torso from view, breasts just two twirls of the paintbrush, arms folded awkwardly over each other in a way that seems to occlude visual access, face crudely drawn, grin sardonic, this seductress does not conform to any conventions of the genre of the female nude.

A Modern Olympia is not an indictment of the possibilities of painting the nude *tout court,* but it is, indeed, evidence that Cézanne was a careful student of Manet's lessons. In the latter's *Olympia,* sex is scattered all over the surface of the image, finding no comfort in the inhospitable figure of the prostitute or in the metonymic substitutes around her.[72] Flowers are both a signifier of Olympia's sex and an indication of her male caller; the cat is explicitly phallic at the same time that it is a displacement of the female pubis; the black maid (traditionally the locus of the implied base sexu-

28. Gustave Courbet, *Woman with a Parrot,* 1866. Oil on canvas, 129.5 x 195.6 cm. Metropolitan Museum of Art, N.Y., H. O. Havemeyer Collection, bequest of Mrs. H. O. Havemeyer, 1929. 29.100.57.

29. Édouard Manet, *Young Lady in 1866,* 1866. Oil on canvas, 185.1 x 128.6 cm. Metropolitan Museum of Art, N.Y., gift of Erwin Davis, 1889. 89.21.3.

ality of the white nude in the Western tradition) is clothed; Olympia's clenched hand, which purports to cover and conceal, functions instead to reinforce the presence of her dangerous sexuality. And the body itself, mingling passages of carefully studied realism with broad areas of barely articulated form and inserting a suggestion of androgyny into a space normally reserved for the depiction of fetishized femininity, is hardly unambiguous either.

Cézanne's *Modern Olympia* took up this problematic, offering another body that was wholly inadequate to the task of representing, and thus containing, desire. But it did so in a qualitatively different way from Manet's painting: here, the erotic is not produced in the shuttled course of displacement between the clenched hand, the phallic cat, floral bouquet, and black maid. If pleasure is dislocated from the body and its substitutes, it is relocated in a wholly more mobile signifier: the paint-loaded brush as it moves over the picture surface. To say that Cézanne's girl on the bed has nothing going for her would be naïve, to put it another way. If the form of her body leaves something to be desired when it comes to late-nineteenth-century conventions of the nude, the way she is painted has something to offer: she is a lick of paint, almost a single stroke of the brush, and the paint itself is an oily impasto not apparent in other parts of the painting (pl. VII).[73] If she is meant to provoke a sensual response she does so not by her form but by the very *matière* that composes her figure.

THE EROTICS OF PAINT

This is the context in which we should understand Cézanne's exploration of the bather theme, which he began in earnest in 1874: in terms of a move away from presenting the erotic in terms of a theatrical interaction of bodies, this transfer of the signifier of desire from the bodies represented to the brushstroke, the material trace of the artist. We can see this operation at work in a series of bather compositions started in 1874—in other words, in the earliest sustained work on bathers that the artist produced—in which a shadowy figure appears in the bushes, turning the three women into modern-day Susannas (figs. 30–32). In contrast to a group of earlier works, all done around 1870, such as *Pastorale* or *The Temptation of Saint Anthony* or even the less overtly literary *Male and Female Bathers,* the interaction of the genders here is reduced to these few strokes of the brush or the pencil, almost slipping out of visibility, consumed by or morphing into the thicket of marks that constitute the foliage. As this composition would evolve, in works such as *Three Bathers* of circa 1875, the shadowy face of the desiring figure (or leering one, depending on how tendentious you allow me to be) is totally obliterated by a set of rubbed-in strokes atop the tree trunk, making the exaggerated poses of the female figures less obviously motivated, since they no longer signify the innocent's horror at being watched. By the time we get to a work like the Matisse *Three Bathers,* the process of obliteration is complete: no trace of the man in the bushes appears. We are left instead with a painting that seems to revel in the virtuosity of brushwork that holds the figures in place, structurally, like a firm embrace.

I am certainly not trying to argue that hidden in all of Cézanne's bushes are leering Lotharios or even that we should imagine that the relocation of the sign of eroticism from scenario to brushstroke follows, metaphorically, this one obliterated encounter between man-consumed-by-bushes and women-on-the-canvas. It probably does not matter that I find the pleasure sig-

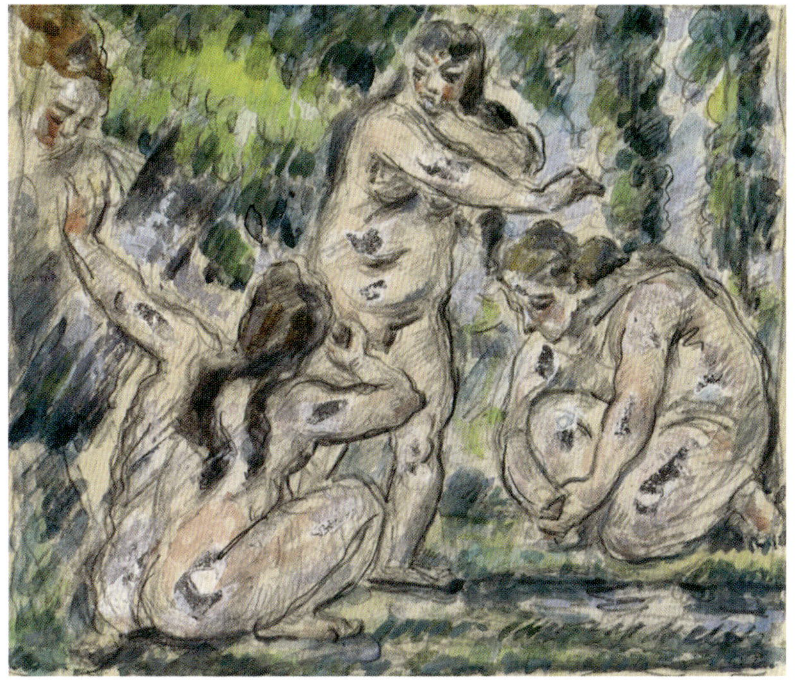

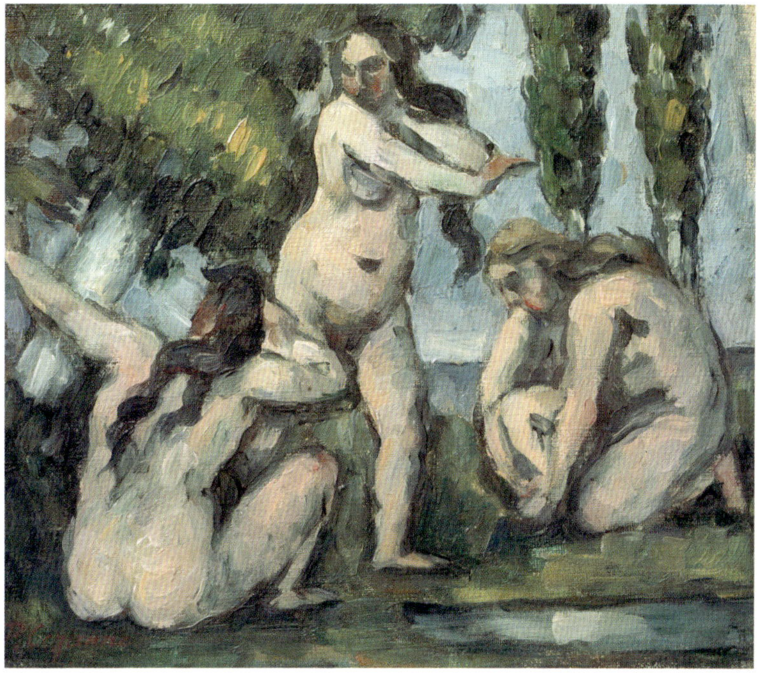

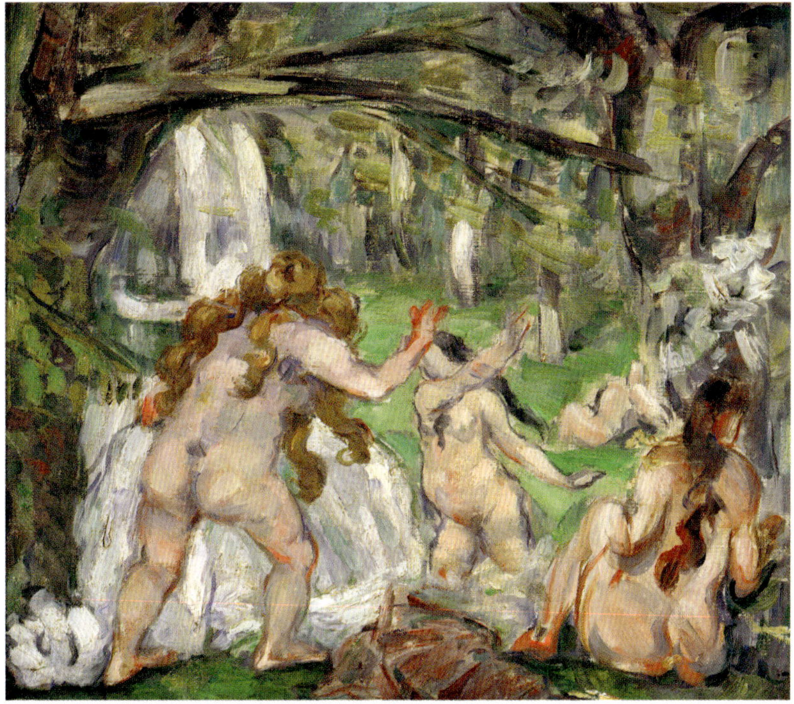

30. (*above left*) Cézanne, *Three Bathers,* ca. 1874–75. Pencil, watercolor, and gouache, 11.4 x 12.7 cm. National Museum of Wales, Cardiff.

31. (*above right*) Cézanne, *Three Bathers,* 1874–75. Oil on canvas, 19 x 22 cm. Musée d'Orsay, Paris.

32. (*left*) Cézanne, *Three Bathers,* ca. 1875. Oil on canvas, 30.5 x 33 cm. Private collection, U.K.

nified by these strokes to be more onanistic than anything, the result of the repetitive friction of brush meeting canvas in a process that seems, by its very distance from any conventions of the genre, to be open-ended and even endless (although, as I argued in the first chapter of this book, I am reasonably convinced that this quality was, in part, what motivated stories of Cézanne's "artistic impotence" that circulated in the last ten years of his life). Nor does the brushstroke in question have to be, to my mind, the paint-loaded, oily impasto that occurs in *Three Bathers* in order to carry the weight of this signification. Rather, Cézanne's erotics of paint, as I call it, was a matter, above all, of *matière,* of the sensuality of the medium and of the process of making a painting. In the Art Institute of Chicago's *Bathers* of 1900–1904, for example, a work done in concert with the Philadelphia *Bathers,* the surface oscillates with color: blocky vertical strokes and commas of clear blues and translucent greens, with occasional dabs of yellow in the sky, and an orangey-brown on the bodies and in the tree trunk on the right. Tree branches meander and split across the surface, and there are some tentative, exploratory contours in the central compositional void that seem to remain as a mostly abandoned idea. In the lower third of the canvas, bodies emerge, barely, from the primordial stuff of paint on the surface, fusing with the trees and the sky and the surrounding grass and foliage in disconcerting ways, only just defined by the multiple and open-ended contouring marks of deepest blue pigment. Again, on this thinly painted surface, there are moments of thickened paint, primarily in the grass-green areas around the figures and along the left vertical edge of free-floating leaves. In a work like this, and in countless others that Cézanne did in the same mode, it is neither the bodies, even in their "*déformations*" as was the fashionable term at the turn of the twentieth century, nor a luscious impasto à la Rubens that allows the scene to be understood in terms of a history of the nude. Rather, it is Cézanne's material rhetoric of touch. The strangeness of works like these is rooted in the radical dissonance of signifier and signified: the sensuality of the paint handling, the way Cézanne coaxes his oils to act like watercolor in terms of translucence and liquidity, the seduction of the mark itself, come to replace the depicted body as the source of visual pleasure—to replace the body but not to occlude it; that is to say, not to deny the body in a radically formalist gesture but to claim the body out there as a function of the physical will of the body making the marks out of which it is (barely) constituted and as a function of the facticity of the stuff out of which it is made.

If both Garb's and Clark's accounts suggest ways to access such a reading of these works without wholly offering one, it may be because both are limited by their reliance on psychoanalytic models that privilege sight, rather than touch or other sensory experience, as their organizing term: for Clark, it is the Oedipal scenario, with its emphasis on the visual discovery of difference, and for Garb it is the notion of the Lacanian gaze (or, more properly, a feminist revision of that notion). In their privileging of the imago as a crucial element in psychic development, neither can account for the eroticism of the bathers outside the terms of the figural, and thus they treat the materiality of the paintings as simply a metaphor for the visual operations of desire.

The dangers of such an approach can be encapsulated, it seems to me, in one of Luce Irigaray's statements, to the effect that "The moment the look dominates, the body loses its materiality."[74] These words seem particularly apposite in relation to Cézanne's painting of *baigneurs* and *baigneuses.* Where

Tamar Garb has imagined Cézanne's painting to have emerged precisely from this clash between the look (i.e., the drive to capture optical sensations) and the body (which dissolves under the pressure of the formal imperative to capture sensations), Irigaray allows us to conceive ways that the body—in the sense of the pleasures of the body, its erotics, not necessarily its form—is not erased from even the most illegible of Cézanne's canvases but is expressed in completely unexpected terms, terms that do not depend on any imagined (and, in fact, imaginary) visual encounter between painter and model. Irigaray's revision of Lacan starts from a fundamental break with psychoanalysis, which conceives of femininity in terms of lack—the male child recognizes his mother from what she does not possess. For Irigaray, by contrast, female sexuality is essentially complete, the two lips of her genitals forming a perfect autoerotic whole that can only be interrupted—violently—by entering into heterosexual relations. In contrast to male sexuality, she writes, woman's sexuality is tactile and plural, the geography of female pleasure is multiple and diverse; it can, however, never be represented as such because social practice continues to construct woman as use value for man, and within such a phallogocentric realm any attempt to "liberate" female pleasure is illusory.[75]

It is tempting to imagine that one could simply apply Irigaray's language of eroticized topographies of the body, of tactility as the site of sexual pleasure, to an interpretation of Cézanne's paintings, so that the painting's skin of flurried marks, and the touch of the brush on the canvas, would now represent the eroticization of the medium. That, however, may approach too closely the sort of metaphorization—a language of resemblance—that has limited prior accounts of these works, so that the skin of painting becomes the metaphor of the body's skin, Cézanne's brushstroke becomes the caress, etc. Rather, one might attend to the sorts of structural conditions that Irigaray identifies as corresponding to this other notion of sexuality, a notion in which the materiality of the body is not constantly erased under the pressure of the visual. In describing this battle, she writes: "Within this logic [of the Oedipal scenario], the predominance of the visual . . . is particularly foreign to female eroticism. Woman takes pleasure more from touching than from looking, and her entry into a dominant scopic economy signifies, again, her consignment to passivity: she is to be the beautiful object of contemplation."[76] Later on in her famous essay, "This Sex Which is Not One," she states: "[Women's] desire is often interpreted, and feared, as a sort of insatiable hunger, a voracity that will swallow you whole. Whereas it really involves a different economy, one that upsets the linearity of a project, undermines the goal-object of a desire, diffuses the polarization of a single pleasure, disconcerts fidelity to a single discourse."[77]

What would be gained, then, by understanding the erotics of Cézanne's bather paintings as operating not under the conditions of normative, heterosexual, masculine desire but under the conditions of this other conception of sexuality, one that rails against the predominance of the visual and especially its "discrimination and individualization of form"? Would, then, the deformation and dissolution of the figure that operate in many of Cézanne's paintings be conceived not as the inadvertent outcome of his optical search but rather as a reconception on Cézanne's part of how eroticism could be translated into painterly terms, into the analogical language of paint? What would be gained by imagining this series of pictures according to the "different economy" that Irigaray describes, "one that

Detail of fig. 33

upsets the linearity of a project, undermines the goal-object of a desire, diffuses the polarization toward a single pleasure, disconcerts fidelity to a single discourse"? Would, then, the strangeness of Cézanne's engagement with his motif—the fact that he painted bathers over the course of more than thirty years, the fact that his paintings of bathers are repetitive, marked by recurrences and recombinations of figures, poses, compositions from one to the other without, it is important to say, operating according to the conventional developmental logic (sketch-study-finished work)—seem less strange, and would it thus allow us to absorb those small, intimate paintings into our understanding of the operations of Cézanne's bathers as something other than mere precursor? Would it allow us to understand the discomfort Zola had with Cézanne's painting of the nude, expressed by proxy in *L'Oeuvre,* where Lantier can never create his "masterpiece" of nudes bathing by the Seine? And would it allow us to process Cézanne's laughing rebuttal to Zola, who he accused of knowing nothing about painting ("When a painting isn't realized, you pitch it in the fire and start another one!")?

Beyond the metaphorical dimension of eroticized surfaces of pleasure, then, Irigaray points to other structural conditions of signification that may be understood as part of the erotic address of Cézanne's bathers.[78] Rather than imagining the works as pre-Oedipal fantasies, a notion common in the history of Cézanne criticism (through repeated emphases on the paintings' "Arcadianism") and reiterated by Clark in his own interpretation of the bathers as fantasies of the body's disalienation from the world, from nature and from the mother's body, as fantasies of sensory continuity of body and space—as fantasies of the undoing of gender or, more properly, of femininity—Irigaray offers the tools to recognize the pictures as sites in which we might be seeing a structurally Other inscription of eroticism in painterly terms.[79] And, as we shall see in the next chapter, this radicalization of painting the nude was understood by Cézanne's critics and contemporaries—though, often, they could only express their recognition through the language of artistic biography.

PLATES

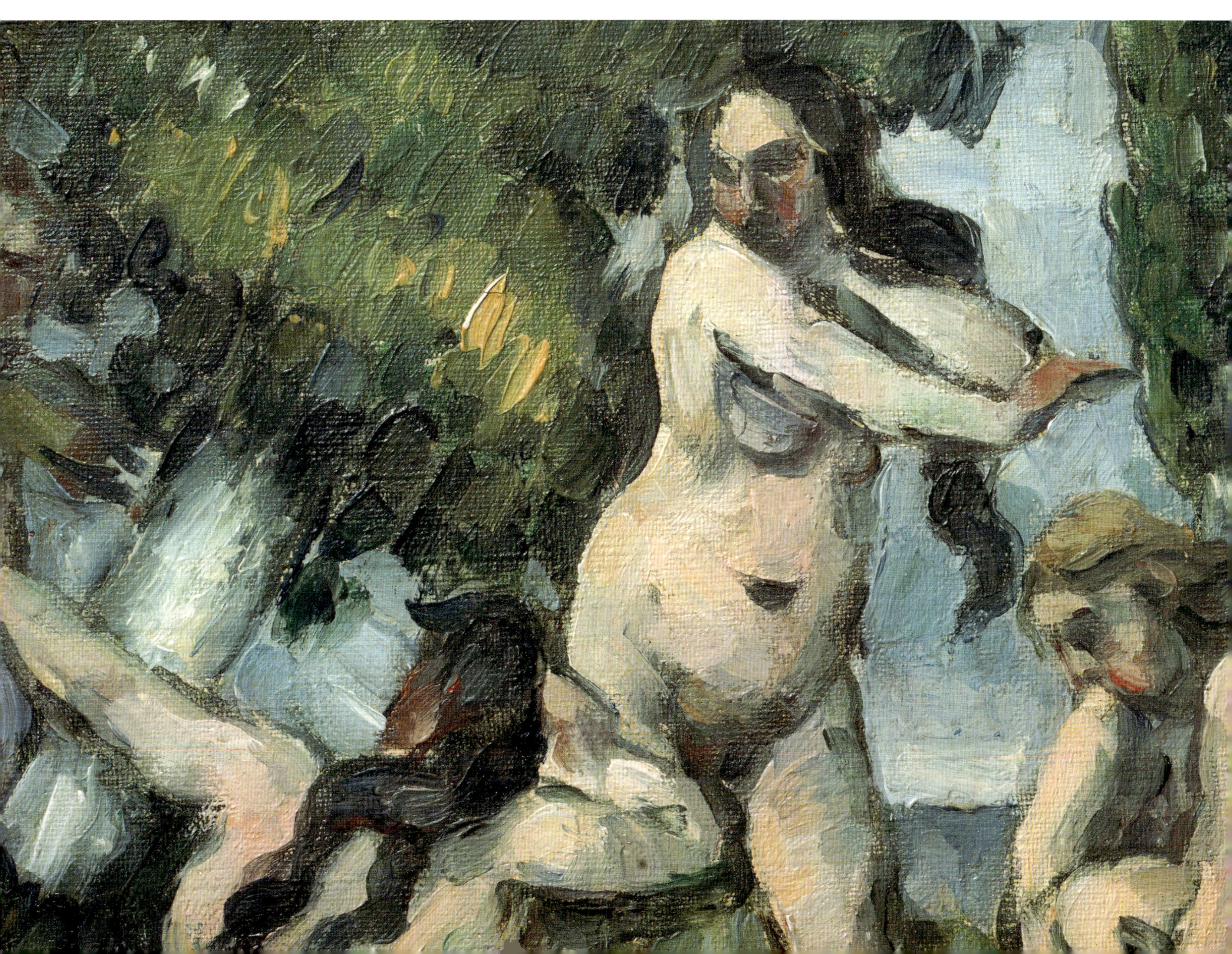

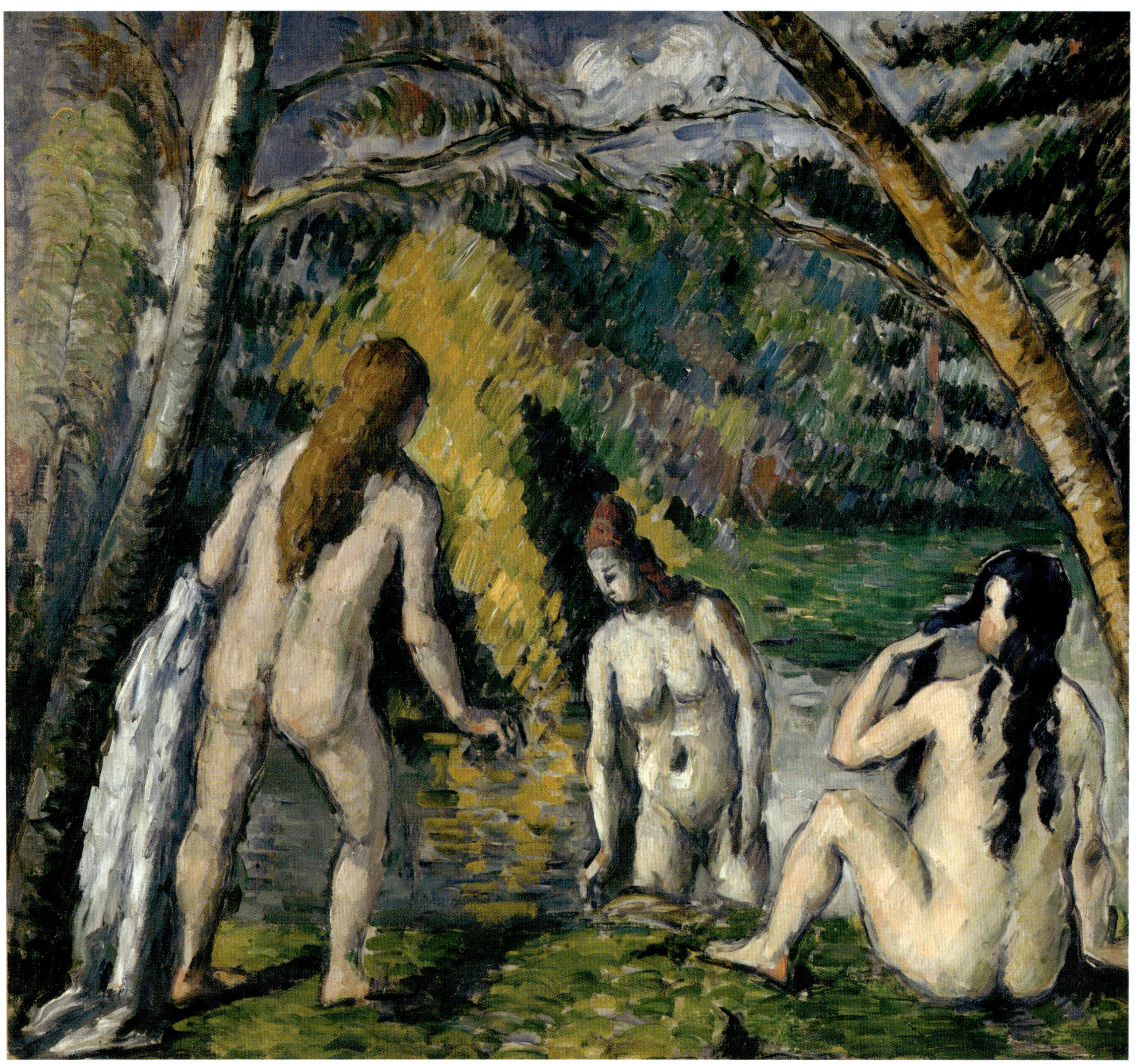

PLATE I. Cézanne, *Three Bathers,* 1876–77. Oil on canvas, 52 x 54.4 cm. Musée du Petit Palais, Paris.

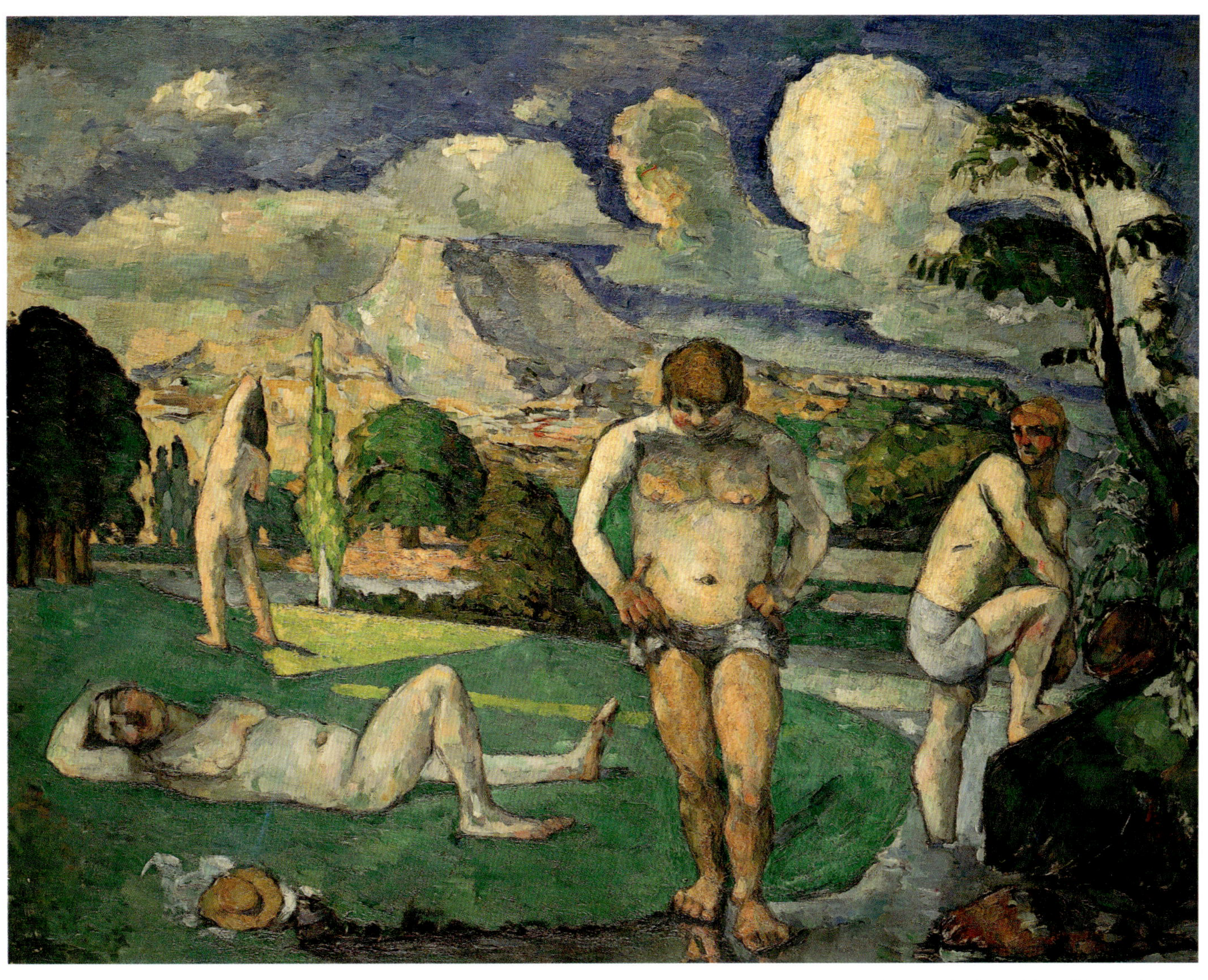

PLATE II. Cézanne, *Bathers at Rest III*, 1876–77. Oil on canvas, 82.6 x 101.6 cm. Barnes Foundation, Merion, Pa. BF906.

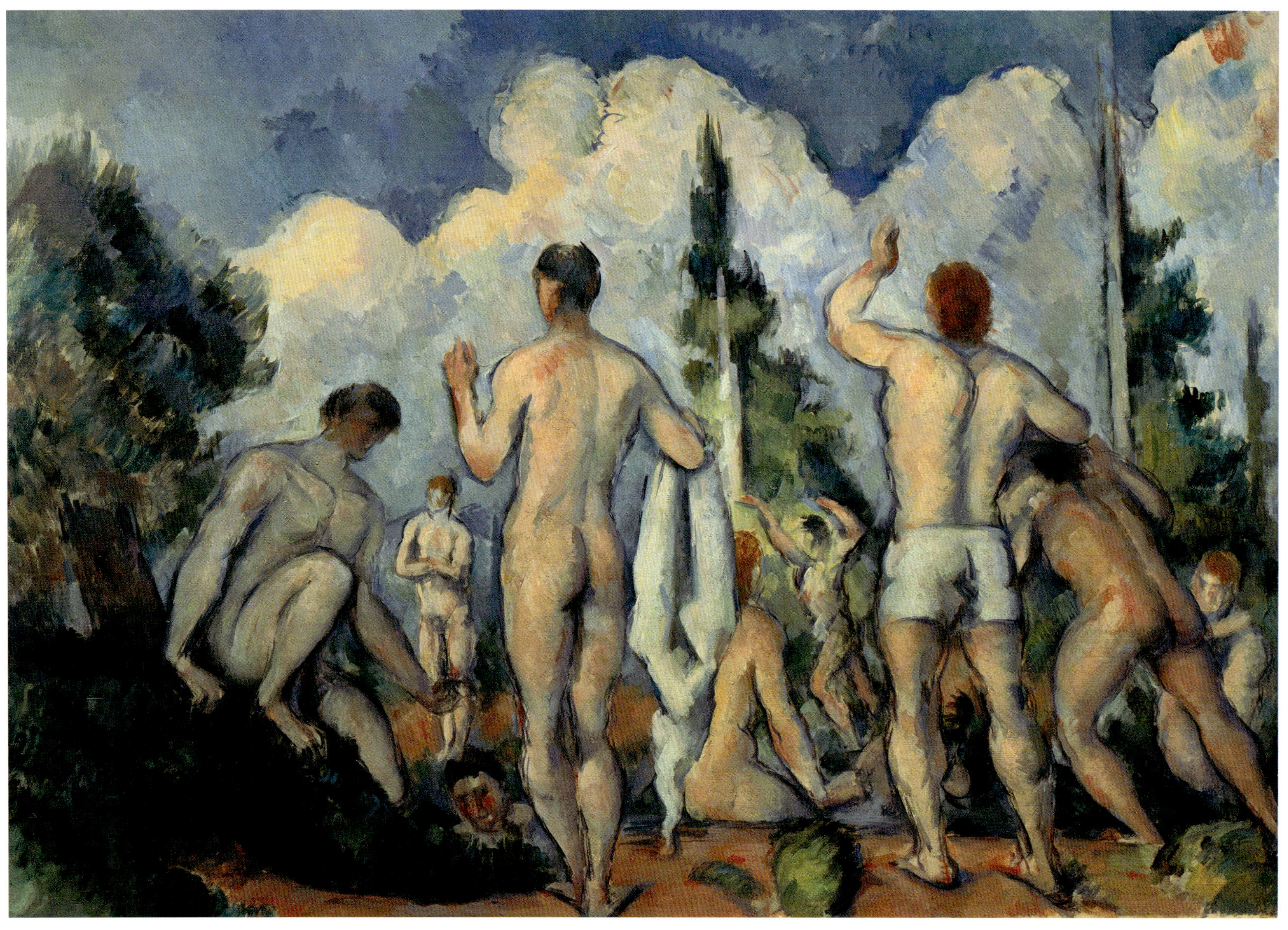

PLATE III. Cézanne, *Bathers,* ca. 1890. Oil on canvas, 60 x 81 cm. Musée d'Orsay, Paris.

OPPOSITE LEFT AND RIGHT

PLATE IV. Cézanne, *Bathers,* ca. 1890. Detail of plate III.

PLATE V. Cézanne, *Bathers,* ca. 1890. Detail of plate III.

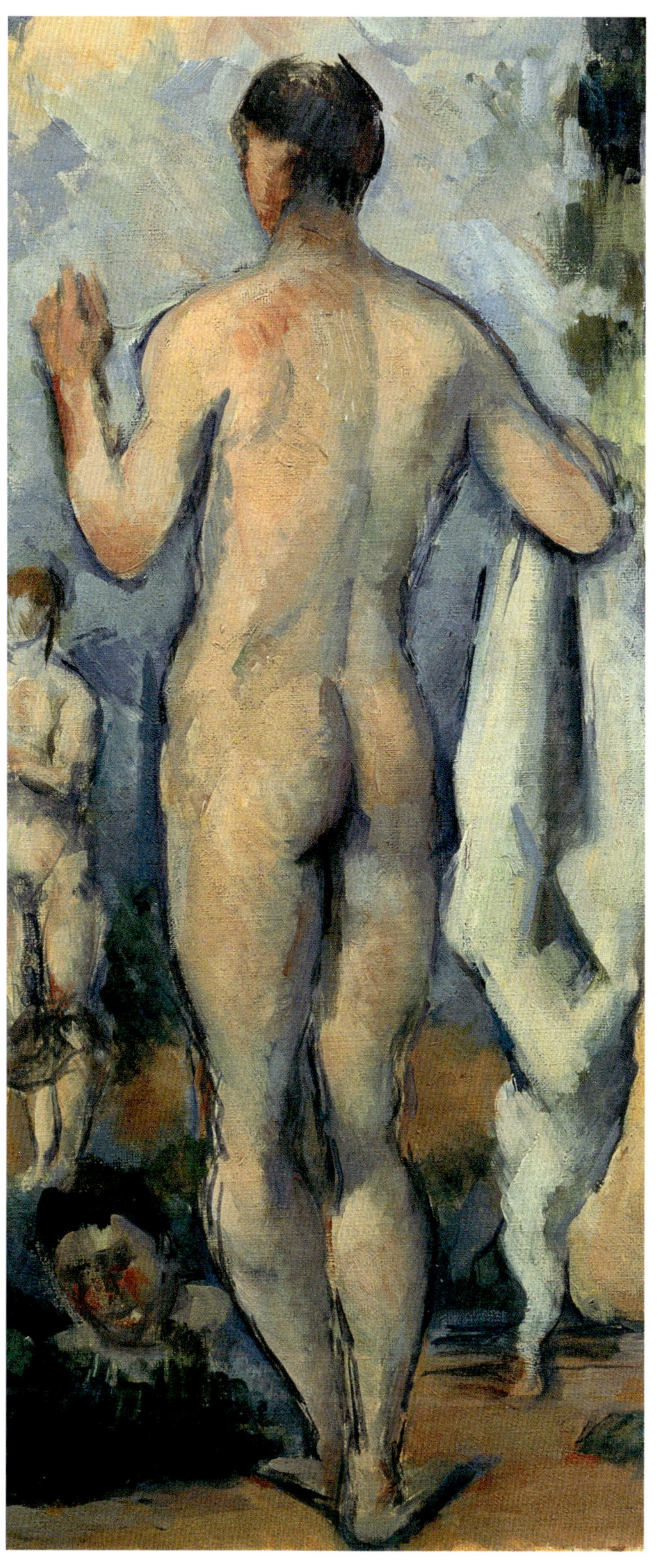

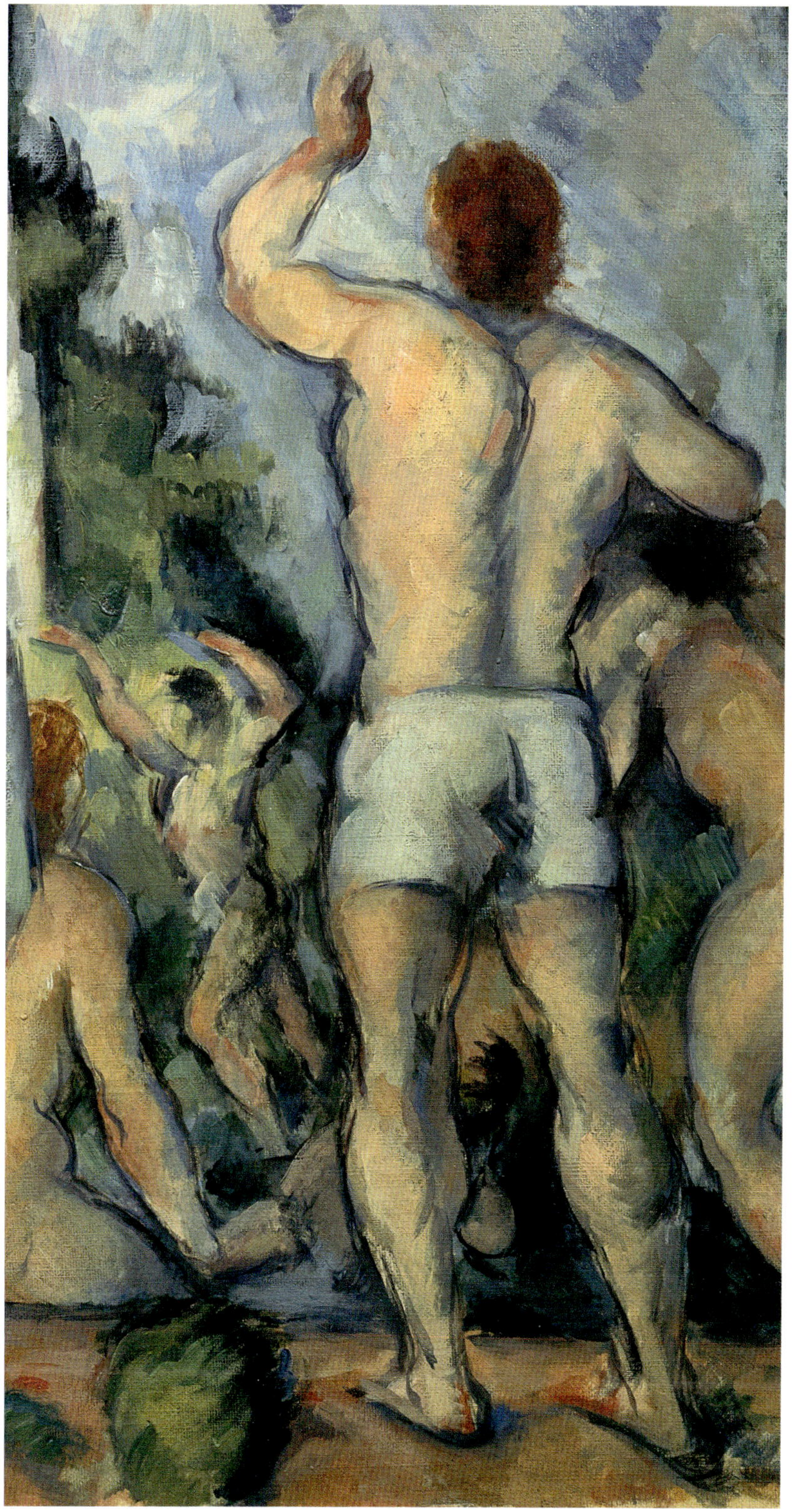

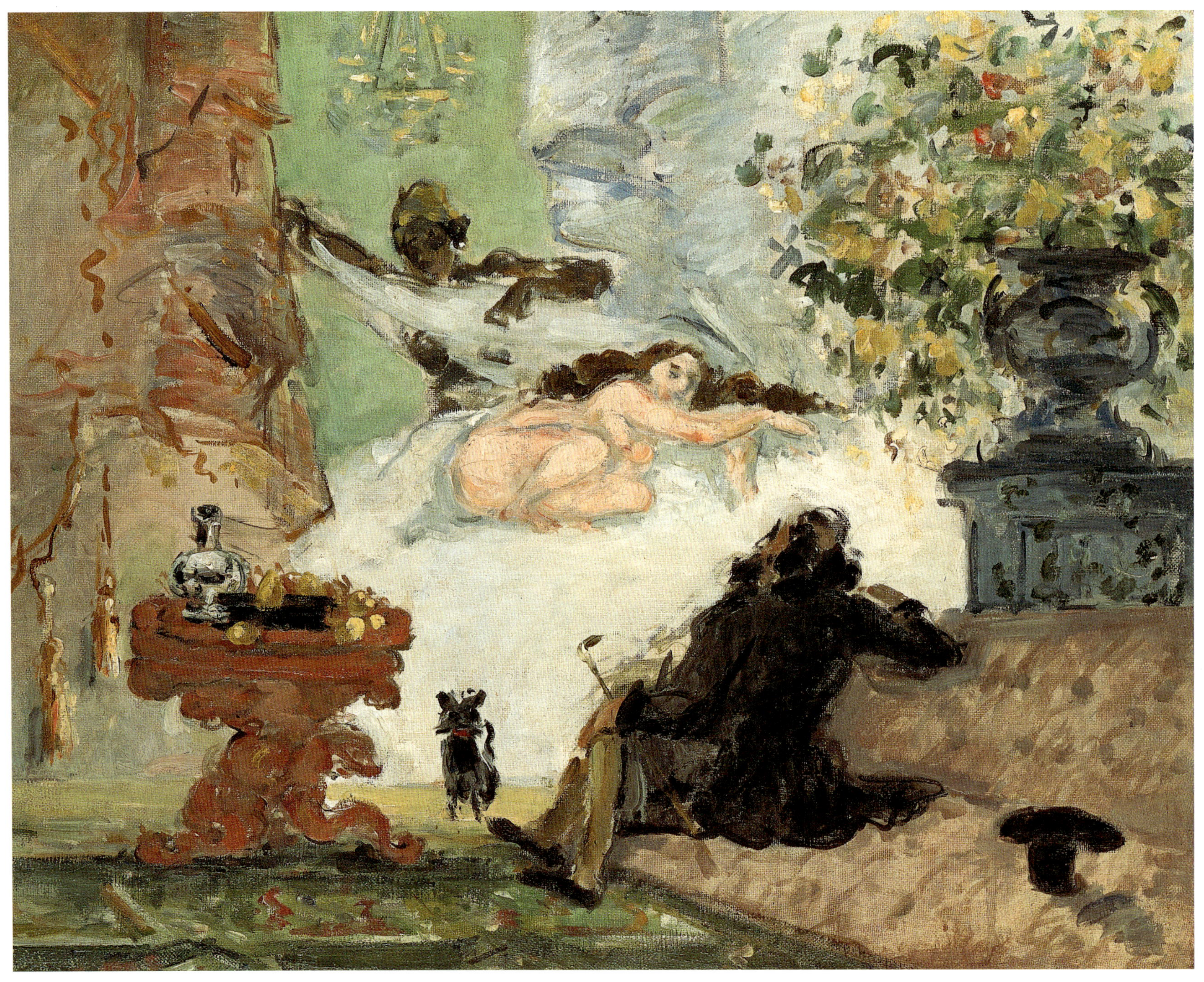

PLATE VI. Cézanne, *A Modern Olympia,* 1873–74. Oil on canvas, 46 x 55 cm. Musée d'Orsay, Paris.

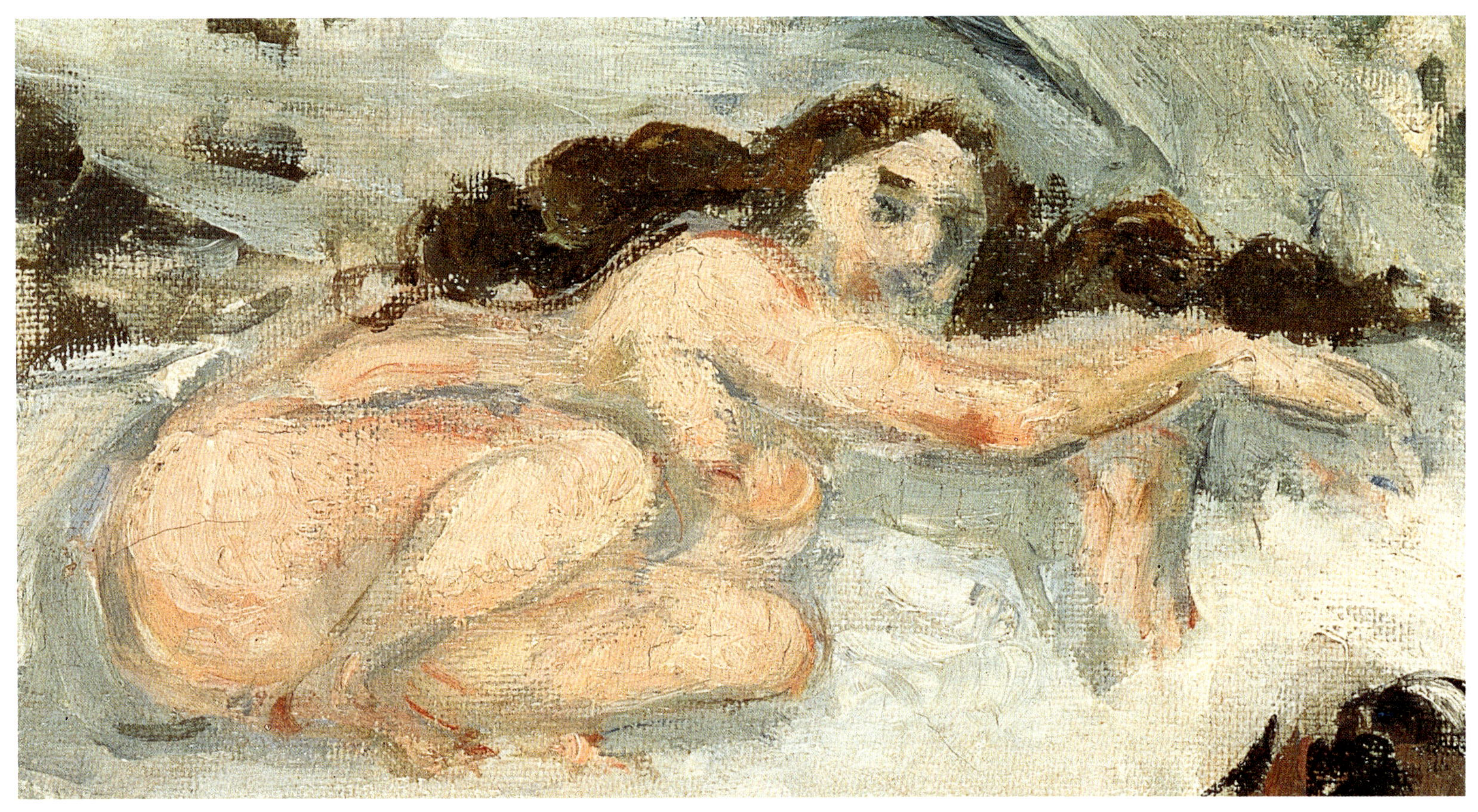

PLATE VII. Cézanne, *A Modern Olympia*, 1873–74. Detail of plate VI.

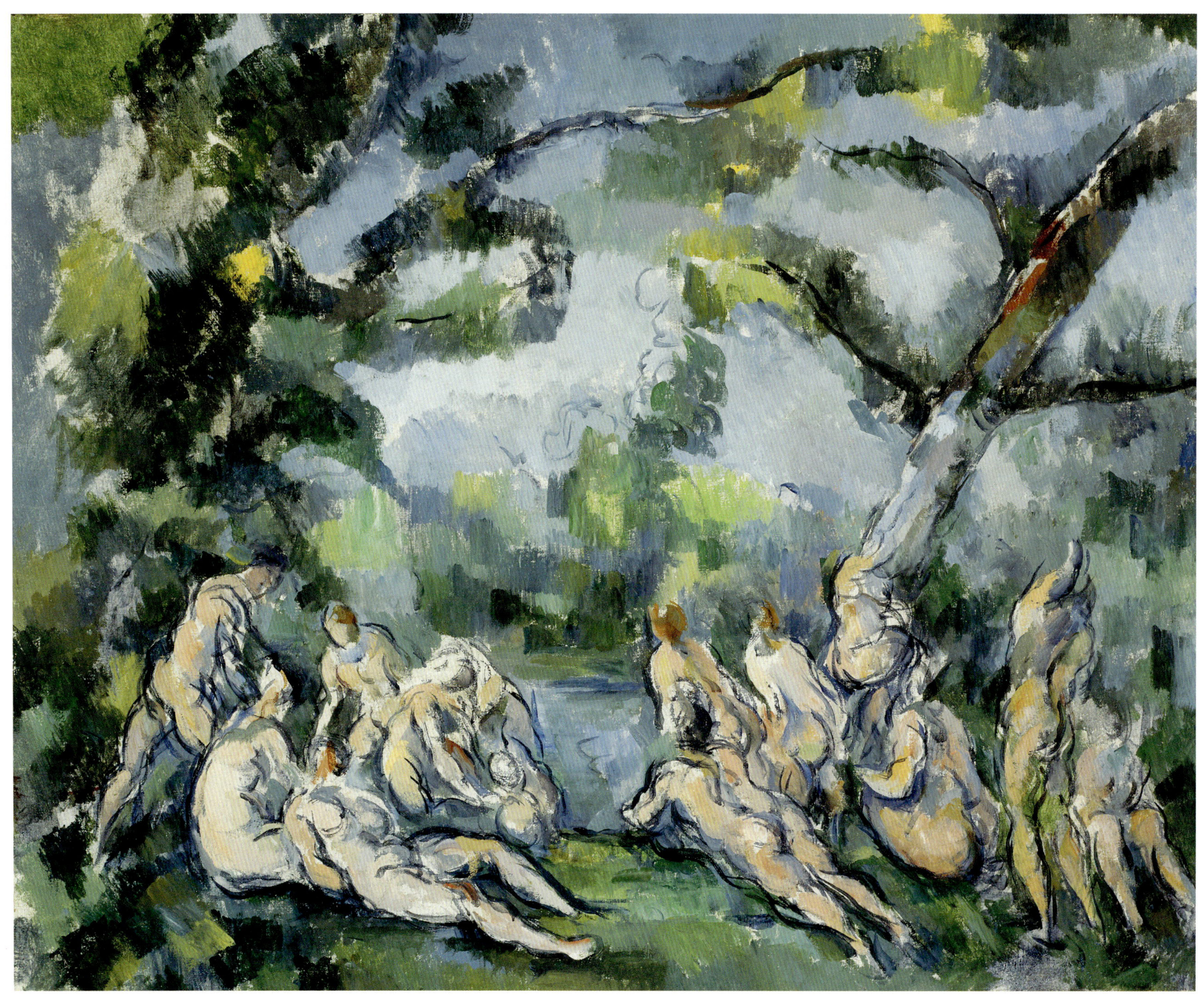

PLATE VIII. Cézanne, *Bathers,* 1899–1904. Oil on canvas, 51.3 x 61.7 cm. Art Institute of Chicago, Amy McCormick Memorial Collection. 1942.457.

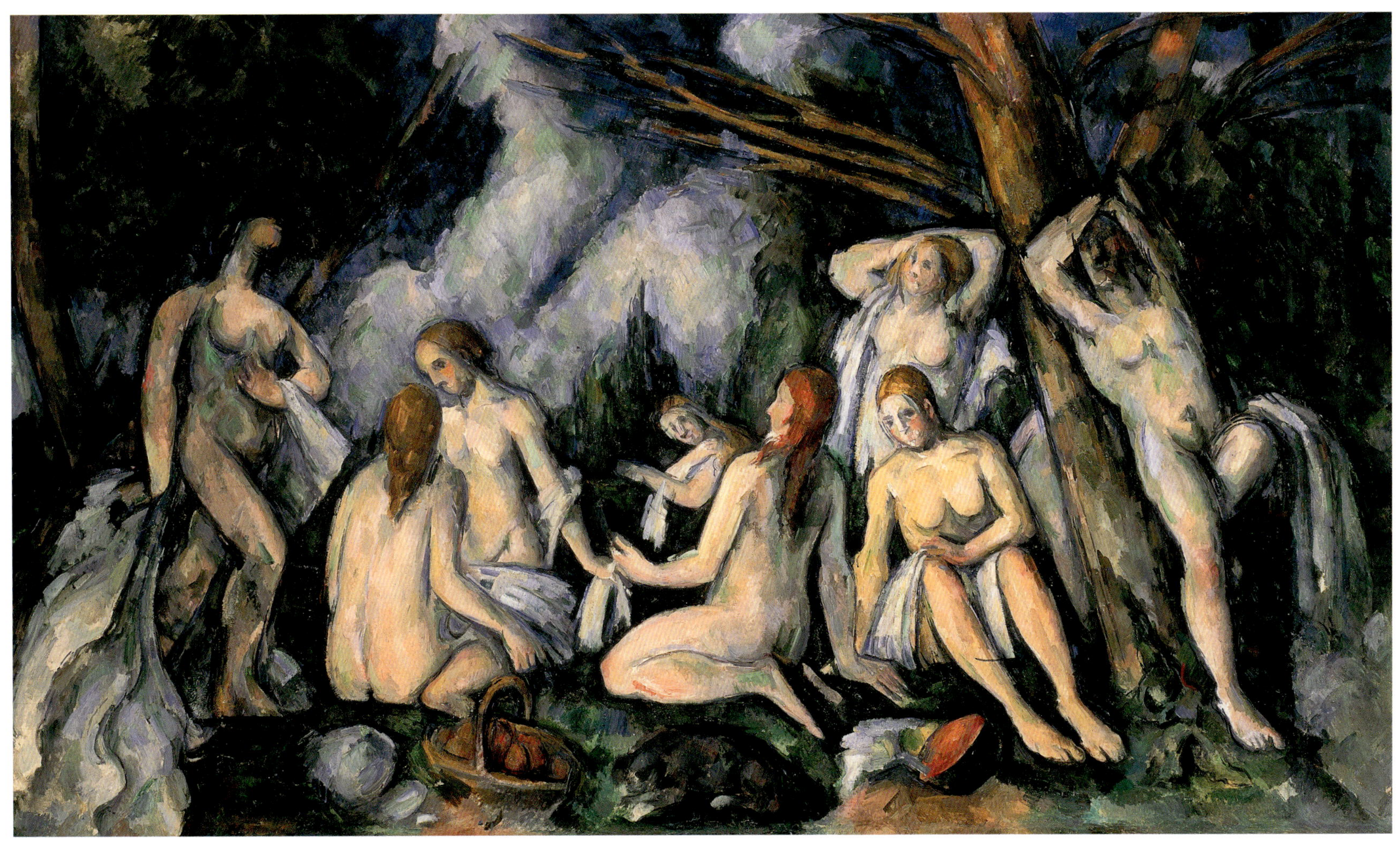

PLATE IX. Cézanne, *Large Bathers,* 1895–1906. Oil on canvas, 133 x 207 cm. Barnes Foundation, Merion, Pa. BF934.

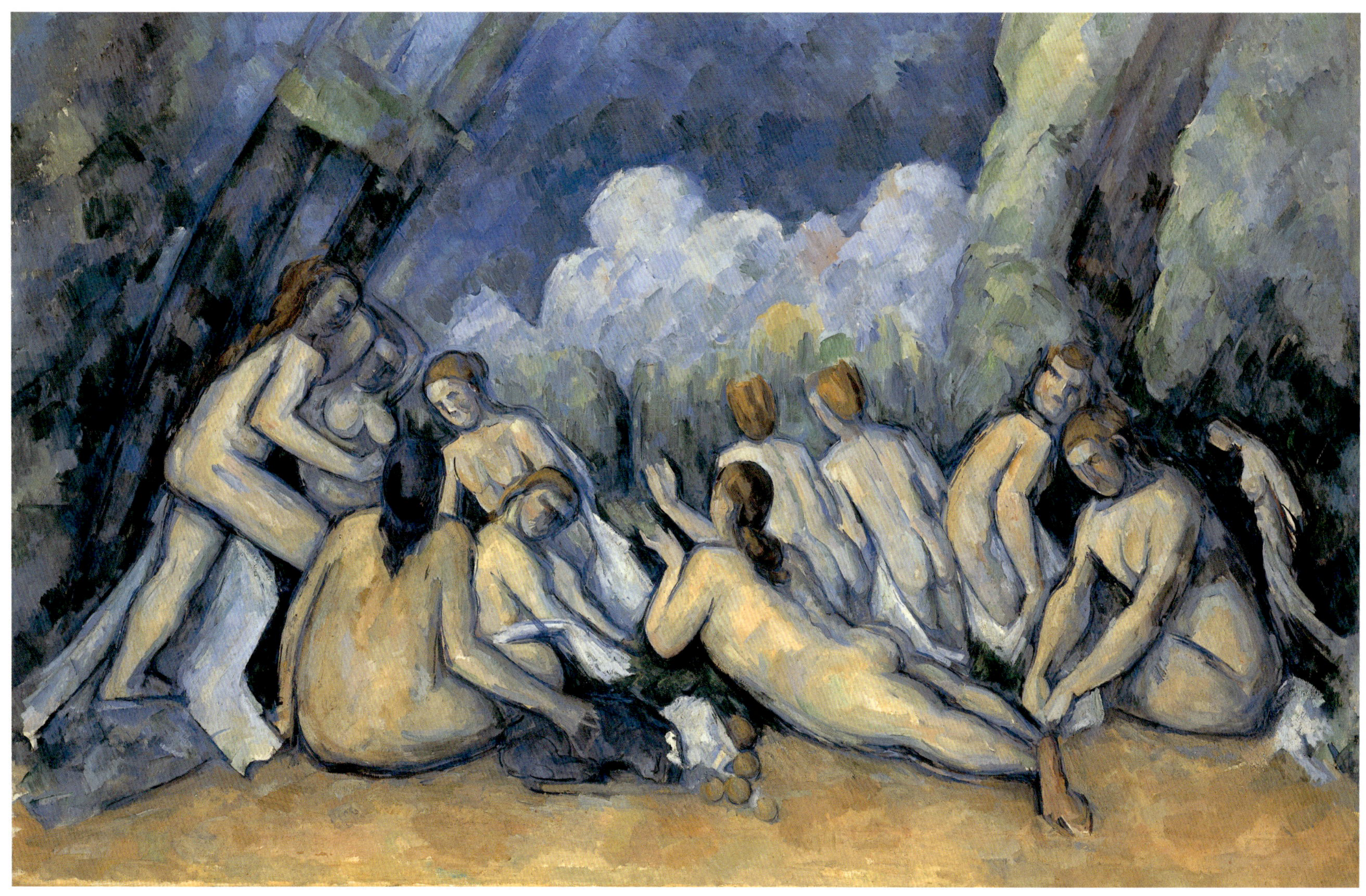

PLATE X. Cézanne, *Large Bathers,* 1894–1905. Oil on canvas, 127.2 x 196.1 cm. National Gallery, London.

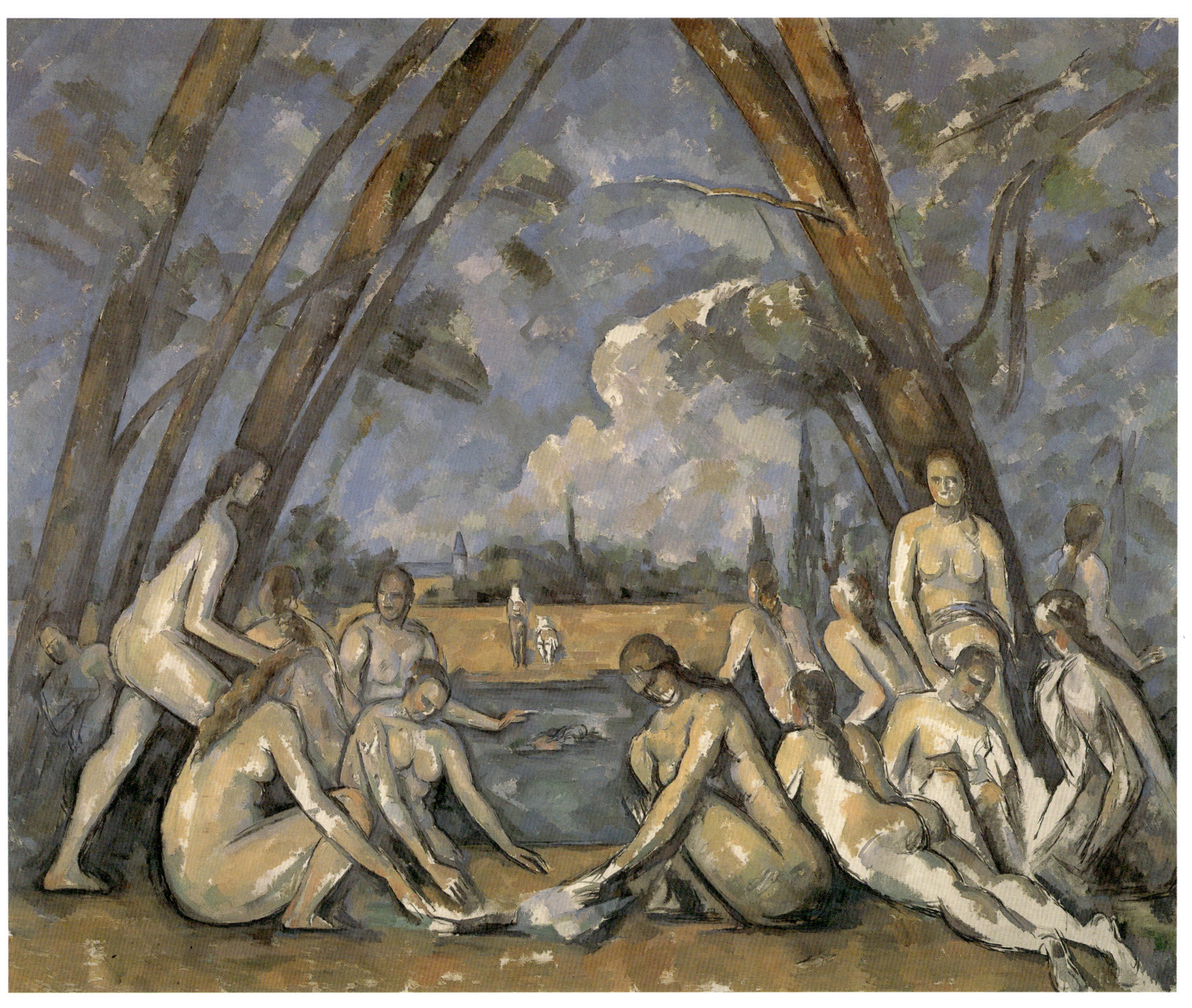

PLATE XI. Cézanne, *Large Bathers,* 1906. Oil on canvas, 210.5 x 250.8 cm. Philadelphia Museum of Art, purchased with the W. P. Wilstach Fund, 1937.

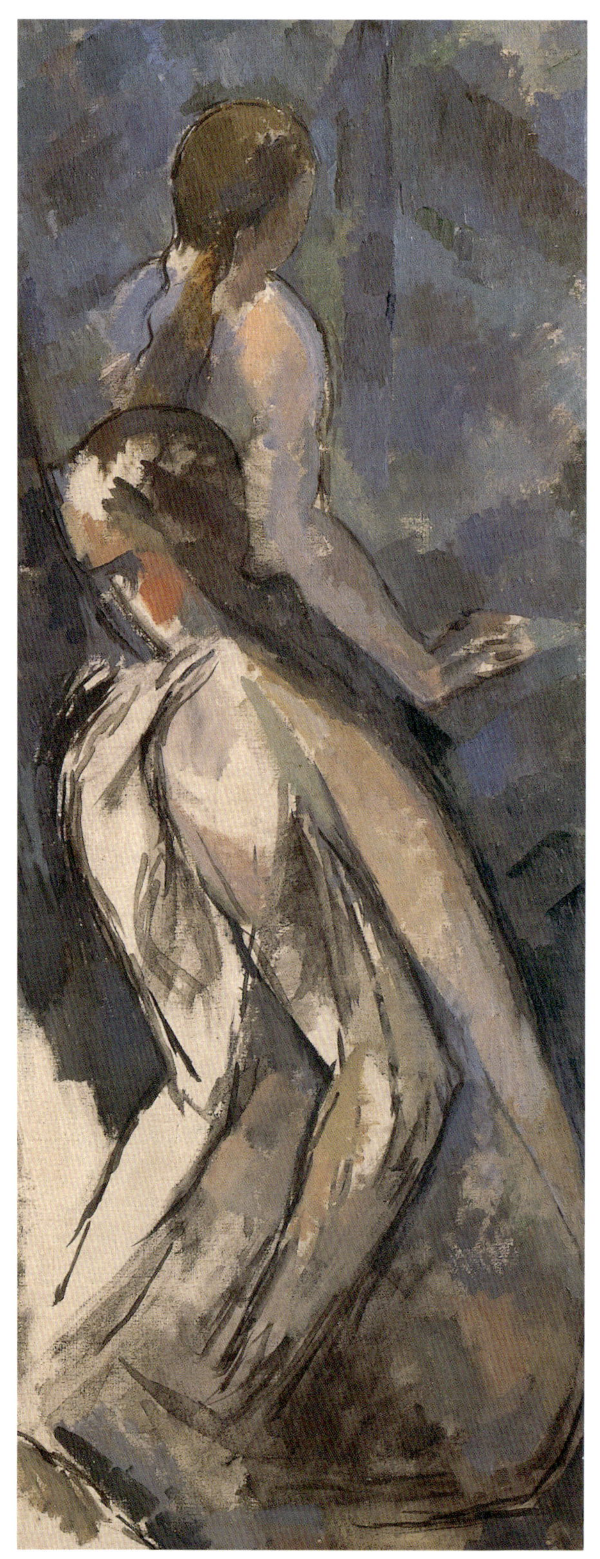

PLATE XII. Cézanne, *Large Bathers,* 1906. Detail of plate XI.

OPPOSITE
XIII. Cézanne, *Large Bathers,* 1906. Detail of plate XI.

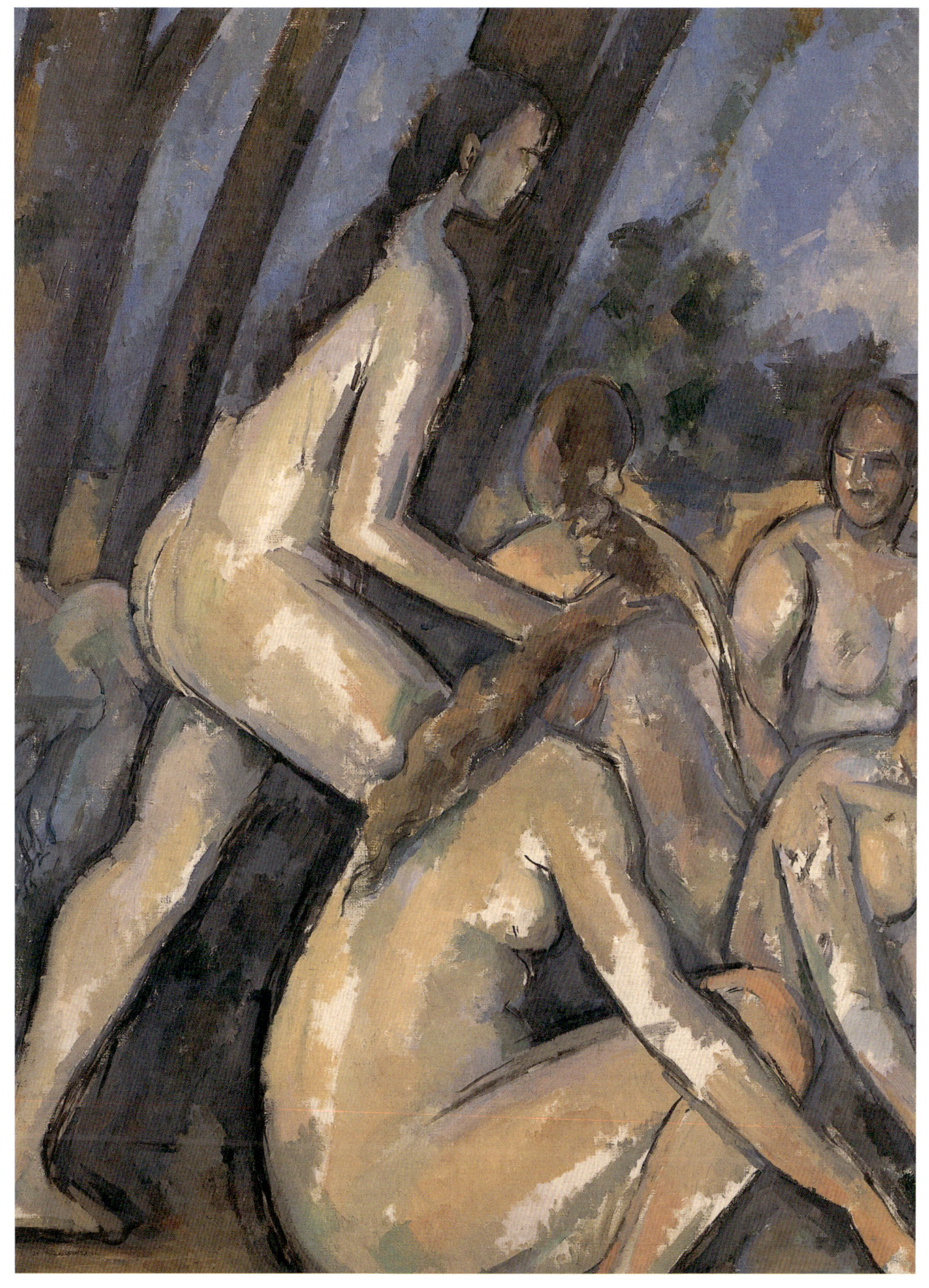

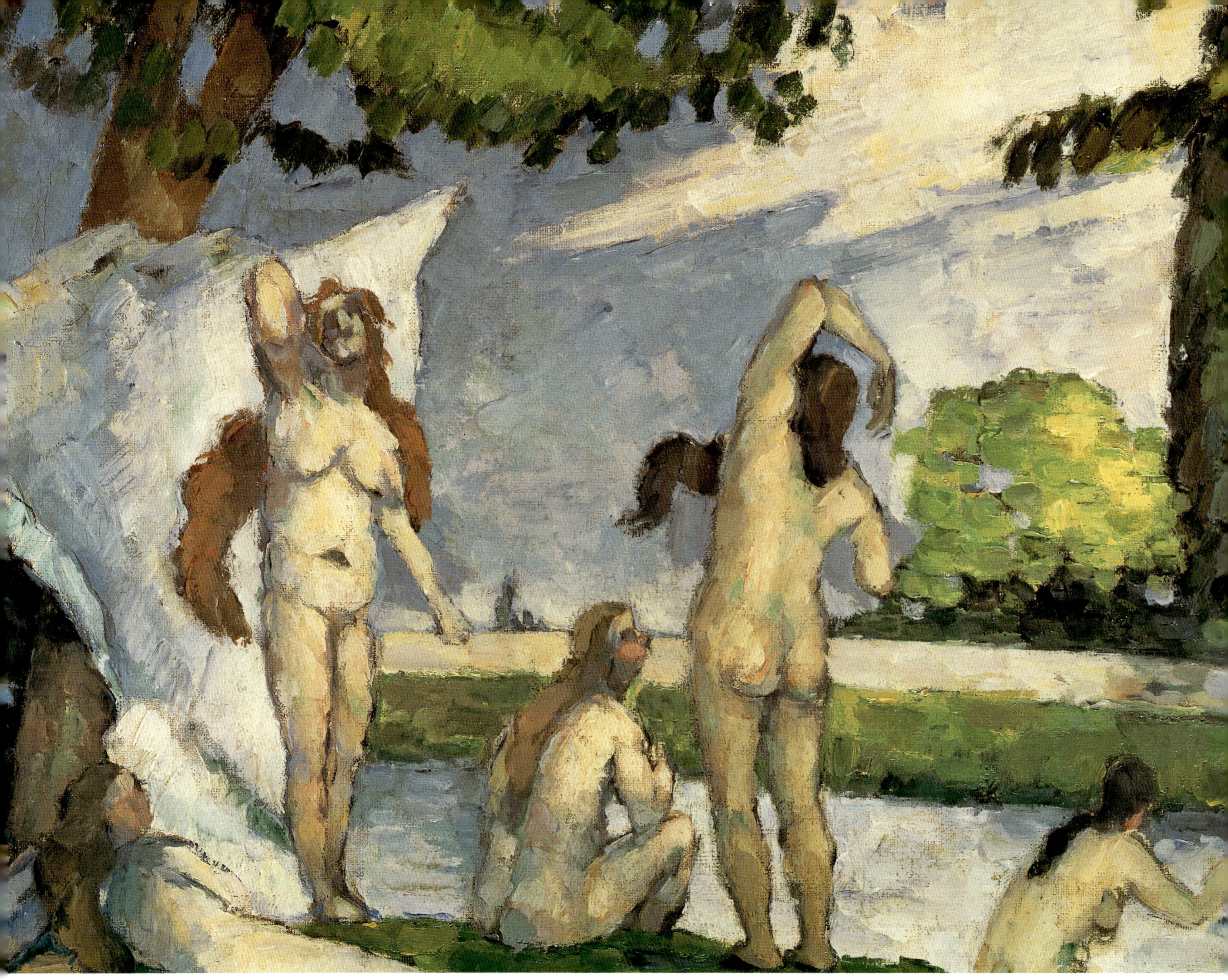

3 *BAIGNEURS/BAIGNEUSES:* MAKING A DIFFERENCE

Detail of fig. 43

THREE BATHERS (1874–75) IS A SMALL PAINTING (fig. 33). Writers on Cézanne's bathers tend to avoid talking in detail about such small works, seduced, perhaps, by the fact that the *Grandes baigneuses* are the artist's only monumental paintings in any genre and thus deserve the lion's share of attention. But *Three Bathers,* like many of Cézanne's small-scale essays on the theme, is neither a study for the larger canvases nor subordinate to them: Cézanne's working method, one characterized by a process-driven and open-ended or even circular impulse, does not allow one to speak of studies and finished works, of *esquisses* and *machines.* Rather, each canvas is a world unto itself, though linked genealogically to a body of work that provides it with meaning. To focus only on the *Grandes baigneuses,* in other words, in a study on the bathers, would be to leave out qualities that are essential to the elaboration of the theme in Cézanne's oeuvre: the intimate, the proximal, the tactile, that range of sensory experience that derives from closeness. All these have been overshadowed by issues of the shape of things and bodies, the optical, the structurally imperative, by those qualities that seem to predominate in the *Large Bathers.*

Three Bathers hangs slightly high on the wall of the Musée d'Orsay. In order to see this painting, you must stand very close to it, so that the frame—richly carved, very traditional, and several inches wide—does not get in the way. Surrounded by tourists who are convinced that the "secret" of an impressionist painting is that, when seen from a distance, the flurry of painted marks will cohere into an almost-perfect realism, standing this close to a canvas in the gallery seems odd; it seems almost too intimate an experience than is appropriate for such a public place. From this close up—from the viewing distance insisted on by the work itself—the painting does not resolve into anything like photographic veracity: on the contrary, one's understanding of the bodies is overwhelmed by the facticity of the brushstrokes, their luscious and oily appearance, their almost sculptural presence on the surface. By tracing the contours of this impasto, one discovers the three women depicted here, as well as the trees, sky,

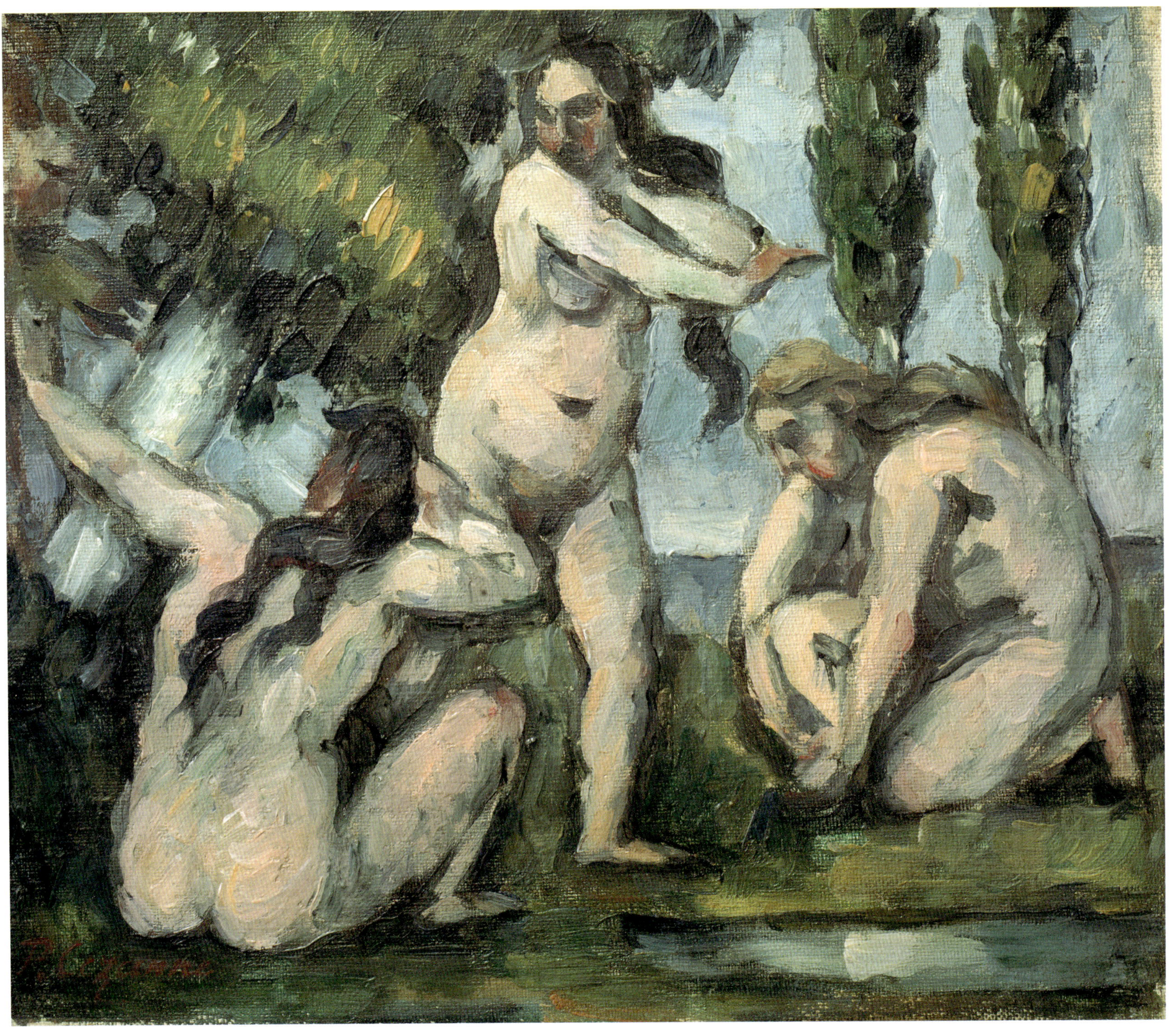

grass, and water. The bodies are more thickly painted than the rest of the painting. Attention has been paid to an irrational light that bounces off their ponderous forms, and one senses, given the traces of blues, greens, browns, and purples that are shot through the yellowish-pink tone Cézanne employs for their flesh, that he has returned to their figures continually while painting the surrounding landscape, as if unable to tear his eyes and his brush away from their carnality. But even as the bodies seem to have captured the greatest share of his painterly caress, the sky, foliage, and grass are hardly subordinate to them: the sky does not form the backdrop to the figures but was painted in afterward, and the brushstrokes that define its bluish expanse define the contours of the bodies, too, especially the torso of the central woman. It takes effort to see the figures for the brushstrokes, just as it takes effort to see the background for the leaves. Likewise, the figures exist in a sort of tension of priority with the rhythm of the composition, a rhythm formed by the counterpoint of the hatched regularity of the markings that make up trees and sky and the sweeping arabesque of the bathers' startled gestures, from outstretched arm to cascading hair to arched back, through hair and arm and back again. These women are not quite subordinate to the composition. Rather they drive its logic.

It is in these frictions, I would argue—in the tension between brushstroke and body, between background and object, between composition and content—that the eroticism of the pictures is produced. Neither a product of the theater of the figure and its role in the Oedipal drama, nor an inadvertent outcome of a modernist imperative, nor a product of a sublimatory impulse, the erotics of Cézanne's bathers are the result of a quite self-conscious engagement with a long-standing, art historical conversation about visual pleasure and the nude body that was especially pressing at the end of the nineteenth century. Cézanne's is an erotics of paint: a product of his visible touch on the painted surface, of the buildup of pigment, of the reworking of contours, of the play of the brush over the expanse of the canvas's skin. And as such, it was a radical shift, for it was not simply that paint was deployed in a way that would *augment* the erotic charge of a scene—the way one might understand Rubens's great lashes of saturated color in *The Judgment of Paris,* or the play of the brush, like a thousand flickering tongues, over Boucher's *The Dark-Haired Odalisque* or Watteau's *Judgment of Paris,* or the porcelain-smooth, "licked" surface of Ingres's *Grande Odalisque* (figs. 34–37). While these practices may form a prehistory of Cézanne's own—and indeed, Rubens, the Rococo artists, Ingres, all these were important touchstones for his understanding of his medium—their use of paint as a material substance was part of a presentation of figures who could, in their very forms, their anatomies, and poses sustain an erotic and pleasurable viewing.[1] Cézanne's approach to the nude, by contrast, detaches one metaphorical signifier of erotic pleasure—the visible material of paint—from another—the representation of idealized, beautiful, pleasure-producing bodies. The erotic is no longer bounded by the object of fantasy but dispersed, made to exist as part of the process of painting rather than contained in the final image, circumscribed by a woman's form.

To say that Cézanne's rhetoric of *matière* was a *signifier* of the erotic and not an effect of his will to sublimate the erotic or an inadvertent by-product of his formal investigations would imply that, to some degree at least, his manipulations of the genre of the erotic nude were readable within the critical context of

OPPOSITE

33. Cézanne, *Three Bathers,* 1874–75. Oil on canvas, 19 x 22 cm. Musée d'Orsay, Paris.

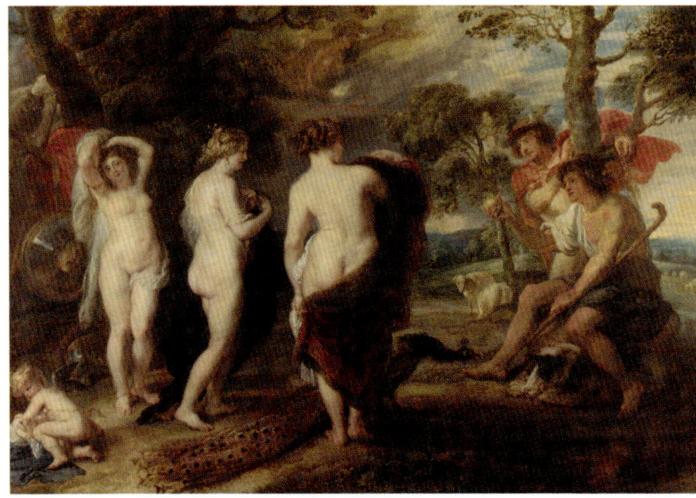

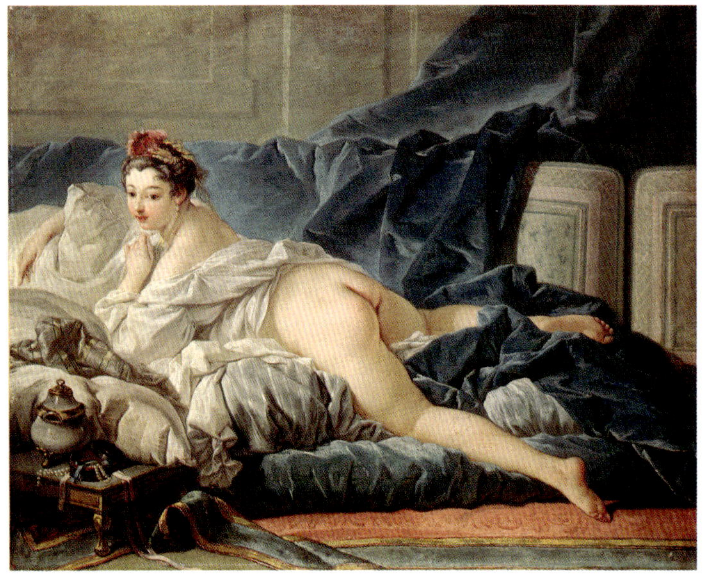

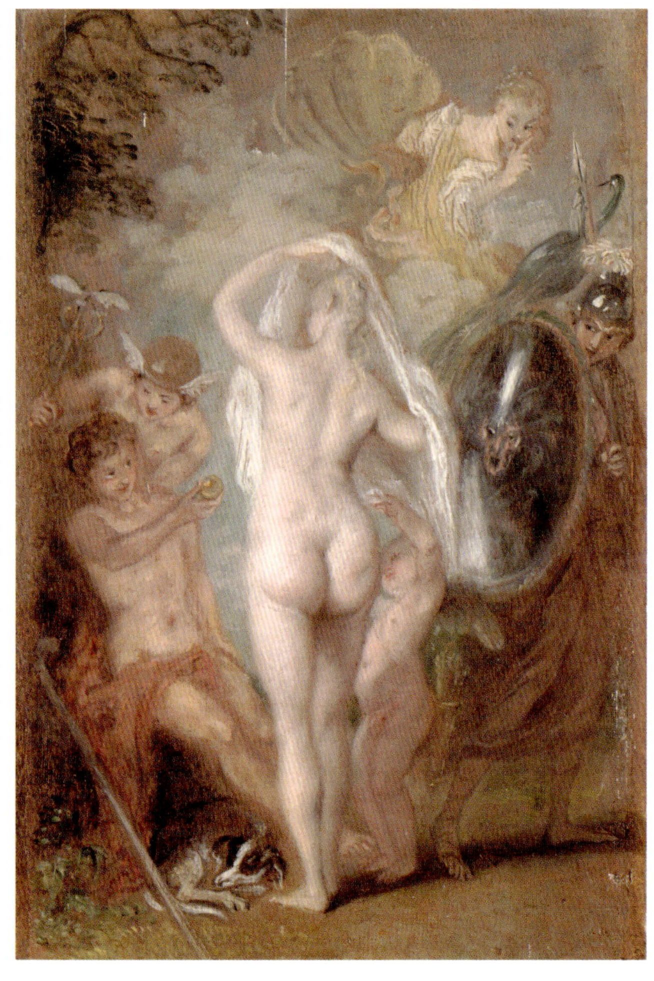

34. (*above left*) Peter Paul Rubens, *Judgment of Paris,* ca. 1632–35. Oil on oak panel, 144.8 x 133.7 cm. National Gallery of Art, London.

35. (*left*) François Boucher, *Dark-haired Odalisque,* 1745. Oil on canvas, 53 x 64 cm. Musée du Louvre, Paris.

36. (*above right*) Antoine Watteau, *Judgment of Paris,* ca. 1720. Oil on wood, 47 x 31 cm. Musée du Louvre, Paris.

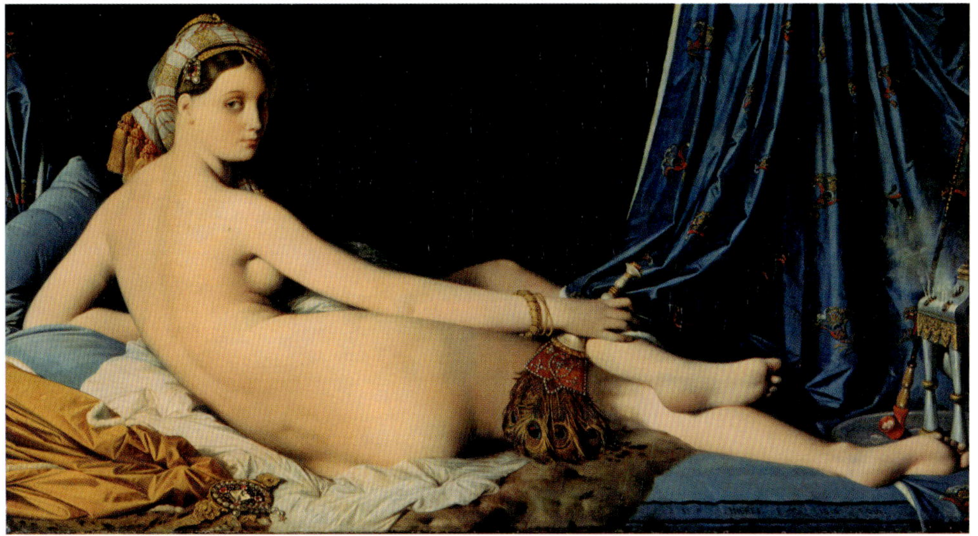

37. Jean-Auguste-Dominique Ingres, *Grande Odalisque*, 1814. Oil on canvas, 91 x 162 cm. Musée du Louvre, Paris.

the time. And as long as we are willing to pay particular attention to the absences and silences and overdeterminations of the contemporary criticism, we will find that to be true. First, we might turn our attention to the effort Cézanne's early critics—these included Bernard as well as Joachim Gasquet, Gustave Geffroy, and J.-K. Huysmans—made trying to explain a confounding fact: that these paintings, in which neither the bodies depicted nor the qualities of finish seemed to have anything in common with the terms of the genre of the female nude as it was understood in the late nineteenth century, seemed still to belong, in some complicated way, to that category, and seemed to share its libidinal content. The full range of Cézanne's gaucheries, which included both the forms of the bodies as well as the reworked contours, clotted impastos, and unpainted passages in these paintings, were the things that made these images impossible to read as erotic and yet also made it necessary to read them as such: for how else to understand these works, which seemed to new eyes entirely *inachevé,* naïve at best, failed at worst, and yet the object of Cézanne's continued, even obsessive, interest? And, most interestingly, the critical attempts to make sense of this conundrum were largely undertaken in terms of the writing of his biography: narrative tropes of his isolation and his sexual anxieties and fears were deployed in order to explain Cézanne's formal interventions in the genre of the female nude.

The second signal that Cézanne's erotics of paint registered with his contemporary public has to do with the treatment of the male nudes, the *baigneurs,* by these same critics. For if Cézanne had wrenched the signifier of the erotic from the confines of the figure and put it into play instead in a free-floating group of marks (the artist's brushstroke and the other signs of subjective engagement with the motif, the gaucheries), what was to prevent the male bathers, which were depicted with the same types of painterly eccentricities as their female counterparts, from being understood as eroticized as well? The result was that much effort was spent in the early years of Cézanne criticism arguing that those pictures were qualitatively different from the *baigneuses,* primarily because they sprang from the painter's memories of youthful camaraderie or from his plein-air encounters with soldiers bathing in the river near Aix rather than from his imagination. Again, biographical constructions of Cézanne play a crucial role.

BAIGNEUSES: CÉZANNE'S FAILURE

The sheer confusion with which Cézanne's contemporaries—even his most fervent supporters—faced his paintings of the nude cannot be overstated. We are repeatedly counseled in contemporary writings on Cézanne that if one were looking for the representation of an idealized female body, one would do well to look elsewhere than Cézanne's *baigneuses.* Karl Ernst Osthaus, for example, writes of his visit to Cézanne's studio, where he encountered the Philadelphia *Bathers*:

> On the easel could be seen a barely started still life, as well as the most important work of his later years, *The Bathers.* The tall tree trunks were already bent, forming a cathedral vault below which unfolded a bathing scene. *The connoisseur of noble female beauty can perhaps console himself with the thought that the nudes in this painting are not of an elevated descent; in any case, the person who takes into account that the artist has set out to capture the image of nature merely for its value as colored space . . . will find the strange arrangement easier to understand.*[2]

Osthaus's words suggest the extent to which a formalist interpretation of Cézanne's bather paintings—the idea that the artist has "set out to capture the image of nature merely for its value as colored space"—is a small comfort for the strange forms of the figures contained therein, with their heavy-bottomed, flat-footed weightiness and oozing boundlessness. But compare Osthaus's restrained expression of distaste with Julius Meier-Graefe's outright disdain for Cézanne's deformed figures: "His 'academies' look like lumps of rough-hewn flesh," Meier-Graefe wrote in 1904. "Anatomy seems to be treated with lordly contempt; and yet these blocks of flesh live. Not that one would ever think of touching such flesh; one wants to drink it in with one's eyes."[3] If there is revulsion expressed here—the horror of touch—there is desire, too, a sense that these figures hold a seductive power over the viewer. One is permitted to wonder, faced with such responses to Cézanne's *baigneuses,* whether the measure of such erotic power is precisely the figures' failings.

In fact, the *baigneuses* were consistently discussed in terms of failure—a failure of execution, a failure of discipline, a failure of imagination, a failure of realization ("realization" being Cézanne's own term, indicating the ability of his painting to measure up to his vision). And yet, this language of failure deployed by writers on Cézanne was not motivated, it seems to me, by an outright condemnation of the works but rather by an inability to account for the underlying sense of eroticism of these paintings, which seemed to live up to none of the standards of beauty or technical finesse expected of the genre of the nude.

For many critics, Cézanne's *baigneuses* were understood as an inadequate pursuit of a realist goal: unable to disengage themselves from the terms set forth by impressionist criticism, perhaps, with its emphasis on pleinairism, critics found the artist's eccentric working method—his failure to work from a live model—to be the obvious source of the paintings' gaucheries. In response, perhaps, to the dense, graceless flesh of the London *Bathers,* with their truncated limbs, illegible faces, and eccentric anatomy, Roger Fry for one could claim that Cézanne's "power of conjuring up a credible image to his inner eye . . . has by now become extremely feeble" because "for so many years, [his] fear of models deprived him of all observation of nature."[4] Likewise, in a review of the 1907 Salon d'Automne, Émile Bernard's disapproval of Cézanne's deviations from accepted technique was obvious: "Cézanne does not have knowledge of the human body and has not learned its lessons; he naïvely goes forth, squeezing illogical forms onto a canvas of patient and logical brushstrokes, forms which are illogical because they are ignorant and without structure."[5] And the source of these illogical figures was, to Bernard, also obvious—the refusal to use models ("[Cézanne] did not grasp their form through knowledge and regular use of the model").[6]

Myriad reasons were supplied for Cézanne's resistance to normal studio practice. Gustave Coquiot's comments, published first in 1914, repeat the common theme of Cézanne's fear of working from posed women:

> He did not even have the resource of a model; . . . in Aix it would not have been possible to have a female model pose for him, let alone at the studio of an old man! Once, Cézanne brought a woman from Marseille, but this sparked such an outcry that Mlle Marie Cézanne was the first to intervene, and he never tried again. In fact, he himself was very ill at ease in front of the nude woman; and it was with a real relief that he availed himself again of his old Academies from his time in Suisse's studio and of the engravings in the *Magasin pittoresque,* which were the best and least troubling models for painting his *Bathers.*[7]

Coquiot cites many reasons for Cézanne's unorthodox method of painting the human form, ranging from the conservative society in Aix and the implied objection of even his sister to his own discomfort in front of naked women. In this, he was hardly original, however: such stories had circulated widely since the early 1900s, thanks in large part to the writings of Émile Bernard.

Émile Bernard's first mention of the pictures of female bathers appears in his earliest text on Cézanne, published in 1891, in which he refers to an unidentified composition of *baigneuses,* describing the figures as "female nudes in a strange blurry decor, their elegance more suggestive of sixteenth-century Dianas than anything else."[8] Though seemingly untroubled by the radicality of Cézanne's approach to the nude at that encounter, Bernard would refer to the apparent insufficiencies of Cézanne's work in an article three years later, claiming in Cézanne's defense that the gaucheries and eccentricities of his master's painting were signs of sincerity and purity; he maintained that "one must accept the oeuvre entirely and for what it is, or misunderstand it absolutely; only an artist can appreciate the science of such carefully divided colors, of such subtleties, of such sensibilities, of such a fragile style, loose or wild, of such boldness which is not at all brutal, of such apparent roughness which is nothing other than refinement and beauty."[9] The elegance and refinement to which he earlier referred may have faded in Bernard's eyes by 1905, after he had seen Cézanne's work on his *Large Bathers.* He then avowed "were I to be taken for a fossil, nonetheless I would dare declare that in my eyes Cézanne's *Bathers,* where there is neither idea, nor drawing, nor color, do not constitute the last word in painting."[10]

Bernard's ambivalence toward Cézanne's art in general and his bathers in particular must preface any reading of *Souvenirs sur Paul Cézanne,* which was published in 1907 and had an immediate impact on writings on the artist. It is in this text, which includes the author's most extensive discussion of the bathers to date, that Bernard attempts to explain *why* Cézanne's knowledge of the human body was deficient. It was not, he maintains, simply the result of poor artistic training or an ill-judged decision to substitute tonal for value modeling, as he had claimed in his 1907 Salon d'Automne review; rather, he goes to some trouble to insist, it was Cézanne's fear of women that left him resourceless when it came to painting the series of female bathers. Bernard describes his encounter with the *Large Bathers* (possibly the Barnes version, in front of which Bernard took his famous photograph of an elderly Cézanne) on a visit to Aix in 1905:

> There was also, on a mechanical easel that he had just had installed, a large canvas of female nudes bathing that was in a state of total disorder. The drawing in it struck me as rather deformed. I asked Cézanne why he didn't use models for his nudes. He answered that at his age one had the obligation not to make a woman undress to paint her, that it would be permissible for him, if absolutely necessary, to call on a woman in her fifties, but that he was almost certain he would never find such a person in Aix. He went to his portfolios and showed me some drawings he had made in the Atelier Suisse in his youth. "I've always used these drawings," he said to me. "It's scarcely sufficient, but I have to at my age." *I divined that he was the slave of an extreme sense of decorum, and that this slavery had two causes: the one, that he didn't trust himself with women;* the other, that he had religious scruples and a genuine feeling that these things could not be done in a small provincial town without provoking scandal.[11]

This, then, is the first (rather understated, perhaps) articulation of Cézanne's anxieties about painting the nude model. Not simply a profound sense of decorum, not simply the practical difficulties of finding a small-town woman willing to pose, but something more troubling—the fact that "he didn't trust himself with women," a turn of phrase that invokes images of barely controlled passion toward them—was stopping Cézanne from carrying out his artistic goal. Artistic insufficiency is explained, in Bernard's 1907 account, by sexual anxiety.

Bernard's formulation was repeated (and exaggerated) by other critics, starting almost immediately after the publication of *Souvenirs sur Paul Cézanne.* Élie Faure echoed the theme, locating Cézanne's discomfort in painting from the model in the fact that "this great sensualist feared women more than anything. . . . Like all those who desire women too much, he affected a contempt towards them that was nothing but an homage to their power. Knowing nothing of them, he believed that they took everything, and fled from them, in order not to have to face them with useless resistance."[12] Joachim Gasquet, who once said that "nude flesh made [Cézanne] giddy, he wanted to leap at his models; as soon as they came in he wanted to throw them, half-undressed, onto a mattress. He was excessive in everything," would have agreed with Faure's conclusion that Cézanne's problem lay in his excessive passion for women and not outright misogyny, as many other writers believed.[13]

To say that these writers resorted to Cézanne's biography to make sense of his paintings of the nude—that they relied upon stories of the artist's sexual anxieties to justify his anatomical and formal deviations from accepted standards of the genre—would not be entirely correct. For the texts I have been citing here were, in large part, the same texts from which Cézanne's biography was pieced together. In fact, it would be more legitimate to say that Cézanne's biography was not simply relied on to explain the strange look of his female nudes but was *constructed* in order to do so. And it should not come as a surprise that this explanation of the formal qualities of Cézanne's exploration of the genre had less to do with the artist's actual working method than with the critics' desire to come to terms with these odd paintings.

That the largely accepted explanation of Cézanne's deviation from normal studio practice served a purpose other than objective, journalistic accounting of the artist's method is suggested in a text by Ambroise Vollard. Vollard claimed that "[Cézanne's] dream would have been to have nude models pose in the open air; but that was unfeasible for many reasons, the most important being that women, even when clothed, frightened him."[14] He goes on to say, however, that "[Cézanne] made an exception only for a female servant who had previously worked for him at the Jas de Bouffan, an old creature with a rough-hewn face of whom he remarked admiringly to Zola, 'Look, is that handsome? One would say she's a man!'" When Vollard, on another occasion, expressed surprise that Cézanne was searching for a model to pose for him, Cézanne allegedly responded that, not to worry, he would get some old crow ("une très vieille carne"), and proceeded to paint two portraits and a nude study of the woman.[15] That the painted nudes traditionally identified as resulting from this painting session with the "vieille carne" depict a figure neither particularly old nor particularly ugly points out the irony of Cézanne's remark (fig. 38).[16] Given the evidence of these two studies, it seems clear that Cézanne was neither unable nor incapable of working from the live, naked, female model.[17] (His large number of portraits of women, including his wife, his servants, and others, would seem to suggest that he was not particularly fearful of working from clothed female models, either.)[18]

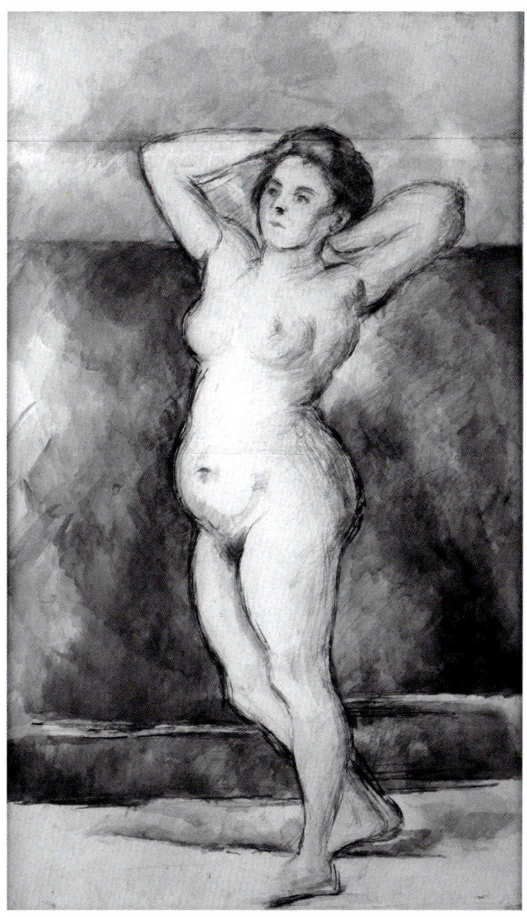

38. Cézanne, *Standing Female Nude*, 1898–99. Watercolor, 89 x 53 cm. Musée du Louvre, Paris.

If Cézanne's failures of execution (his incapability of rendering a figure in any conventional way) were borne of the failures of his working method—which were borne, in turn, of his irrational fears of women—they were compounded by his recourse to other sources of his imagery. If Bernard was the first to suggest that Cézanne's excessive passion toward women made working from the live model impossible, he also claimed that Cézanne's only legitimate alternative—copying from the works of other artists—was deeply flawed. He writes:

[Cézanne] had Charles Blanc's books on the Spanish and Flemish schools, and he paged through them assiduously. Unfortunately this work is mediocre and the reproductions in it are worse than bad. . . . I was incensed by the grotesque distortions that these wood engravings made of the masters' paintings, so that you couldn't recognize them at all. Cézanne, who had only seen the Louvre and was ignorant of most of the originals, believed that the copies were faithful and admired them. I came to understand, finally, that he believed certain of the faults introduced by the engraver or the copyist to be true. I shared my opinion with him and he seemed to doubt it.[19]

Bernard clearly draws on stereotypes of the provincial—as naïve, as unsophisticated, as almost childlike in his inability to understand the limitations of his knowledge and experience—in this passage. Not only is Cézanne's reliance on an inadequately illustrated book at issue but also his incapacity to even recognize the book's failures.[20] That Cézanne's bathers might look the way they do because the artist intended them to was impossible to conceive, and thus two explanations—both matters of biography—were constructed in order to rationalize the insufficiencies of his bodies: the idea that Cézanne's figures appeared the way they did because of his lack of recourse to the model as a consequence of his sexual excesses and the idea that the artist did not know any better than to imagine that his only recourse—Blanc's book—was inadequate for his purposes.[21]

If the failure of Cézanne's *baigneuses* was the result of the failures of his working method, it was also, for the critics, the result of a more fundamental failure: more than the practical exigencies inhibiting his figurative works, it was the feebleness of Cézanne's imagination that was most troubling. Not only was it the case, according to Bernard, that "he did not know how to draw without the model, a serious obstacle to all valid creation," but worse, "Cézanne's imagination was impoverished, he possessed only a very fine sense of composition."[22] As Guila Ballas has demonstrated, this was not a remark easily forgotten. Only one week after the publication of Bernard's *Souvenirs* Camille Mauclair referred to Cézanne's "total lack of imagination and taste" and his "inability to create a figure or a composition," while in 1910 Élie Faure would speak of Cézanne's "pauvreté d'invention" and Fry would later comment on "his fundamental inaptitude of invention."[23]

IMAGINATION AND THE IDEAL

For Bernard, at least, Cézanne's lack of imagination was clearly linked to another of his failures: his inability to achieve the ideal. Partly an influence of the Symbolist moment, but clearly also the sign of a growing conservatism on Bernard's part, the determination that beauty should be removed from immediate or mundane reference, the belief in the elevated quality of the ideal, was clearly also a wish that the subjects painted should be stripped of the complicated, messy, illogical, and often ugly desires that motivated them. When Bernard described Cézanne's approach to his painting subjects in a 1904 text, he emphasized Cézanne's progressive disengagement from his initial communion with the motif as the mark of his exemplary practice:

Such is his working method: at first, complete submission to the model; carefully, the establishment of the composition, discovery of the contours, the proportional relations; then, through very meditative sessions, the animation of colored sensations, the elevation of form towards decorative composition and of color towards the most harmonious pitch. Thus the more the artist works, the more his work distances itself from the motif, the more he distances himself from the opacity of the model which served as his point of departure, the more he enters into a purified form of painting [*la peinture nue*] which has no other goal than itself; the more he abstracts his image, the more he simplifies it with fullness, after having conceived it narrowly, consistently, hesitantly.

Little by little the work grows, comes into being as the result of a pure conception.[24]

The process of abstracting the motif, of submitting it to the rules of representation, should have been, according to Bernard, a way of progressively emptying or purifying the object of the painter's investment in it. The resulting work would achieve a sort of unadulterated aesthetic disinterest.[25] (It is not surprising to note that in Bernard's description, disinterest in the motif is another way of saying defense against the motif: he speaks of Cézanne's ability to distance himself from the "opacity" of his model, which implies its resistance, its unknowability, and therefore its potential threat, perhaps. Suggestive, it seems to me, when that model is imagined to be a woman.)

Bernard's discomfort in the subsequent years, faced with the distorted forms, gaucheries, and emphatic unidealism of Cézanne's *Large Bathers* was the result in part of his sinking feeling that the master whom he had set out to extol was severely lacking in his ability to make certain types of painting. His effort to locate this deficiency in an image of Cézanne as a sexually anxious man is telling. Bernard realized with horror that the distance between an ideal depiction of the female nude and Cézanne's own "deformed" specimens was the measure of Cézanne's passion for his subject.[26] However, it was not simply the fact that Cézanne's *baigneuses* failed to live up to this notion of the disinterested, aestheticized, ideal but the *way* they failed that most troubled Bernard. For it was precisely the eccentricities of technique and the inadequacy of bodies that accounted for their failure. This is certainly the lesson not only of Bernard's writings on the artist but also of another crucial text: Bernard's own series of bather paintings, done in the shadow of his admired elder in the 1890s.[27]

It is not clear which of Cézanne's *baigneuses* Bernard might have seen before 1891, at which time the latter's first written words on the paintings appeared, but he undoubtedly encountered them at Père Tanguy's color shop and in the collections of fellow artists and *aficionados*, including Victor Chocquet, Camille Pissarro, and Henri Rouart.[28] Whatever the case, Bernard's knowledge of Cézanne's paintings seems to have been extensive enough to prompt his own exploration of the theme in a series that begins with a group of paintings likely intended as a triptych or larger assembly of pictures: *Bathers with a Red Cow* (ca. 1889) (fig. 39), *Bathers with Waterlilies* (ca. 1889), and a third *Bathers* composition, currently in a private collection (fig. 40). The first two were dated by Bernard as having been done in 1887, but MaryAnne Stevens has convincingly argued that all three were undertaken at the same time, perhaps 1889 as indicated by the date on the now-lost canvas (although an even later date would not be unreasonable).[29] About nineteen other compositions on the theme of the bathers painted in a wide range of "modern" styles were completed at some point after these.[30]

To compare, say, Bernard's *Seven Bathers,* one of these later images, which is admittedly his most Cézannian canvas from this series, with works such as Cézanne's *Five Bathers under the Trees* or *Three Bathers,* one may initially note similarities in the treat-

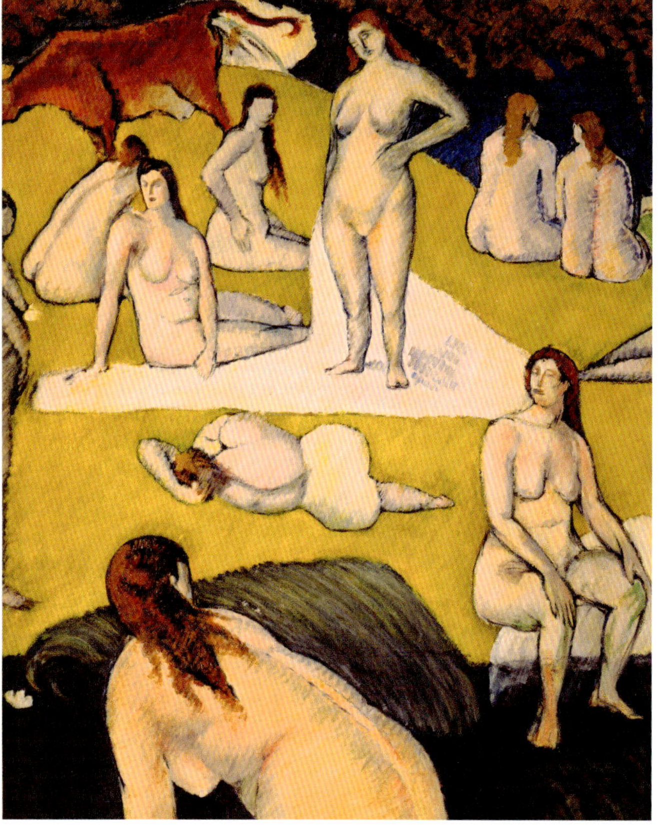

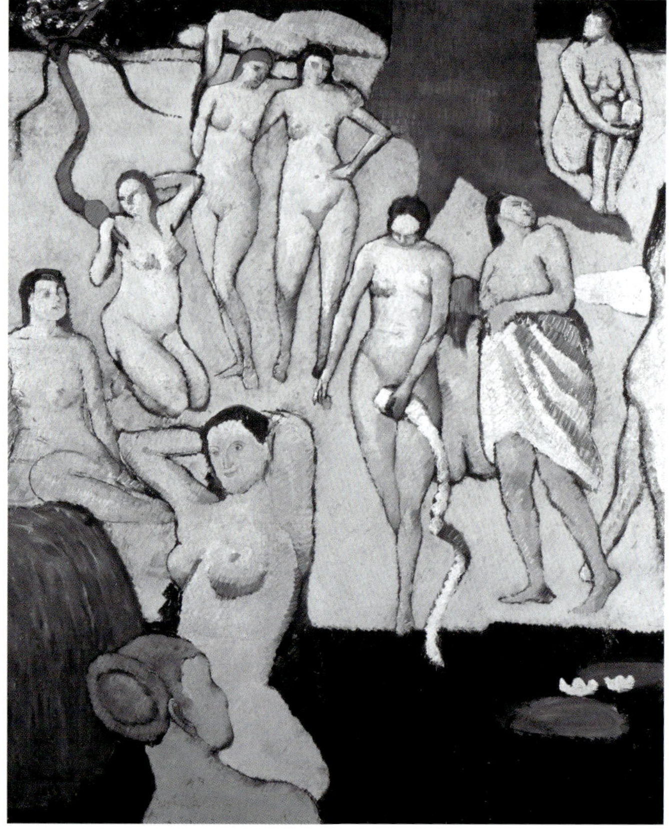

39. Émile Bernard, *Bathers with a Red Cow*, ca. 1889. Oil on canvas, 72.4 x 92.7 cm. Musée d'Orsay, Paris. © 2006 ARS/ADAGP, Paris.

40. Émile Bernard, *Bathers*, ca. 1889. Oil on canvas, 73 x 92 cm. Private collection. © 2006 ARS/ADAGP, Paris.

ment of the subject of the nude figure in an idyllic landscape, in paint handling and facture (insistently parallel strokes of vividly colored paint), and in figural type (heavy-bottomed, thick-waisted, unconventional nudes with emphatic outlines and flattened forms) (figs. 41 and 42).[31] There are, in fact, striking resemblances between certain of Bernard's women and certain of Cézanne's: the bending figure in the lower left corner, whose unnaturally long arm is anchored to the lower edge of the canvas, seems to be related to the striding figure that shows up in a number of Cézanne's bather scenes from the period 1876–77, including *Three Bathers* and *Four Bathers* (1876–77).[32] The central, brown-haired figure seen from behind with her left arm bent over her head in Bernard's picture is a familiar character from Cézanne's oeuvre—she is first seen in *The Temptation of St. Anthony* around 1870 and recurs in the pastoral compositions of both male and female bathers in the 1870s and 1880s, including *Five Bathers under the Trees*. The figure along the upper left edge of Bernard's painting, sitting to the right of the tree trunk, with one arm bent over her head and the other holding a hank of her hair, seems to be at least in part related to the seated figure on the left-hand side of this same Cézanne painting as well.

Whatever the similarities, it is the differences between the two practices that are most illuminating here. The facture of Bernard's work, for example, reveals only a superficial understanding of Cézanne's painting process, consisting of parallel strokes of paint simply laid over broad areas of flat, pure color, such as the bluish-green touches over the expanse of yellow that covers more than a third of the painting, indicating a grassy field. Bernard's are not constructive strokes, in other words; one must instead look for the source of this aspect of his technique in Paul Gauguin, his mentor and collaborator between 1886 and 1891.[33] Despite the negligible difference in the sizes of the paintings, there is a vast divergence in their scale, which is partly a result of the smaller brushstroke used by Bernard than that used by Cézanne and partly the result of the far greater particularity of Bernard's painting in relation to the fairly cursory indications of Cézanne's.[34] Bernard's painting, besides incorporating a larger number of figures than either the *Five Bathers under the Trees* or *Three Bathers,* also insists on a far greater detail in those figures, especially as it involves the articulation of their

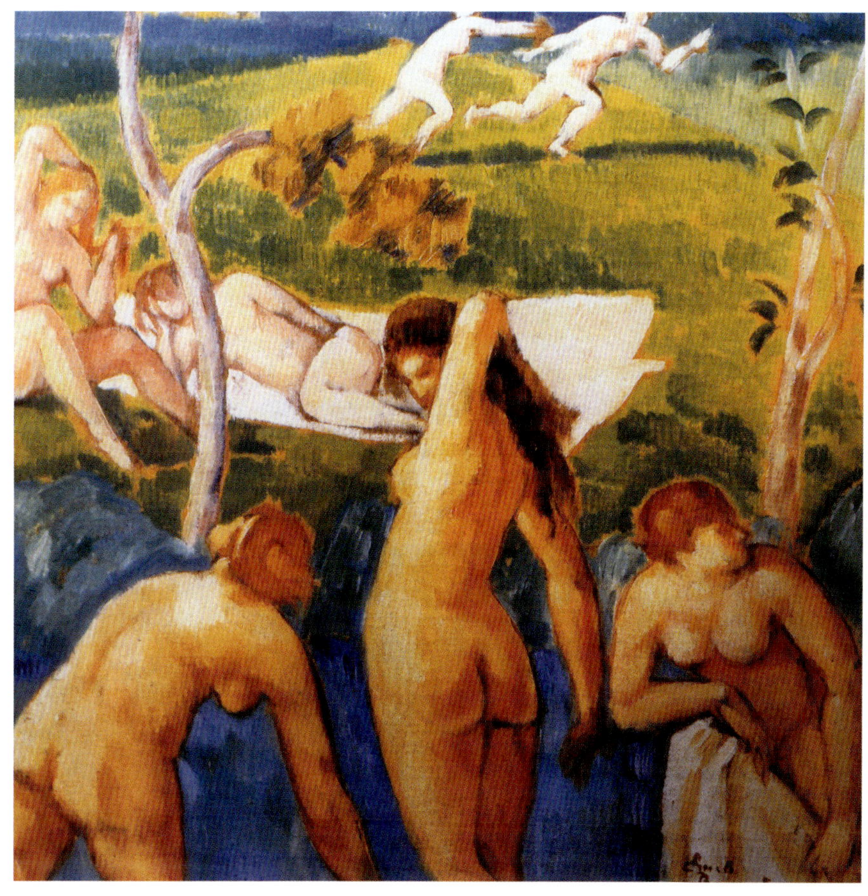

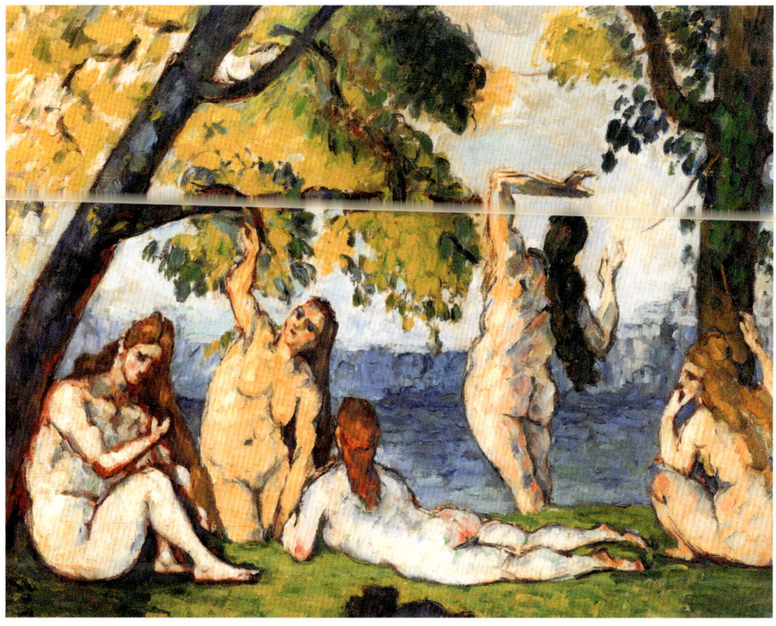

41. (*above*) Detail of Émile Bernard, *Seven Bathers,* c. 1889. Oil on canvas, 61 x 63 cm. Private collection. © 2006 ARS/ADAGP, Paris.

42. (*left*) Cézanne, *Five Bathers under the Trees,* ca. 1875. Oil on canvas, 60 x 73 cm. Private collection, Paris.

three-dimensionality. The shading and contouring of the central figure's back, for example, is utterly unlike the far less specific treatment of the back of the striding figure on the left-hand side of Cézanne's *Three Bathers.* There are also significant contrasts in the approach to composition and spatial construction among the three works: Cézanne refuses, for the most part, a foreground, arranging his figures in a frieze-like arrangement within a fairly narrow pictorial band in the middle plane of his canvases, thus compressing the sense of spatial expanse, where Bernard anchors his central figures to the bottom edge of the painting and deploys figures over three distinct planes, each one separated from the other by a seemingly significant distance resulting in a relatively open pictorial space.

The figures themselves, too, seem only distantly related on closer inspection. Cézanne's, of course, are marked by those formal "inadequacies," those gaucheries, that Bernard was to lament in his writings: in *Five Bathers under the Trees,* one might point to the dwarfed leg, improperly foreshortened, of the right-hand bather, or the flattened-out lower half of the reclining figure, or the reddened, heavy outline of the left-hand bather, or the endless reworking of the contour that links sharply bent elbow to armpit to curiously lumpy waist in the central bather. In *Three Bathers* we may turn to the same inadequate foreshortening of the leg of the right-hand bather, her equally withered arm raised to her hair, the spatial confusion of the torso of the central figure such that her breasts seem fused to her belly, or to the insistent gracelessness of the striding figure, with her thick-waisted heaviness, for examples of that with which Bernard would later express his dissatisfaction.

Bernard's figures seem to correct these "mistakes." Gone are the more striking formal eccentricities of Cézanne's figures—note the correctly foreshortened calf of the seated bather halfway up the left-hand side of *Seven Bathers,* for example—and gone, too, are the reworkings and hesitations of contour found in the Provençal artist's images. Bernard's contours, rather, are sharp and crisp, relatively speaking, and while they do not have the heaviness of his more properly *cloisonniste* works, such as *Bathers with a Red Cow,* they are closer to that work than to Cézanne's quivering *cerne.* Bernard's bodies are normalized in other ways as well. For example, the figure leaning forward and holding a bit of drapery in the lower right-hand corner of the canvas has the same half-moon, pendulous breasts as the central figure of *Three Bathers,* but hers are not fused with her belly as the latter's are and thus somehow seem more breastlike. The figure in the left foreground of *Seven Bathers,* leaning into the water, has a figure that displays some of the heavy, thick-waistedness of Cézanne's striding figure from *Three Bathers,* with a similar prominent shadow of a spinal column running down her back; Bernard, however, "corrects" the androgyny, or rather the ambiguity of gender, of Cézanne's figure by placing a curious, almost perverse breast that shows through her right armpit, in a move meant to secure, once and for all, the femaleness of this figure viewed from the rear.

Bernard's attempts at "normalizing" Cézanne's figures extend beyond anatomical correction, as the case of the added breast suggests: there is obviously something more at stake here. The seated figure holding her hair in Bernard's work, for instance, when compared to her counterpart in Cézanne's *Five Bathers under the Trees,* is clearly of a different, more conventionally seductive breed, for while the latter's pose closes off access to the figure—this bather's left arm crosses over her breast so that she may touch her

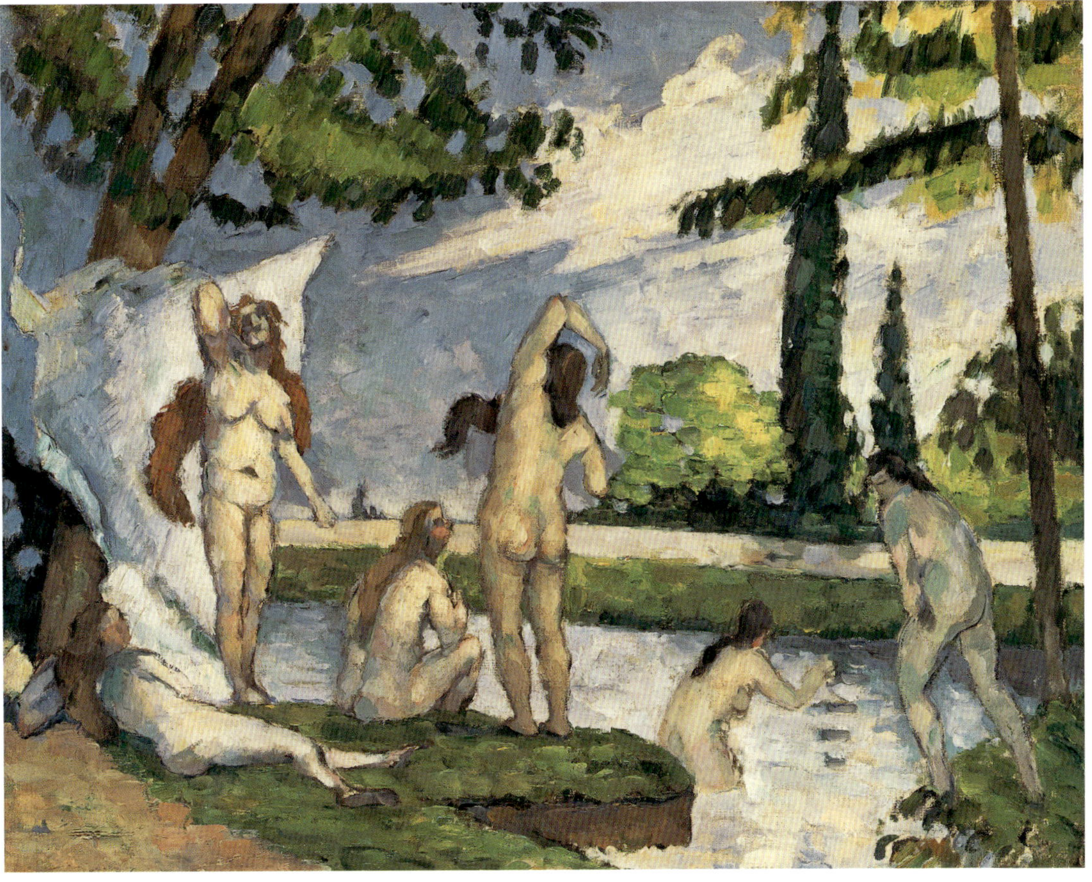

hair—Bernard's figure is posed so as to open herself for visual display, with her left arm bent over her head and her breasts fully revealed. (Notable as well in this contrast is the splay-legged pose of the Bernard figure as opposed to the closed thighs of the Cézanne figure.) Most striking, however, is the central foreground figure of *Seven Bathers:* while Cézanne's use of the pose tends to obscure the figure's sexual characteristics—see the central, standing figure in his *Bathers* (1875–76) for instance, in which only the slightest narrowing of the torso indicates a woman's waist, and a touch of blue paint against her left contour seems to emphatically *deny* the possibility of a breast coming into view (fig. 43)—Bernard returns the pose to a more conventional gesture of seduction. His temptress's arm bends dramatically over her mass of hair, revealing a perfectly pert breast along the left contour of her body, while her other arm (this one curiously disengaged) frames the curve of her arched back. Her waist is nipped in, her buttocks swell, her chin is turned downward, as is her gaze. She is, in other words, the perfect image of coy, demure, and alluring female sexuality.

43. Cézanne, *Bathers,* 1875–76. Oil on canvas, 38.1 x 46 cm. Metropolitan Museum of Art, N.Y.

All of these differences, these "corrections" that Bernard makes in relation to the example set by Cézanne, add up to something curious, almost paradoxical. Bernard takes Cézanne's women and makes them straightforwardly erotic, even titillating. That is not to say that he turns Cézanne's figures into a series of Salon Venuses; Bernard's painting mines some part of the by-now conventionalized characteristics of avant-garde painting of the nude. But look at the changes he effects: the figures are more highly detailed, not just a flurried accumulation of painted dabs, and they exist in a more easily readable space without being entirely embedded in the pictorial surface. That is to say, Bernard's figures refuse the more radical gaucheries of Cézanne's, they are anatomically correct, with a clear and firm contour, they are not overwhelmed by clotted pigment and violent brushwork. They are clearly female—none of the Provençal's ambiguous lumps and tenuous femininity—and coquettishly seductive. What other reason is there, Bernard seems to ask, for painting the female nude?

Bernard's reworkings of Cézanne's compositions, then, are evidently attempts to reinvest the female bathers with a certain and clear sexual charge. It would not, in fact, be unreasonable to assume that Bernard disapproved of Cézanne's *baigneuses* simply because they lacked the eroticism the subject seemed to warrant. However, we know that this is not the case. We know, to the contrary, that Bernard's discomfort with them is expressed in his writings as an uneasiness with the overflowing desire out of which they seemed to him to spring—in Cézanne's fear of working from the female model, in his excessive desire for women. Bernard was *not,* in the end, reinvesting these figures with the sexuality that he believed they *lacked* in their earlier, Cézannian incarnation. He was, rather, relocating an eroticism that he already felt to be present from the eccentricities of the painted mark to the bodies depicted, reterritorializing the signs of desire that Cézanne had deterritorialized, containing them in a more acceptable, fetishized form. Rather than circulate freely over the surface of the canvas, the marks of desire should be bounded, says Bernard, by bodies that are worthy of their attention. The problem for Bernard was not that Cézanne imagined the genre of the nude in erotic terms; rather it was that he had rendered the language of that eroticism almost illegible.

CHASTE MEMORY

Despite the visibility of the motif of the male bather in the artist's oeuvre, few of the artist's most important early commentators discuss the paintings and of those that do, none talk about them at any length. Émile Bernard in his early writings on the artist mentions the male bathers in passing and then only to remark that he has not seen any of them (a highly unlikely claim); Maurice Denis, who wrote an article that was as influential in England as it was in France, thanks to its republication by Roger Fry in the *Burlington Magazine,* does not mention the male bather pictures at all; Fry, in his study of the artist, mentions the Barnes bathers without actually specifying its subject matter; and Vollard mentions the *Bathers at Rest III* but only in the context of its refusal by the Luxembourg after Caillebotte's death in 1883.[35]

And what of those who did mention the male bathers? Leaving aside the majority of workaday critics who expressed typical but uninteresting outrage following the exhibition of *Bathers at Rest III* at the impressionist show in 1877, Georges Rivière provided the only positive and thoughtful commentary when he wrote: "M. Cézanne is, in his works, a Greek of the classical era; his canvases have the calm, the heroic serenity of classical paintings and ceramics, and the ignoramuses who laugh in front of the *Baigneurs,* for example, are like barbarians criticizing the Parthenon."[36] Gustave Geffroy, writing in 1894, described the *Bathers at Rest III* as "coagulated and luminous, [taking] on the brilliant and bluish-white look of a thickly decorated *faïence*."[37] Comments such as these, when they appeared, were curiously neutral in their approach to the images in question; all seem to talk *around* the naked men. This was a sort of looking away: not a word on the nude bodies, on their sources in art history, on their strange interaction on the canvas.

Notwithstanding this lacuna in the criticism, from the moment of the appearance of Paul Cézanne's paintings of male and female bathers in the 1870s onward, almost all commentators have insisted on distinguishing those works that feature women planted in the foliage of their natural surroundings from those which feature men. They have done so despite the clear formal similarities that exist among the *baigneuses* and *baigneurs* and despite the existence of a very large number of paintings in which the identification of the gender of the depicted figures is speculative at best. How have they justified such a segregation of types? They have done so, in large part, by claiming that the works had two very different sources, the men in Cézanne's memory, the women in his imagination.

Locating the source of the *baigneurs* in Cézanne's nostalgic memories of youth or in his objective observation and, simultaneously, locating the source of the *baigneuses* in his imagination was a way for early critics of Cézanne's work to claim that the motivations for the one series were qualitatively different from the motivations for the other: while the *baigneuses* were seen to be the evidence of Cézanne's erotic fantasy, the *baigneurs* emphatically were not. Why the need for such insistence, especially given, on the one hand, that in classical and academic traditions, the male nude was thought to signify the lofty aspirations and abstract truths of higher culture, not sexuality and desire, and on the other hand, that Cézanne's eccentric figurative style seems, on the face of it, hardly erotic at all? First, because the depiction of the male body at the end of the nineteenth century, in the context of a painterly rhetoric of contemporaneity and naturalism, inevitably posed certain problems for both artist and viewer. And second, because one of the features of Cézanne's painting of the nude was a dislocation of the signifier of the erotic—sited formerly in the object of desire—to the formal qualities of the painting process itself: the brushstroke, the evidence of the artist's touch, the eccentricities of figuration. In turning the sign of the artist's erotic investment in his motif into a free-floating signifier no longer grounded unambiguously in the female body, Cézanne's technique prompted his earliest critics to squirm at the possibility that his images of the male nude were not entirely heroic nor appropriately disinterested.

A MORALITY TALE

Is it hard to imagine that Cézanne's paintings of *baigneurs* were the cause of a certain discomfort for his late-nineteenth- and early-twentieth-century commentators and that this discomfort had more than a little to do with their subject matter? The male nude, after all, had existed as a representational vehicle for grand historical and mythological themes, a category of painting increasingly relegated to an attenuated academicism by the last third of the nineteenth century.[38] All but disappeared, then, the genre was only revived in realist circles, briefly, in the 1860s, in the work of Frédéric Bazille and Auguste Renoir, in images like Renoir's *Young Boy with Cat* of 1868–69 and Bazille's *Fisherman with a Net*

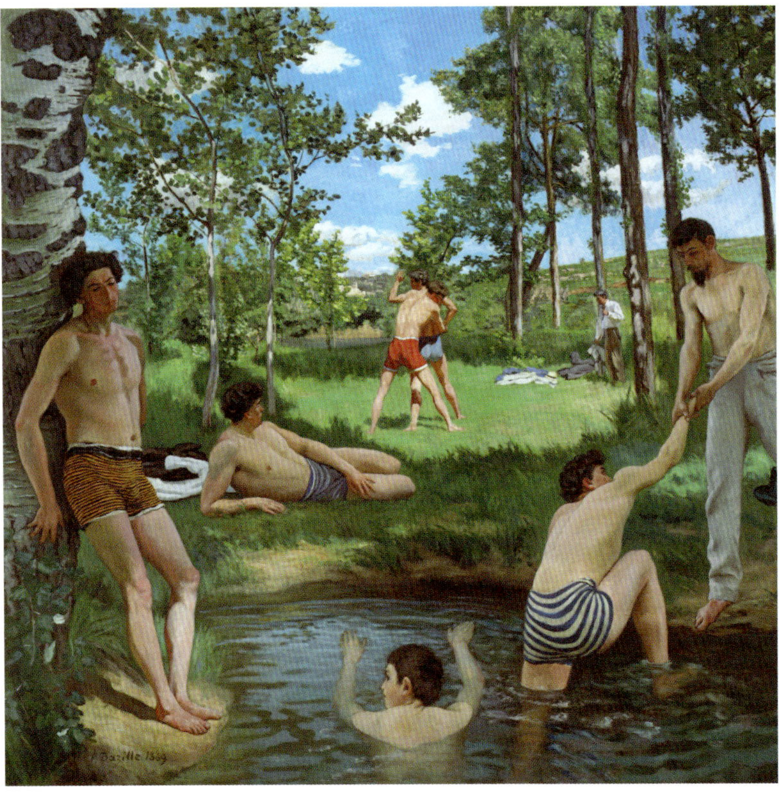

44. Fréderic Bazille, *Summer Scene,* 1869. Oil on canvas, 160 x 160.7 cm. Fogg Art Museum, Harvard University, Cambridge, Mass., gift of Mr. and Mrs. F. Meynier de Salinelles. 1937.78.

of 1868 and *Summer Scene,* of the following year (fig. 44).[39] Of these, Bazille's *Summer Scene,* especially—a work that held great interest for Cézanne—has something to tell us about the challenge of painting the naked male body during this period.

More troubling to a nineteenth-century audience looking at Bazille's or Renoir's paintings in the 1860s than the mere the reappearance of the male nude would have been, I imagine, the guise in which he made his entrance: not as an idealized, timeless hero but as a modern individual or at least as a naked body in a contemporary setting—not as a god in drapery but as a boy in a bathing suit. It was precisely this desire to make modern a traditional motif that rendered the images so jarring: Renoir's reconception of the mythological figure of Cupid within the context of modern life painting, like Bazille's rearticulation of contemporary leisurely activity through the structures of classical models, was especially problematic given the limits of the acceptability of the naked body in nineteenth-century visual culture. As Whitney Davis has proposed, in this period "male nudity had to be constructed as innocent, a conventional Adamic nakedness that a viewer *happens* to see rather than the new nakedness oriented toward the viewer *in order* for him to see it."[40] While certain painters of the period accommodated these proscriptions by presenting the male figure in acceptable, modern life scenarios centered primarily on labor or sport—think of Gustave Caillebotte's working men in *The Floor Scrapers* or even Gustave Courbet's *Wrestlers* (figs. 45 and 46)—the slightly ridiculous bathing trunks of Bazille's men in *Summer Scene,* far from reclaiming the decency of the image, mark these bodies as deliberately naked rather than innocently nude, and their seemingly aimless activity creates a painting at which we are invited to look for the sake of looking.[41]

How then to read the languorous pose of the bather on the far left side of Bazille's *Summer Scene,* leaning with his back against a tree, face turned away and eyes dreamily averted, right hand caressing the tree trunk, a transposition of a classic Saint Sebastian pose now removed from both its original spiritual narrative and its venerable art historical lineage? Or the figure lying on the grass, propped on one elbow with his hand so casually, but not so casually, placed on his thigh—a gesture that brings to mind Manet's *Olympia* but that is in fact a borrowing from images of classical river gods, like the one that motivated the figure of the reclining gentleman in Manet's other painting, the *Déjeuner sur l'herbe*? While these references to Manet might imply that Bazille's painting shares some of the *Déjeuner's* conceptual intent, in fact Manet's pastiche operated on the premise that the original source for the central grouping, the river gods in Raimondi's engraving after Raphael's *Judgment of Paris,* made exactly no contribution to the "meaning" of the final painting outside of the utter arbitrariness of that source. Manet was resolutely *not* saying that modern men and women were "like" these classical models. Bazille, on the other hand, was: he not only wanted to give his contemporary image a kind of art historical *weight* by tying it to both the short history of avant-garde painting and the longer history of the male nude, but he was also taking quite literally Baudelaire's injunction that painters need to find the "heroism" in modern life.

If Bazille was consciously trying to navigate the strictures around the representation of the male nude in this moment in history, certainly it was no help that one of the sources he borrowed—the Saint Sebastian figure—had been, in the confines of a specific religious narrative, the locus of an authorized homoeroticism since the Renaissance (fig. 47).[42] To put this another way: Bazille's *Summer Scene* may well have been expected to generate a certain critical anxiety because it seemed to contain the marks of "erotic identification" that would be considered out of place in a painting of naked men. Not only was this hinted at, to some extent, in the figures' poses—their passivity and their averted gazes (a trope of academic painting of the female nude, it was a way of representing or constructing the male gaze, or an invitation to look, at the woman's body)—but it was suggested by the visibility of the artist's brushstroke, since the brushstroke was, in nineteenth-century critical language of nude painting, increasingly equated with the caress.[43] In that case, Bazille's impressionist technique was one that raised

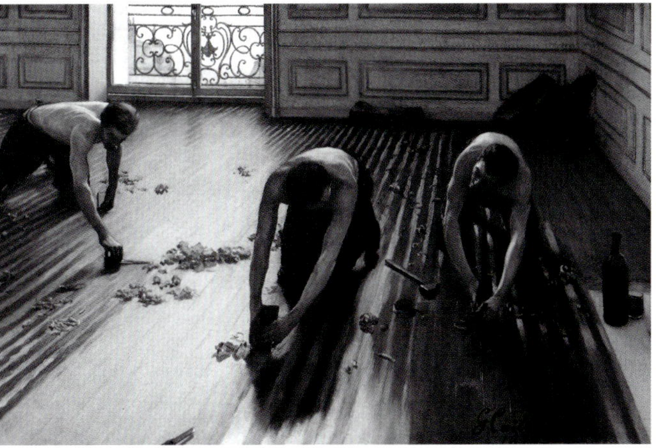

45. Gustave Caillebotte, *The Floor Scrapers,* 1875. Oil on canvas, 102 x 146.5 cm. Musée d'Orsay, Paris.

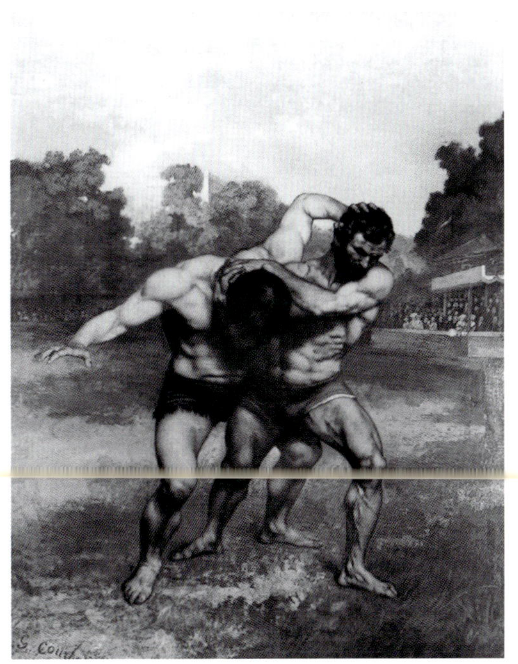

46. Gustave Courbet, *Wrestlers,* 1853. Oil on canvas, 252 x 198 cm. Szépművészeti Museum, Budapest.

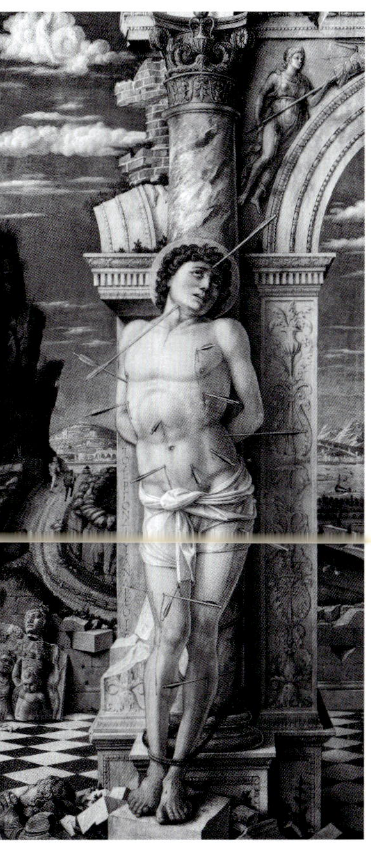

47. Andrea Mantegna, *St. Sebastian,* ca. 1455–60. Tempera on panel, 68 x 30.6 cm. Kunsthistorisches Museum, Vienna.

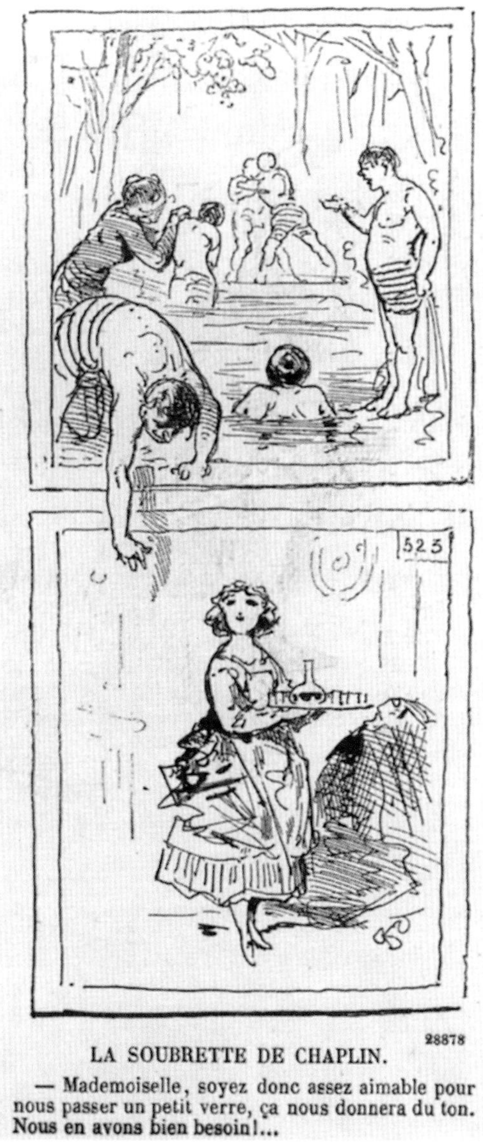

48. Bertall, "Chaplin's Lady's Maid," *Le Journal Amusant,* 1870.

the disturbing issue of the male brush caressing the male body, a not insignificant idea, as we will see in our discussion of Cézanne below.

If indeed Bazille's painting provoked an anxious response in its viewers and critics, what would this anxiety have looked like? Perhaps the answer is to be found in a caricature by Bertall that appeared in *Le Journal Amusant* in 1870, the same year that Bazille's painting was shown at the Salon. Titled "La Soubrette de Chaplin" ("Chaplin's Lady's Maid"), it depicts *Summer Scene* hanging above Charles Chaplin's picture of a pretty young barmaid proffering a tray of drinks, called *Young Woman Holding a Tray* (fig. 48).[44] One of the men from Bazille's picture—the dreamy, languorous one on the far left—reaches down into the painting below and says "Mademoiselle, soyez donc assez aimable pour nous passer un petit verre, ça nous donnera du ton. Nous en avons bien besoin!" (Roughly: "Miss, please be so kind as to pass us up a glass; it will give us some tone. We really need it!")

Like most Salon caricature, it is difficult to read as serious art criticism: after all, its lament is a familiar one, criticizing the work for its failure to employ traditional technique (thus the figures' "lack of tone," presumably both coloristic and anatomical).[45] But I find it interesting that the young man reaches down to the young woman almost as if to distract us from the fact that what we have here is a picture of a group of men who are both basically naked and intensely interested in each other. In the original painting, in fact, the circuit of gazes among the figures is entirely closed: the standing man at the far left looks down, out of the corner of his eye, to the swimming boy, who looks back over at him; the two figures in the right foreground look at each other as one helps the other out of the pond; the reclining figure in the middle ground looks at the man in the trees undressing; and the two wrestling figures, while not looking at each other, have their backs to the viewer as they go about their sporting embrace. Bertall's caricature might thus insert into Bazille's painting what is otherwise disturbingly *absent* from it: a reason around which to organize all of the sensual pleasure of the leisure activities being enjoyed by these men, an interruption of this closed circuit of gazes. In other words, a woman.[46] For otherwise, none is present in Bazille's painting, either as the object of desire or as its subject, either as motif or as viewer. (The latter would have been unimaginable—to paint these naked men for the pleasure of the *female* viewer, that is.) It seems that Bazille's audience was left with the jarring possibility that the beauty of the bodies in *Summer Scene,* the sensuousness of the poses, existed for the delectation of the universal (read: male) viewer.

As it was, this "anxiety," if it indeed existed at the time, can only be measured by silence today. Only Bazille's words assure us that the work was in fact noticed at all among the hundreds of canvases hanging at the Salon: "My painting is in a very good place, everyone can see it and talks about it; many people say more bad than good things about it, but I have made a name for myself, and from now on, they will look at whatever I do."[47] Notwithstanding Bazille's confident optimism, few commentators mentioned Bazille's painting in their Salon reviews and this despite its favorable placement. Only Zacharie Astruc spoke at any length on it, finding in it "the stunning plenitude of light—the particular impression of [having been painted in] the open air, the power of daylight."[48] Astruc discussed the quality of light, the relation of the work to tradition, the value of realism, and the quality of truth in *Summer Scene.* What is missing from Astruc's words is any mention of the men populating this light-filled scene.

The case of Bazille and his bathers highlights what was at stake in the painting of the male nude for progressive artists in the last third of the nineteenth century: the problem of how to present the male body in a naturalist context, outside the heroicizing structures of neoclassical mythological drama or history painting.[49] But more than that, it raises the question not only of how these paintings could be painted but also of how these paintings could be viewed. This problem of how one (a "one" presumed to be male) was to look at the naked male body in representation is central to any inquiry into Cézanne's bathers.

BAIGNEURS: MEMORY AND REALISM

Cézanne himself took up the painting of male bathers in the mid-1870s and focused his attention on the subject again in the years around 1885–95. He was profoundly influenced by Bazille's *Summer Scene* and in fact used almost every part of Bazille's painting in one or another of his own works.[50] More important than any of his iconographical borrowings from Bazille, however, are his conceptual affinities with that painter—Cézanne's images are strange at least in part because, like Bazille's, they are a tissue of quotations from sources in art history. Figures from classical sculpture or baroque painting show up in Cézanne's compositions like recurring characters, taking up the same poses from work to work in defiance of claims that his method was that of pure and obsessive observation of the natural world.[51]

Echoing these sources from the past, the *baigneurs* seem suspended between an eternal past and the present. The figure holding a bit of deeply cleft drapery who occurs as the central character in a large number of Cézanne's bather compositions, including the Paris *Bathers* of circa 1890 (pl. IV), is based on a classical sculpture of a Roman orator or perhaps on Signorelli's drawing of *The Living Carrying the Dead,* a photo of which was owned by Cézanne (fig. 49).[52] With his serene pose and chiseled musculature, he seems to exist

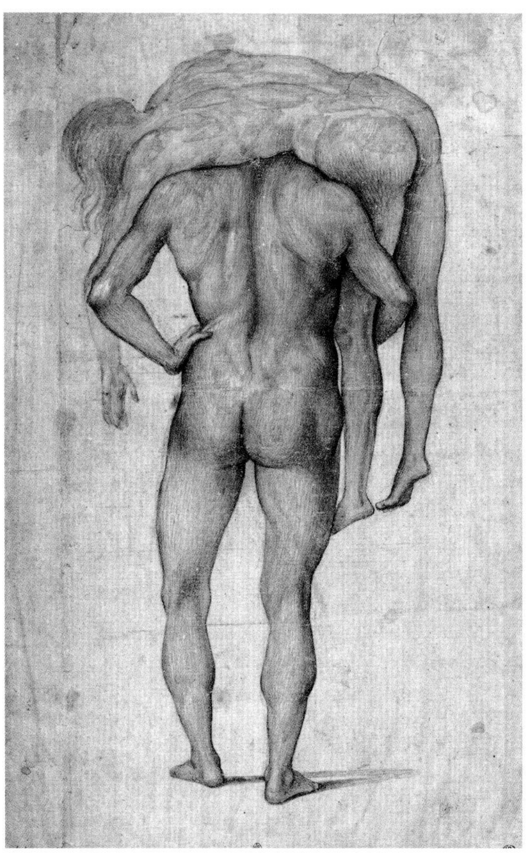

49. Luca Signorelli, sketch of a nude man with a cadaver on his shoulders. Charcoal, wash, and watercolor on paper, 35.5 x 22.5 cm. Musée du Louvre, Paris.

in the timeless, idealizing realm of the classical age. Timeless, that is, until one notices the man standing to his right, wearing white "trunks" (pl. V)—a marker less of contemporary bathing attire than of studio practice, since these were the preferred mode of dress for male models in life drawing classes—or the small figure in the background between them, who waves his arms over his head in a gesture of boisterous play.[53]

Gustave Geffroy, writing in 1895, felt this tension in Cézanne's bather paintings, describing their figures as "erected like statues amid admirable landscapes of warm blue skies, of violently bursting foliage, deep-rooted and delicate, free and blooming like the fruits of nature and at the same time, by the magic of art, deliberate and stylized like the arrangements of an ideal park."[54] There is a certain elision, I believe, in Geffroy's words (more apparent in the original French), between figure and ground: not only does the landscape hover between the natural and the artificial but so, too, do the figures, "erected like statues," within it. Too strange, too emphatically modern in technique to be part of an idealizing, classicizing, Arcadian past, and at the same time too stilted and too overlaid with competing historical references to be utterly contemporaneous, Cézanne's male bathers seem to resist any attempt to place them in a time of their own. This quality of being caught between two moments has not gone unremarked by other critics of Cézanne's work. The male bathers have generally been treated either as studies from nature or as memories of Cézanne's innocent, youthful play with his childhood friends Émile Zola and Baptistin Baille: that is to say, they have been understood as representations of either an idealized past or a witnessed present or, more often, as suspended between the two, in a move that replicates the temporal instability of the images themselves.[55]

For the first of these interpretations—the bathers as studies of soldiers bathing by the river—there is no documentary evidence. While Cézanne did refer, in one of his letters, to a certain M. Rolland who made a tempting offer to pose for him on the banks of the Arc, neither was this Rolland a soldier nor was this plan ever realized.[56] This interpretive trope seems to have emerged among the closely knit group of Cézanne *aficionados* in the 1890s.[57] And though the story was eventually attributed to Cézanne himself—or, at least, in the words that Gasquet attributed to Cézanne in his 1921 book—the claim that the *baigneurs* were the result of these plein-air figure studies did not appear in print until 1910.[58]

As for the second of these interpretations—that the images of male bathers constitute some sort of memory image, nostalgic recollections of a happy and healthy youth—there is scarcely any more "proof." A letter from Cézanne to Émile Zola in June 1859 includes a drawing of three young men (presumably Zola, Baille, and the artist himself) frolicking around a swimming hole, although the sociability and athleticism depicted there, not to mention the fact that it was done almost twenty years before the artist's most concerted work on the theme, make it difficult to understand it as a "clue" to unlocking the meaning of the series (fig. 50). Nor, for that matter, was the drawing available to scholars until 1937 when John Rewald first published the letter.[59]

More influential for the elaboration of this interpretation, which linked the images of *baigneurs* to Cézanne's youth and his joy in bathing with his friends in the lakes and streams of Provence, were the early chapters of Zola's *L'Oeuvre.* Although, as discussed in chapter 1, it is a subject of debate to what extent Zola's book was a roman à clef, it is clear that for certain portions of his fiction, Zola relied on details culled from his own life and his relationship with a number of close friends, including Cézanne.[60] For example, he recounts Lantier's adolescence:

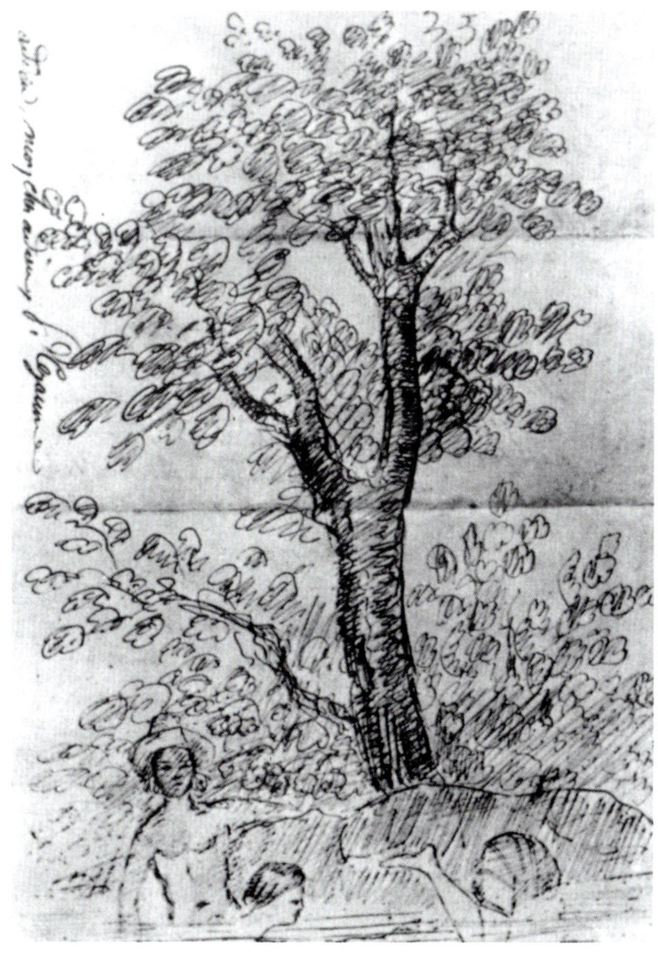

50. Cézanne, *Bathers under a Tree,* letter to Émile Zola, June 1859. Bibliothèque nationale de France, Paris.

In summer especially their dream was the Viorne, the mountain torrent that waters the low-lying meadows of Plassans. They could swim when they were scarcely twelve, and they loved to splash about in the deeper parts of the stream; they would spend whole days, stark naked, lying on the burning sand, then diving back into the water, endlessly grubbing for water plants or watching for eels. They practically lived in the river, and the combination of clear water and sunshine seemed to prolong their childhood, so that even when they were already young men they still sounded like a trio of laughing urchins as they ambled back into Plassans on a sultry July evening after a day on the river.[61]

It may be that the mere repetition of such "recollections" in writings otherwise devoid of references to the male bathers was enough to suggest a source for the paintings.[62] Élie Faure, for example, in his 1910 text on the artist, implies such an association between Cézanne's paintings *in general* and his childhood memories:

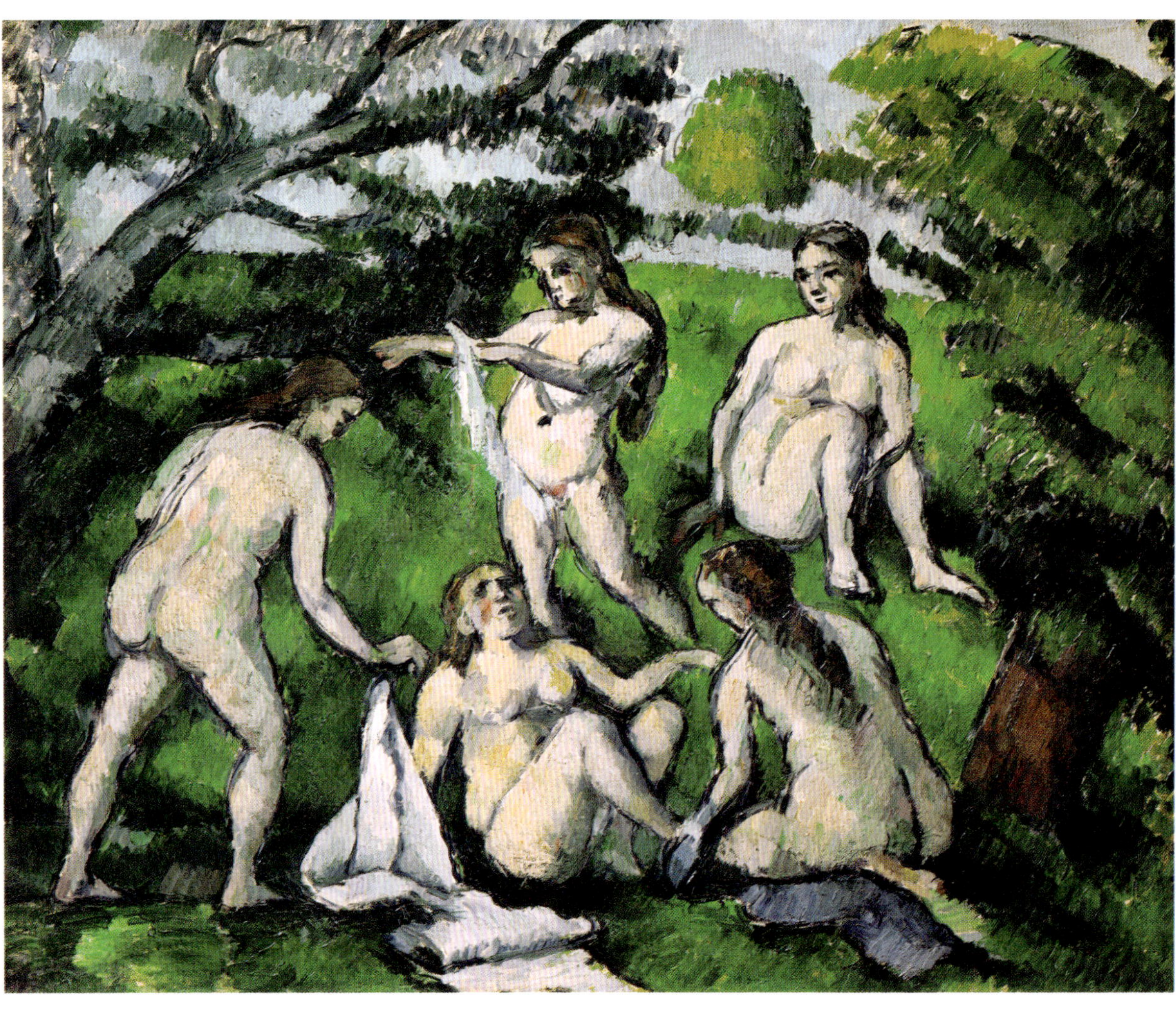

51. Cézanne, *Five Bathers,* 1877–78. Oil on canvas, 45.5 x 55 cm. Musée Picasso, Paris.

There was something divine in their pagan childhood, we have all experienced it, whether or not we understood its effect on us, we have felt the passage of that blast of brutal intoxication which swells in the earliest books of the poet, . . . and in the painter's strange blue and green canvases, in which the shudder of space and of water stirs the world and murmurs about the nude figures assembled under the boughs of the trees. Together the two would start out along the roads where the dust lets out a cry under their footsteps. During the heat of the day they splashed about in the Arc, swimming, diving, rolling on the warm moss to dry themselves, diving in again, naked in the water and the sun until the air grew cool. Often they stayed away from home for two or three days, sleeping under a shed or on the leaves in the motionless nights of summer that cool into morning. They returned with sunburnt skins, smarting feet, and red earth under their nails.[63]

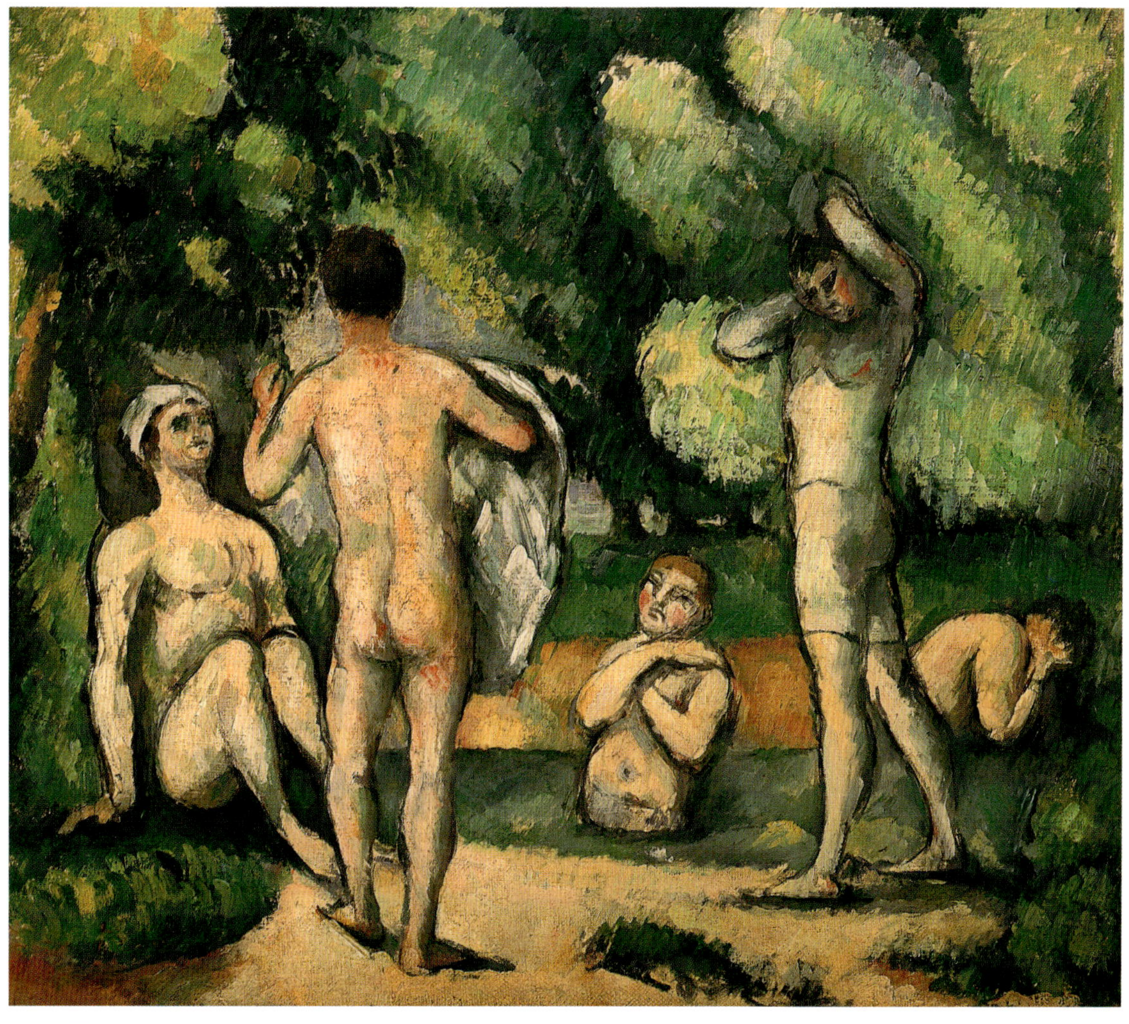

52. Cézanne, *Male Bathers,* 1879–80. Oil on canvas, 34.5 x 38.1 cm. Detroit Institute of Arts.

It was only later, however, that the *specific* connection between descriptions of his youthful play and the paintings of bathers were finally made explicit, first by Alfred Neumeyer in 1959 and afterward by Kurt Badt, Meyer Schapiro, and others.[64]

The problem, of course, with insisting that Cézanne's female and male bathers were conceived entirely differently—the one a product of the artist's overheated imagination, the other the result of lived experience, whether past or present—is that there is as much continuity as difference between the *baigneuses* and the *baigneurs.* Perhaps more. In comparing specific paintings of male and female bathers—for example, *Five Bathers* of 1877–78, once owned by Picasso, and *Male Bathers* of 1879–80, now in Detroit—one is struck by their resemblances (fig. 51 and 52). The images share above all a cursory treatment of the bathers. Little is provided by way of anatomical or

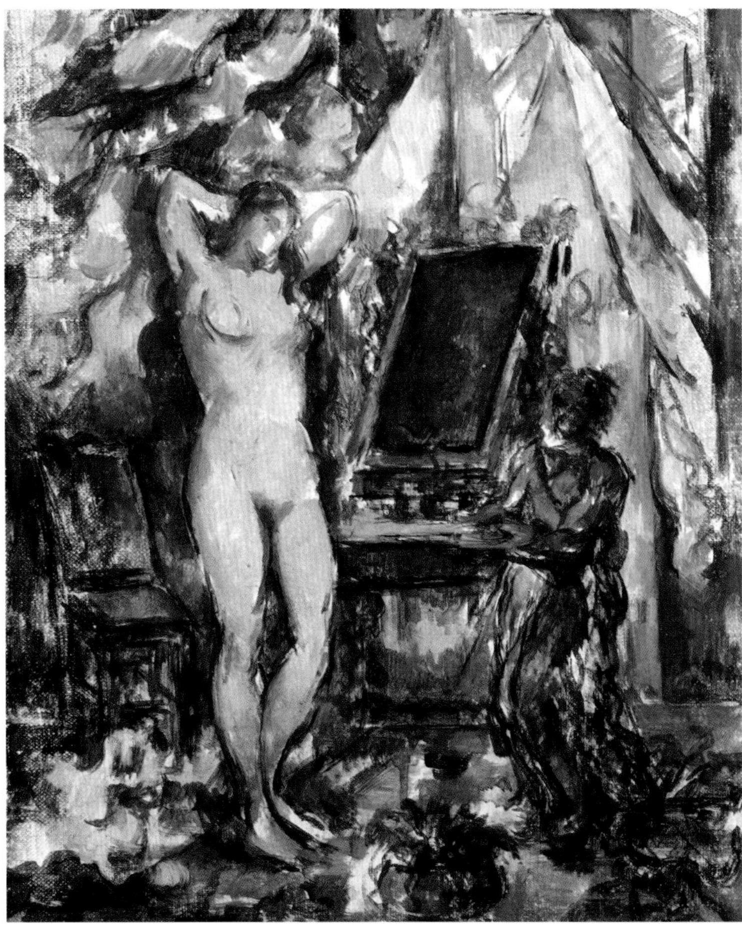

53. Cézanne, *La toilette*, 1885–90. Oil on canvas, 33 x 25.4 cm. Barnes Foundation, Merion, Pa. BF12.

physiognomic particularity. Traces of reworking of body contours remain visible on the canvas, their volumes wedded to the two-dimensional canvas support by a web of short, parallel, "constructive" brushstrokes. Spatial relations among the group are ambiguous. The palette is remarkably similar in both canvases as is a vague sense of communality or sociability. One might also note the pose adopted by the standing male figure on the right-hand side of the Detroit *Baigneurs:* his seductive stance is one repeated throughout Cézanne's oeuvre, as Krumrine has made clear, translated fluidly from male to female figure and back again and often associated with sexual temptation.[65] (Compare the figure of the female nude in *La toilette* [1885–90], for example [fig. 53].) Between the clearly male bathers and clearly female bathers, too, there exist as well a great number of works—such as the Art Institute of Chicago *Bathers* —in which it is much more difficult to definitively identify the gender of the figures depicted. This overdetermined effort to segregate the paintings into *baigneurs* and *baigneuses*—as well as to distinguish the sources of what were claimed as two separate series of works—has been motivated, it seems, by a critical anxiety over the radical technique that Cézanne employed, one in which the material qualities of paint came to take the place of bodily integrity as the locus of erotic charge.

Take, for example, the case of J.-K. Huysmans's writings on the bathers: in the chapter devoted to Cézanne in *Certains,* Huysmans writes of "nude bathers [*baigneuses nues*] defined by lines that are demented but throbbing—to the greater glory of the eye—with the ardor of a Delacroix without refinement and without delicacy of touch, whipped into a fever of botched colors, shrieking in relief, on canvas so loaded it sags!"[66] There is a certain displacement operative in the insistence on applying an intensely sexualized, almost orgasmic description of Cézanne's *baigneuses* not to the forms of the figures but the lines surrounding them (in French, *cerner*)—in other words, onto a purely formal element of the work. By reading the sexual charge contained in the image of *baigneuses* into the material makeup of the painting Huysmans shows us the extent to which Cézanne's painting of the nude was more about the erotics of paint than the erotics of the body. But more than that, Huysman's comments demonstrate the extent to which these signifiers of desire could be almost entirely *separated* from the depicted bodies in Cézanne's work. For his description, while referring specifically to "*baigneuses nues,*" does *not* refer to paintings of female bathers but rather was written in response to Cézanne's *Bathers at Rest III*, an image of male nudes.[67] Huysmans, having seen the painting at the 1877 impressionist exhibition, twelve years before the publication of his description of the work in *Certains,* surely cannot be faulted for his hazy memory of the scene, especially since the figures depicted in this painting themselves seem to blur the distinction between *baigneurs* and *baigneuses:* look, for example, at the rearmost figure, seen from the back, with arm twisted over head in a pose of (conventionally) female seduction, or the reclining figure in the foreground whose pectorals are suspiciously breastlike and whose pose is remarkably odalisque-esque. But for the writer to remember the erotic charge of the very application of paint in his description and not remember the gender of the figures depicted suggests, perhaps, that he *did not want* to remember—it suggests that maybe Huysmans's recollection of *baigneuses* was a way of managing the eroticism that had, in reality, been signified in a painting of male, not female, nudes.[68]

The elision taking place in Huysmans's comments reveals what was at the root of attempts to claim that the *baigneurs* were distinct from their female counterparts. The need to separate the *baigneurs* and the *baigneuses* into two distinct series did not derive simply from the fact that the female bathers were thought to be rooted in the erotic imaginings of the artist and thus that the motivation for male bathers had to be located somewhere else, namely in nostalgic memory or objective observation. It was, rather, that the signs of the *baigneuses*' erotic content were not only figurative but formal: the signs were the anatomical distortions, built-up surfaces, and reworked contours that marked these images.

Such is the logic at work in Theodore Reff's contention that Cézanne developed his figure compositions "in two parallel series, corresponding to their twin sources of inspiration. The female bathers emerged from the early romantic pictures of erotic pleasure or tension; . . . they continued to express a sensual ideal. . . . The male bathers embodied memories of youthful excursions with Zola and Baptistin Baille in the countryside around Aix and of summer days spent swimming in the Arc River."[69] Behind the division of Cézanne's figure paintings into clusters of *baigneurs* and *baigneuses* is a desire to "normalize" the *baigneurs,* to remove from them any trace of the erotic which was seen to penetrate their female counterparts. This division was effected via Cézanne's biography, by locating the source of the male bathers in one part of his lived experience—his youthful escapades, his walks along the Arc—and of the female bathers in another—his fears and anxieties about women.

The stakes of this biographical picture of Cézanne are made clear in the comments of Bernard Dorival and Richard Kendall, to cite but two instances. Dorival, for example, makes the following claim for the *baigneurs:*

> The theme of the *baigneurs* thus represents for [Cézanne] an event, a state of the soul, a moral value that he cherished more than anything. These were the memories of the happy moments of his youth, moments of physical recreation that he evoked with nostalgia. Even more, these memories were tied, in his memory, to the richest experiences of friendship he had ever had. Which led to a double nostalgia: that of physical well-being and that of the awakening of the intellectual and creative faculties as a result of these friendships. These escapades in the Provençal countryside, such as those described by Zola, constituted a veri-

table Golden Age of their adolescence. . . . But this earthly paradise is strictly masculine. It is a virile world where the friends dream of conquests—of Paris, symbol of their destiny, of women, also . . . Thus we could say that the theme of the *baigneurs* is founded on three emotions: nostalgia, friendship, and virility.[70]

Richard Kendall, on the other hand, makes a case for the male bathers as a coincidence of the sort of nostalgic memory that Dorival describes with a kind of realist intent:

[Cézanne's] memories of bathing in the river Arc with his schoolboy friends seem to have established a vision of earthly delight and physical fulfillment which continue to illuminate the later series of male nudes. The male bather pictures are generally more tranquil as compositions and less problematic as reconstructions of actual events than their female counterparts, and Cézanne even underlines their plausibility by providing some rudimentary swimming-trunks and bathing towels. In physique, too, the men are more orthodox and athletic than the women, reminding us that some of them (according to Gasquet) were based on soldiers glimpsed beside the river near Aix.[71]

In both cases, two things are clear: first, whether the source for these images is memory or objective observation, they are purported to spring from an actual *event,* from something seen. And second, these compositions of bathing men are emphatically and unambiguously *virile* in their effect; they create a masculine world of easy, homosocial interaction from which springs not only pleasant recollections of a happy youth but also, as Dorival emphasizes, the root of Cézanne's creative endeavors. Kendall uses the word "plausible" to describe the male bather paintings in relation to their female counterparts, implying not only that these are scenes that could actually have happened but suggesting as well that Cézanne took pains—by adding swimming trunks and towels to his figures, for example—to make manifest the claim to realism.

This insistence on *virility* is, ultimately, an insistence on the normative nature of Cézanne's motivations: the heterosexuality of his desire in the face of images that might otherwise hint at homoeroticism. One might return to Meyer Schapiro's comments, cited earlier in this chapter, to see this operation—this construction of Cézanne, through his paintings, in an image of "safe" masculinity—at work. Says Schapiro: "The male nudes go back to an important part of Cézanne's boyhood to which he often returned in memory: the enchanted days spent with Zola and other friends on the bank of the river"—so far we are in familiar territory, but he goes on—"swimming, playing, talking, and reciting verses—verses in which women were the objects of romantic fantasy."[72]

Schapiro's interpretation echoes Bertall's caricature of Bazille's *Summer Scene:* just as Bertall had one of Bazille's men reaching out to the woman in the next painting in order to introduce a female around which to organize this scene of male sensual pleasure, so, too, does Schapiro introduce a female element in order to turn Cézanne's paintings of male nudes from potentially homoerotic to comfortingly homosocial. The male nudes depicted by Cézanne can themselves hardly be the object of erotic or romantic imaginings in Schapiro's interpretation, because we are "seeing" them, in effect, in the act of fantasizing about women.[73] The activity Cézanne is purported to represent in his *baigneurs* is not simply a virile one but an explicitly heterosexual one. For this to be the case, the suggestions of the erotic that permeate the *baigneuses* had to be inoperative in the *baigneurs;* Schapiro effects this by attributing not simply to Cézanne, but to his represented male figures, the predeliction to fantasize about women.

That an insistence on the *baigneurs* as representations of either nostalgic memories or as insistently contemporaneous instances of observed reality was a way of managing certain sexual anxieties produced by Cézanne's formal method is clear. It was easy, for example, for Joachim Gasquet to have Cézanne say about his frustrations over his *Large Bathers:* "I have tried, when the soldiers are bathing, going along the Arc and observing the contrasts, the colors of flesh against the greens. . . . But that's something else, that doesn't help me, that can't help me with my good women. . . . But wait, good heavens! what a mannish look this one has. . . . They're still in my eye, those recruits."[74] It was easy, in other words, for the putative realism of the male bathers to infect the conception of the female bathers; in a way, one might say that Gasquet's scenario provides a comforting explanation for the strange look of Cézanne's female figures. In no case, by contrast, could the fantasy and desire motivating the female bathers ever be conceived, in the early literature and even often today, as penetrating the male. Cézanne's biography was relied on—and in some cases written—in order to ensure that this was the case.

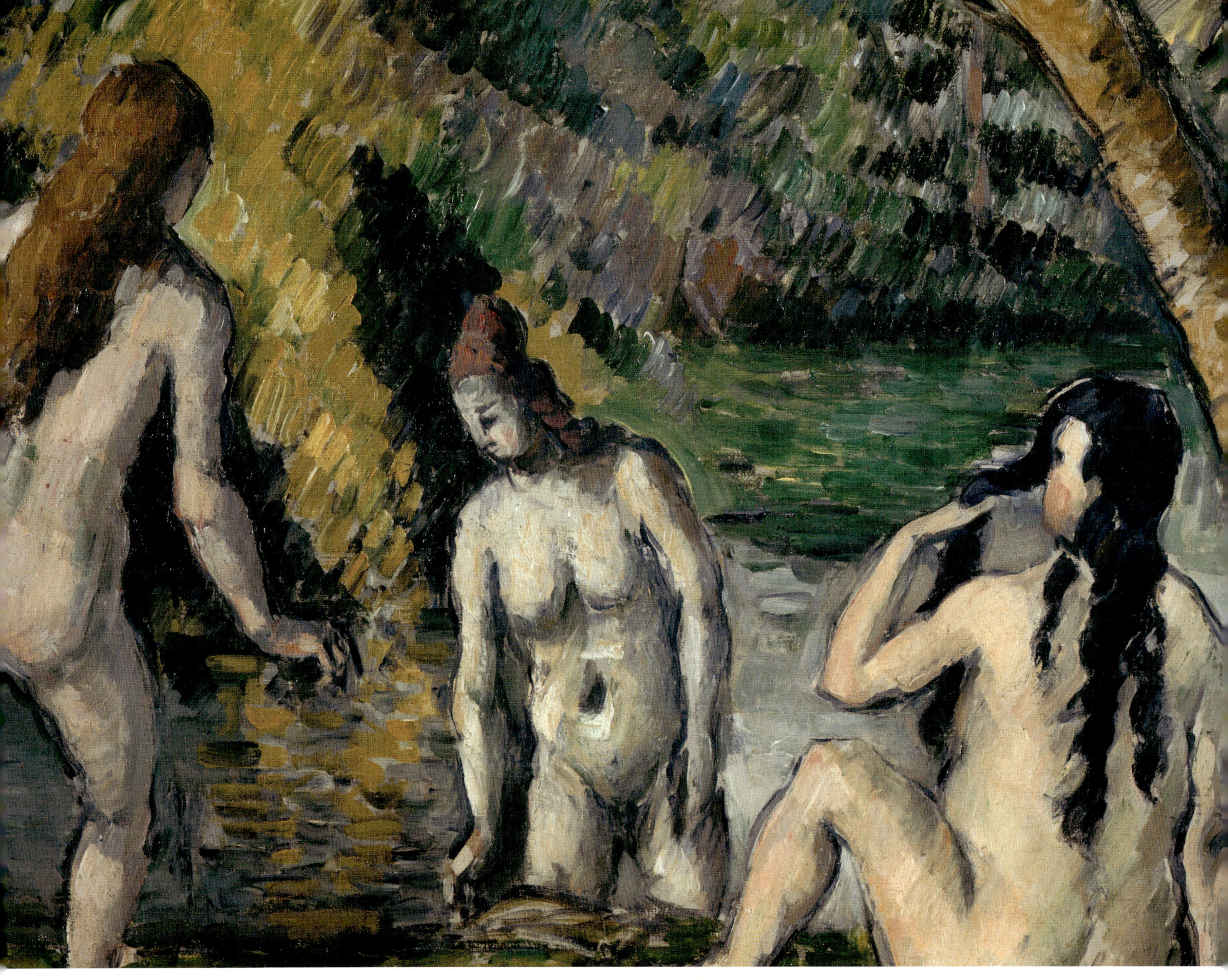

4 MATISSE'S DOUBT/DOUBTING MATISSE

Detail of pl. 1

Look . . . at one of Cézanne's pictures: all is so well-arranged that no matter at what distance you stand or how many figures are represented you will always be able to distinguish each figure clearly and to know which limb belongs to which body. If there is order and clarity in the picture, it means that from the outset this same order and clarity existed in the mind of the painter, or that the painter was conscious of their necessity. Limbs may cross and intertwine, but in the eyes of the spectator they will nevertheless remain attached to and help articulate the right body: All confusion has disappeared.

MATISSE, "NOTES OF A PAINTER"

HOW SHOULD WE UNDERSTAND THESE WORDS, written by Henri Matisse in 1908? By the time he wrote his "Notes of a Painter," he had achieved a certain comprehension of Cézanne's work, both through the close study of Cézanne's *Three Bathers*, which he had acquired in 1899 at great personal cost, and through frequent visits to the 1904 and 1907 retrospective exhibitions at the Salon d'Automne.[1] At that latter show, he would have been confronted with a work like the Philadelphia *Large Bathers*: looking at this painting, it is impossible to perceive in Cézanne's bodies the kind of cohesion that Matisse describes. Indeed, given the strange amalgamated figure on the right-hand side of this canvas, whose buttocks and legs turn into the shoulders and arms of her neighbor, or the figure on the left, whose face is subsumed into the hand of the striding figure and the back of the woman behind her, one would have to conclude that Cézanne's bodies operate in exactly the opposite way. They do not provide a comforting cohesion but instead a discomforting, even uncanny, sense of dissolution. They certainly were experienced as such by their viewers, who lamented the awkward gaucheries of their depiction; when Bernard described the drawing he saw in them as "*assez difforme*," he referred not simply to their distance from accepted technique but to their refusal of bodily integrity as well.[2] Faced with this picture, how is it possible to understand Matisse's insistence that "you will always be able to distinguish each figure clearly and to know which limb belongs to each body"? How can he write that "limbs may cross and intertwine, but in the eyes of the spectator they will nevertheless remain attached to and help articulate the right body"?

It might be tempting to view Matisse's perverse reading of Cézanne's bathers—perverse in the way that it speaks in blatant contradiction to the visual evidence of the image—as a sort of willful blindness, akin to that of J.-K. Huysmans, as we saw in the last chapter, or any of the range of turn-of-the-century critics who were confounded in their attempts to articulate the strangeness of Cézanne's approach to the genre of the nude. Or one might conclude that Matisse's text is a productive misreading of Cézanne's practice, something akin to Harold Bloom's notion of "misprision."[3] Matisse's reasons for articulating this view of Cézanne's work were, however, more complicated than that: they represented neither an inability to face the radicality of Cézanne's practice nor a misunderstanding of it that was then put to productive use but were rooted, on the contrary, precisely in Matisse's own sensitivity to and very accurate assessment of the latter's project. Matisse's stubbornly erroneous description of Cézanne should not, in other words, be taken at face value. Rather, it should be read through and across his own paintings of the erotic nude.

Matisse once said, when asked why he never went to see Cézanne in Aix, that "the artist puts his best into his paintings. Tough luck for those for whom that isn't enough. The artist's words don't count for anything, in the end."[4] But it is not true in this case—Matisse's words do count. Only in their negative sense, though; only in what they do *not* tell us about painting—his or Cézanne's.

DISTORTIONS

When Matisse wrote his "Notes of a Painter," it was, in large measure, a way of responding to critics who had attacked his work. Even before the Salon d'Automne of 1905, where his paintings were hung in a room alongside those of Manguin, Marquet, Derain, Vlaminck, and Camoin and dubbed the work of "wild beasts" and where the extreme nature of Matisse's submissions that year—which included *Luxe, calme, et volupté* (fig. 54)—provoked real controversy, Matisse was the target of sustained criticism, especially in relation to his treatment of the human form. As early as 1903, Charles Morice would write of the "useless, inexpressive and ugly distortions [*déformations*] of M. Henri Matisse" that "betray that denial of sincere effort which is a grave insult to art."[5] Camille Mauclair, a conservative critic, wrote that Matisse (along with the other painters showing at the 1905 Salon d'Automne) had abandoned the pursuit of beauty in art, succumbing to a "cult of ugliness" driven by an unquestioning acceptance of the work of Cézanne. What made this work even more surprising, for Mauclair, was the fact that its depictions were coarse but its authors were not untrained or lowborn—in other words, they knew better, and the deliberateness of their images was disconcertingly strange:

> Many nude women were figured there; all were . . . presented with a strange misogyny which sought to render them repellent. . . . The methodical disgrace of the flesh and its forms was stupefying. It was not ignorance or awkwardness: there was an evident decision to falsify nature with the aim of making her ugly. . . . What certain of the exhibitors painted while looking at the nude model was unimaginable in its ugliness and aberration. Yet most of the authors of these fairground daubings are intelligent young people, knowledgeable and well born, and they

well know the attractions and delicacy that a pretty woman possesses.[6]

By 1907, a once-supportive Louis Vauxcelles would respond to Matisse's *Blue Nude* (fig. 55), shown at the Salon des Indépendants that year, by writing that he could not understand the direction Matisse's art was taking: "An ugly nude woman is stretched out upon grass of an opaque blue under the palm trees. . . . The drawing here seems to me to be rudimentary and the coloring cruel; the right arm of the mannish nymph [*nymphe hommasse*] is flat and heavy. . . . This is an artistic effort tending toward the abstract which escapes me completely. M. Matisse, moreover, has made some wood engravings of distorted [*déformés*] and angular nudes."[7] Morice called the same painting

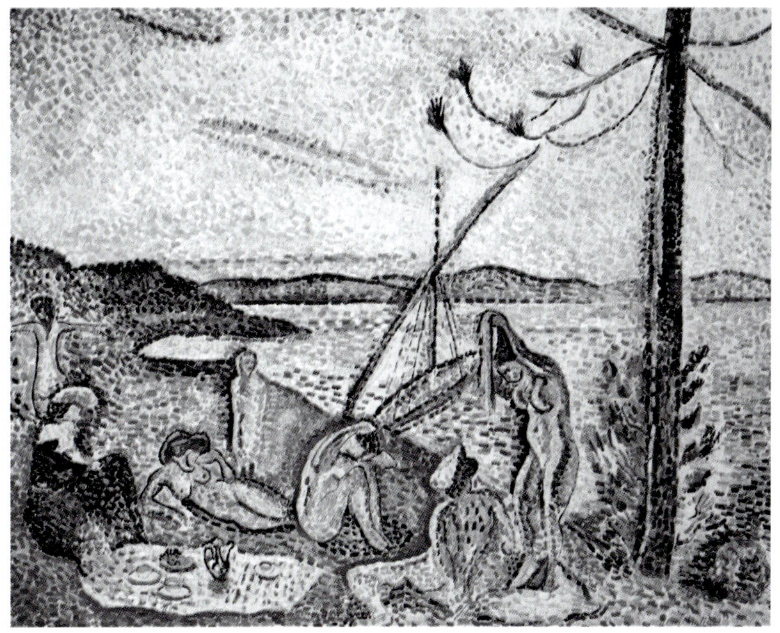

54. Henri Matisse, *Luxe, calme, et volupté,* 1904–5. Oil on canvas, 98.5 x 118 cm. Musée d'Orsay, Paris. © Succession H. Matisse, Paris/ARS.

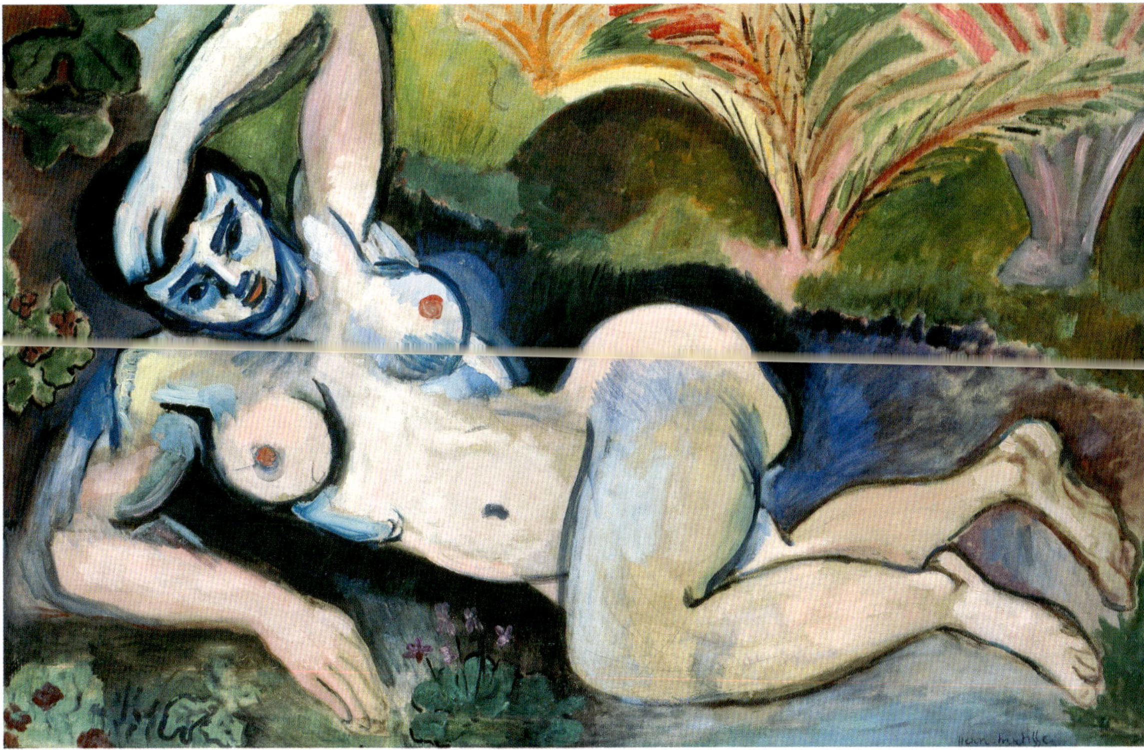

55. Henri Matisse, *Blue Nude: Souvenir of Biskra,* 1907. Oil on canvas, 92.1 x 140.4 cm. Baltimore Museum of Art, Cone Collection. 1950.228. © Succession H. Matisse, Paris/ARS.

an "*académie disloquée*"—a term that brings to mind both its subversion of conventional notions of figuring the nude as well as the overt foreignness, both aesthetic and geographic (or ethnographic), of its supposedly North African model.[8] Such references to Matisse's inadequate drawing and, more importantly, to his distorted and disfigured nudes were commonplace in these years, and these qualities of Matisse's work—his *déformations*—were regularly associated with a kind of barbarism and hatred both of form and of women.[9]

The most important criticism of Matisse's work that arose in the years before the publication of his "Notes of a Painter" was leveled by Maurice Denis, whose review of the 1905 Salon d'Automne decried what he saw as the overly theoretical nature of Matisse's approach that resulted in "painting outside of all contingency, painting in and of itself, the pure act of painting. All the qualities of painting other than the contrast of tones and lines, anything that the intellect of the painter did not himself determine, everything that comes from instinct and from nature, in short all the qualities of representation and of sensibility are excluded from the work of art."[10] These are strange words coming from a man whose formulation regarding the primacy of formal qualities would become a foundational tenet of modernist criticism ("a painting—before being a battle horse, a nude woman, or whatever kind of anecdote—is a flat surface covered in colors arranged in a certain order") and who was an ardent supporter of Cézanne, the figure who was seen as the quite obvious source of Matisse's abstractions from nature by critics at the time.[11] Even stranger was the fact that Denis had been central to the elaboration of the idea of the positive, expressive function of *déformation* in the work of Cézanne and Gauguin: the idea that the particular abstractions and gaucheries that these two artists introduced into their work were the sign of a sincere engagement with their world and with their medium, outside of shopworn academicisms and clichés.[12] In explaining the paradoxical allure of Cézanne's oeuvre, filled with canvases "most often incomplete, scraped with a knife, overloaded with false strokes of *essence,* repainted endlessly, built up to the extent of a relief sculpture," Denis would write that "What is most stunning in the work of Cézanne is assuredly the search for form or more precisely the distortions [*déformations*]: it is there that one discovers in his work the majority of hesitations and anguish."[13]

If, for Denis, Cézanne's *déformations* were the source of his greatest originality and interest, how could it be that these same qualities, which he and most other critics saw as Matisse's most obvious debt to Cézanne (especially in relation to his work on the figure), were so damning, spoke so directly to Matisse's artificiality, insincerity, and—worse—overintellectuality as a painter? My question is certainly not original, and many have sought to explain this apparent contradiction in Denis's attitudes as the result of the extreme abstraction of Matisse's painting—his apparent refusal to retain nature in his work, his willingness to introduce deformations of form and arbitrary color, his painting that seemed at once too beholden to theory and abstract formulae and at the same time too utterly subjective, without purchase in the external world. It is—as the result, in other words, of Denis's desire for a sort of aesthetic "middle path": a mode of painting in which nature was subservient to the artist's sensibility, one in which deformations and distortions and gaucheries could still act as the signposts of an artist's sincere engagement with his project but also in which nature was somehow still *there* in some sense, providing some sense of contingency against and through which the artist would prevail.[14] But this explanation, it seems to me, only partially grasps the significance of Denis's objections. It was not so much the excessive abstractions—the *degree* of *déformation*—in Matisse's paintings but rather their *valence,* their meaning that was at stake. Why Denis considered Matisse's *déformations* to be particularly objectionable can only be understood by recognizing that Denis's notion of expressive distortion was shot through, by the time of this critical encounter between Matisse and Denis, with the critic's increasing valorization of Ingres—one motivated by his reading of Cézanne and driven, ultimately, by a conservative and nationalistic desire to erect a classical lineage for modern painting, in which Cézanne would hold a critical position.

To invoke the names of Ingres in 1905 was perhaps not surprising: he was, by that point, on peoples' minds, as the subject of a major retrospective exhibition at the Salon d'Automne that year. But his currency in 1905 should not blind us to the fact that his was a relatively recent revival: the painter who for years stood for the worst rigidities and artificialities of academicism, the figure of stifling authority, was now being positioned as a revitalizing source for a directionless avant-garde.[15] One only has to look at Cézanne's attitude toward the master to understand the suddenness of this reversal of fortune. Ingres was a constant target of the younger artist's sarcastic humor, perhaps not surprisingly, since he, too, was a son of the south, and his painting *Jupiter and Thetis* was the prized possession of the museum in Aix-en-Provence.[16] That Cézanne signed the decorative panels he painted in the early 1860s on the walls of the grand salon of his father's new country estate "Ingres 1811"—in deliciously self-deprecating contrast to the naïve and almost kitschy rendering of their classicizing subject, *The Four Seasons*—is only the start of it.[17] He had already redrawn Ingres's Jupiter awkwardly copping a feel from Thetis instead of sitting in proud, tumescent glory above a Thetis who crouches in an amphibian pose of beseeching inferiority (figs. 56 and 57). But perhaps most telling was Cézanne's reimagining of Ingres's icon of imperial power, his *Napoleon I on His Imperial Throne* (1806), with his long-suffering friend Achille Emperaire in the place of the little dictator: one deformed dwarf to take the place of another, I suppose—a substitution not without a certain and cruel humor (figs. 58 and 59). And while these exercises might otherwise be read as the acting out of a young, rebellious artist in the formative stages of his career, the publication in 1904 of Bernard's article, which included a series of aphorisms from the artist himself, made Cézanne's continued distaste for Ingres quite apparent: "Ingres is a noxious classicist," he says, "as are all those who repudiate nature or copy it by half-measures, in order to search for their style through the imitation of the Greeks and the Romans."[18]

If, for Cézanne and most other painters of the realist avant-garde from the 1850s forward, Ingres represented the stagnant, antinaturalistic, arcane academicism that was now to be replaced by a painting of modern life and "nature seen through a temperament," it was ironic that in 1905, his exhibition was mounted alongside the retrospective of a painter of that latter tradition: Édouard Manet.[19] And it is no exaggeration to say that in 1905, in the face of an increasingly fragmented and incoherent field of artistic possibilities, critics were desperately hoping that this juxtaposition of Manet and Ingres might clear the way for modern art. "In retrospect," wrote Charles Morice, "the two hangings of Ingres and of Manet constitute the most useful, the most beneficial investigations of

56. Jean-August-Dominique Ingres, *Jupiter and Thetis,* 1811. Oil on canvas, 327 x 260 cm. Musée Granet, Aix-en-Provence, France.

57. Cézanne, study after Ingres's *Jupiter and Thetis,* ca. 1858–60. Brown ink and graphite on brown paper, 15 x 23.5 cm. Musée du Louvre, Paris.

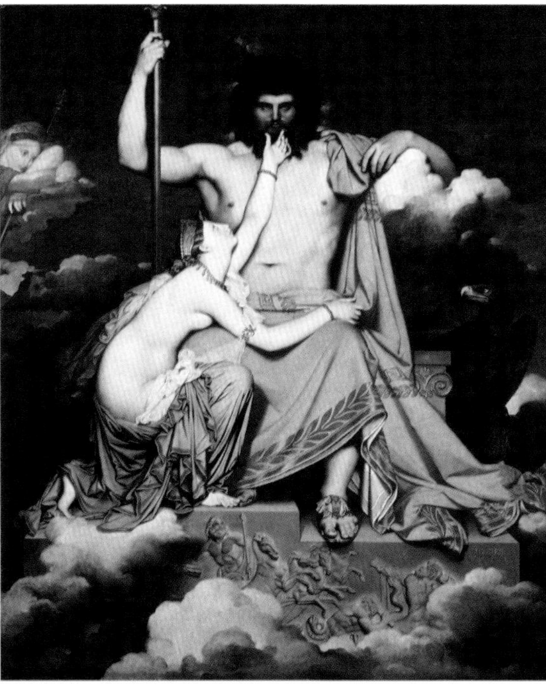

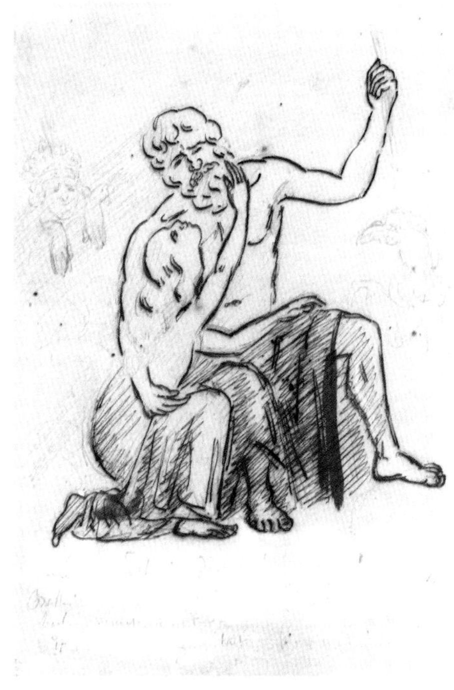

58. Jean-August-Dominique Ingres, *Napoleon I on His Imperial Throne,* 1806. Oil on canvas, 260 x 163 cm. Musée de l'Armée, Paris.

59. Cézanne, *Portrait of Achille Emperaire,* 1867–68. Oil on canvas, 200 x 122 cm. Musée d'Orsay, Paris.

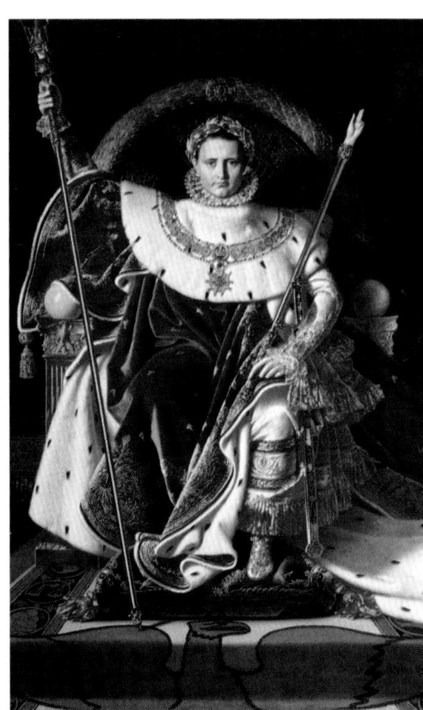

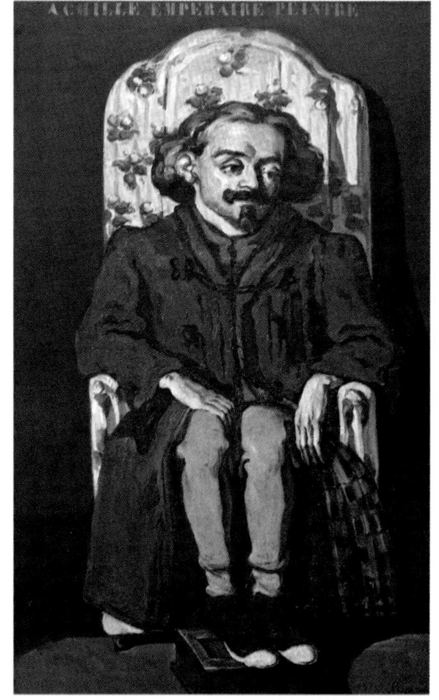

beauty that we have seen in a long time. At least, it is the summary, suggested by the most deliberate opposition that one could imagine, of French painting from a century which achieved its most brilliant glory."[20] So this stark juxtaposition—a confrontation that was now figured as the contrast between a subtle and sensual abstraction and a stark and frank realism—was productive, and though many conservative critics hailed Ingres's presence as the sign of a reversion to classical and academic notions of correct drawing and studied design, a number of other critics were happy to declare Ingres's modernity, period.[21]

Maurice Denis was, we could say, one of this former group. Though Ingres was newly à la mode in 1905, he had figured prominently in Denis's thinking before then, too; in articles starting around 1900 the critic noted a new classicism in recent art, inspired by Ingres and characterized by simplification and synthesis, which "represent[ed] the necessary reaction against the excesses or the frivolities of impressionism, and against the vain theories which consider all expression of individual emotion as a manifestation of Beauty."[22] In this new historical lineage, Cézanne played a central role: "Did Ingres's students not perceive this synthetist reaction? And so after Manet, and Puvis, and Degas, and Cézanne, one returns now, with such fervor, to their Idealism, to the Primitives that they discovered, to the classical Rome that they loved so much, to Raphael, to the Greeks, to Tradition and to Method. That is to say, in short, to the doctrine of M. Ingres!"[23] By 1905, in his Salon d'Automne review, Denis could declare that, at the very least, "No one considers M. Ingres a dangerous reactionary anymore."[24]

If Denis held up Ingres in his writings on the 1905 exhibition as a corrective to a rash of contemporary trends including, most importantly, the arbitrary and subjective abstractions of Matisse, he did so in the face of a critical discourse distracted by the sheer quantity of flesh on display: *The Turkish Bath,* with its writhing accumulation of female figures in various states of bodily disarray, along with eighteen preparatory drawings, formed the centerpiece of the retrospective (fig. 60).[25] Critics were bowled over by the painting's erotic energy; one spoke of the "ecstasy" experienced when faced with the artist's "*morceau nu*" and there was a lot of talk equating Ingres's characteristic arabesque and

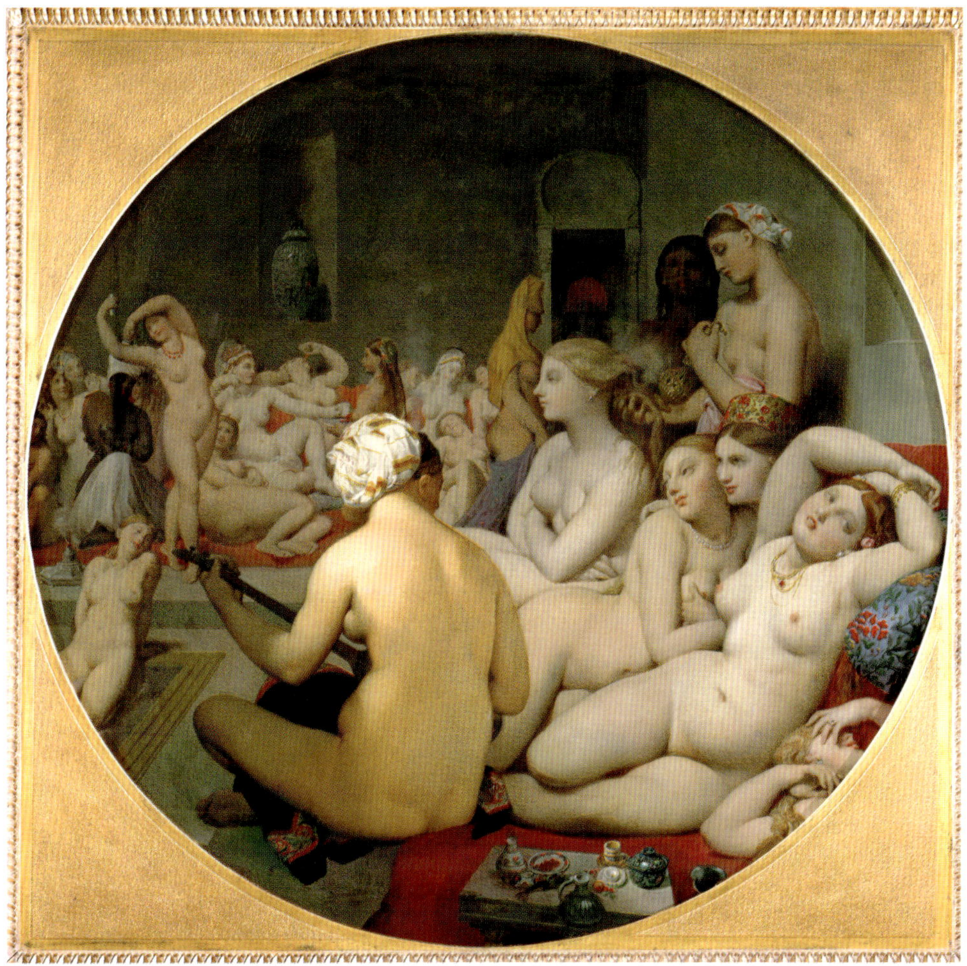

60. Jean-August-Dominique Ingres, *The Turkish Bath,* 1862. Canvas on wood, diameter 110 cm. Musée du Louvre, Paris.

anatomical distortions—his gaucheries or *déformations,* by turn—with eroticized pleasure.[26] Even Henry Lapauze, whose scholarly work on the painting had contributed in no small measure to the early twentieth-century Ingres-mania, could not restrain himself: "Ingres at every stage had a cult of woman, a certain kind of woman, abundant and fleshy. . . . Where better to see him than . . . in his Montauban *croquis,* which show us Ingres as he was, a passionate lover of nature[,] . . . right up to the point when the second Mme Ingres, entering his studio, overheard the enthusiastic old man pointing to his model and exclaiming 'Is she not beautiful! Look at these admirable lines! Look at this supple body, this firm breast, these superb haunches, look!'"[27]

If Lapauze's characterization of Ingres as something of a dirty old man in the studio was, in many respects, typical of the contemporary critical reaction to the exhibition, it was clearly at odds with Denis's preferred image of the artist. So much so that Louis Vauxcelles, a liberal critic, would identify with some precision the political stakes of Denis's Ingres. Identifying a "certain Ingrist snobbery of which M. Maurice Denis . . . has recently become the propagator," he accused Denis, "on the pretext of a return to French classicism," of imposing "not only the magnificent Ingres of the pencil drawings, but also 'Monsieur Ingres,' the terrible dogmatic reactionary."[28] He goes on:

> There is Ingres and Ingres. I take it for granted that our Salon did not wish to exalt the creator of the *Jeanne d'Arc,* that glacial image. . . . Or the pseudo-Hellenism of the *Stratonice.* All the official apostasy of Ingres is invalid. What we love, what is ageless . . . is the lyric and profound realism of the lead-point drawings . . . it is that pagan southerner's sensual love for the beauty of form. . . . What we venerate, what the Salon d'Automne glorifies are the nudes, the odalisques, the bathers, the portraits.[29]

This commentary by Vauxcelles, which claims that Denis desires to promote the *other* Ingres, the one marked not by the contorted, ecstatic bodies of the *The Turkish Bath* but by the glacial classicism of his most academicized images, suggests the stakes of Denis's criticism of Matisse. If Denis was interested in promoting Ingres as a proscriptive example for the development of a contemporary and idealist classicism, it was, in large measure, as a way of securing the meaning of Cézanne's work: it was a way of promoting Cézanne as a contemporary Poussin-by-way-of-Ingres, of understanding his distortions and gaucheries—especially as concerned his figure paintings, which were those images most clearly in the background of Denis's discussion of Ingres's work—as part of this disinterested, objective impulse, in a move that would erase the recurring images of Cézanne's not-quite repressed passions as the instinctual motivation for his strange bathers.[30] (This sets Denis in stark contrast to Émile Bernard, who in these years was developing a narrative around Cézanne's bathers precisely rooted in sexual trauma and conflicted desire; it is perhaps no coincidence that Bernard's transcriptions of Cézanne's theory asserted the latter's dismissal of Ingres's classicism.) Denis's classicization of—and concomitant purification (aesthetic and erotic) of—Cézanne was a way of declaring his (Denis's) own place in this modernist lineage, of claiming Cézanne as the father of his own, deeply reactionary style of painting, a conservative, neo-Catholic symbolism. But just as the critics writing about Ingres in 1905 made it impossible for Denis to separate the abstracted body of Ingres from the sexualized body, Matisse's paintings in these years made it impossible for the critic to separate the classicizing purity of Cézanne's expressive *déformations* from the gaucheries imagined to be rooted in sexual anxieties, repressed passions, and fear of women. This is the source of Denis's seemingly inexplicable reaction to Matisse's work: it was an excess of sex, not an excess of theory, that was at issue.

In other words, it was precisely those things Matisse borrowed from Cézanne's figurative style—the characteristic facture, the tendency of bodies to seep into their neighbors or into the surrounding landscape, the distorted and deformed anatomies, the hesitation and confusion and reworking of form—that indicated to critics Cézanne's erotic investment in his motif. For writers like Émile Bernard, such qualities demanded explanation: the justification for Cézanne's gaucheries, specifically those found in his paintings of the female nude, was located in his fears and anxieties about women, originating in his excessive passion toward them, in the fact that "he didn't trust himself in front of naked women."[31] Thus, the distorted and unidealized bodies on the canvas came to stand as a reminder of the sexual anxiety that was their motivation: Cézanne's thickened, coarse surface of paint, with its reworked contours and scumbled layers of pigment, was linked, via Émile Zola's metaphor of artistic impotence, to an obsessive return of the painter to the object of desire, to the brush's endless caress of the represented body to the point of total pictorial incoherence.

That Matisse's borrowings from Cézanne were coded in terms of the erotic did not go unnoticed by critics, by any means. While in 1904, Charles Morice would contend that Matisse's art showed that he found his pleasure exclusively in "colors, tones and their relations," by 1906, the question of pleasure was put by Morice in explicitly erotic terms when he wrote that Matisse and the Fauves, in their rejection of the anecdotal in their painting of the nude, had emptied it of all *but* sexual interest: "through hatred of painted literature, true thought and feeling are banned from painting. All that is left is the share of the eyes and the hands, elements of a merely sensory sensuality."[32] But it was up to Maurice Denis himself, in his famous condemnation of Matisse's modernist practice that appeared in *La Grande Revue* in 1908 (a text that was written in response to "Notes of a Painter," in effect) to make explicit the connection between what he saw as the base eroticism of Matisse and his followers with Cézanne's formal vocabulary: "they triangulate the human body"—here Denis refers to the sort of faceted, planar, "geometric" approach to form that they had learned from Cézanne—"and, above all, the female body *where, actually, they willingly stress a certain black triangle*" (my emphasis).[33]

Here, then, is the most telling commentary on Matisse that Denis ever wrote: an overt expression of displeasure at the way Matisse mined Cézanne in the creation of images that were crudely sexual. The slippage between "triangulation"—in other words, Cézanne's characteristic formal device—and the black triangle of a woman's pubes should signal to us that Denis's anxiety is precisely rooted in Matisse's reading of Cézanne's *déformations*, his wrenching them away from a classical lineage via Ingres that Denis was attempting to construct. And if, in Denis's earlier lament over the overly theoretical nature of Matisse's painting, one may read a lament over the loss of the coherent subject standing behind the painted mark—the loss, in other words, of "temperament" as the assurance of the subjective authenticity of the signature *tache*—then one might surmise, too, that his condemnation of Matisse's adoption of Cézanne's erotics of paint was rooted in the fact that, unlike Cézanne, Matisse had no legend of sexual traumas and erotic anxieties to justify his mark-making. Biography, again, is crucial here.[34] If Ingres's deformations were the result of his love of women—Denis wrote, in his analysis of *The Turkish Bath* that "at that age [eighty-two, when he painted the picture] M. Ingres still loved women with the candor and the fervor of an adolescent"—and if Cézanne's gaucheries were the result of his fears of women and his Catholic puritanism, Matisse's distortions were unmotivated: and thus, their deliberate rationality was equated with a cold-blooded misogyny—and not only by Denis.[35]

EXCESSIVE SEX

The problem that Matisse posed for Denis's classicizing narrative, in other words, had to do with the fact that his adoption of Cézanne's gaucheries and figurative style vis-à-vis the painting of the female nude—borrowings that were obvious to viewers of contemporary art—made explicit Cézanne's radical idea: his abandonment (or at least demotion) of the figure in favor of the material qualities of painting as a vehicle for the communication of the erotic. For if Matisse borrowed anything from Cézanne when it came to the painting of the nude, it was his eroticization of the medium: the way his distorted and unidealized bodies, thickened, coarse surfaces of color, reworked contours, and brushstrokes that were by turns liquefied and opaque were set free from—operated independent of, or even despite—the fetishized body as the signifier of desire.

While many scholars claim that the period of 1899 to 1907—the years, in other words, between Matisse's purchase of Cézanne's *Three Bathers* and his creation of what is often considered his most Cézannesque painting, *Blue Nude (Souvenir of Biskra)*—was the period of Matisse's closest engagement with Cézanne's work, it was, rather, only in 1907 that he achieved his fullest understanding of the implications of Cézanne's paintings of the nude. *Blue Nude* was completed early in the year and exhibited that spring in the Salon des Indépendants as *Tableau III*, suggesting that it was a manifesto painting of sorts, joining *Luxe, calme, et volupté* and *Joy of Life* in a scandalous threesome. This is clearly a painting that borrows from Cézanne, not least because of Matisse's abandonment of the live model.[36] It also shares a number of formal elements: its blue tonalities, its wedding of figure to landscape so that one seems to motivate the other, its obvious, almost violent reworking of the figure, its sense of unfinish as parts of the underdrawing show through the thinly or at times even unpainted surface, its slashing brushwork, its exaggerated *pentimenti* and heavy impastos in other parts of the canvas (especially around the breasts). At the same time, there are a number of aspects of this painting that are not at all like Cézanne's images of the nude, most importantly the hypersexualization of the body depicted, which, although regularly derided by critics of the time for its androgyny or ambiguity of gender—a criticism that seems likely motivated, more than anything, by the primitivizing qualities of the figure—has full breasts, an hourglass shape, and reclines in a traditional pose of feminine seduction.[37] The anatomy depicted here, as well as the violent contrapposto of its twisted arrangement, in other words, is far from the flattened, flaccid, thick-waisted nudes of Cézanne's bather paintings.

Picasso complained, looking at the picture, that "If he wants to make a woman, let him make a woman. If he wants to make a design, let him make a design.

This is between the two."[38] Picasso is not wrong to identify clashing interests in this painting. However much critics complained of the way the female nude seemed entirely motivated by the decorative imperative of the picture, of the way that her curves were not simply made metaphorically equivalent to her natural surroundings but were, rather, determined by the arch of the palm fronds behind, of the way that she seemed only to function in relation to a linear arabesque, *Blue Nude* is a body that retains a fleshly presence. It has not completely given up the possibility of "making a woman," and as such it is a painting conceived—still—under the sign of the sculptural, in the sense of sculpture's as yet unabandoned retention of a rhetoric of real bodies, of Pygmalion's transformation of inert matter into flesh and blood. And while it is a commonplace in Matisse studies to regard *Blue Nude*'s sculptural effect as precisely the result of Matisse's study of Cézanne, or at the very least as an alignment of Cézanne's classical primitivism with the primitivism of African sculpture, in fact, as we have seen throughout this book, Cézanne's bodies do not operate in the way that the sculptural body had done until this point in time—they do not rely on a rhetorical equivalence of the body-in-representation and the body-in-the-world to communicate their sensual address, in other words. Notwithstanding the assertions that "the conceit of Matisse, shared with Cézanne, was that he could make a body which appeared more well knit and solidly put together than in actual life" or that "the techniques that permitted him to attain the effect of three-dimensionality [in *Blue Nude*] come from . . . Cézanne," in *Blue Nude* Cézanne is not to be found in the fullness and plastic presence of the figure but rather in those elements of design—the fusion of color and line that allow the represented body to become knitted to the composition—that precisely counterweigh her sculptural presence.[39]

This plasticity, this residual rhetoric of real bodies, is not the thing that Matisse derives from his study of Cézanne's bathers but is, rather, the result of his ongoing engagement—one often characterized by rejection rather than unproblematic embrace—of Rodin.[40] That Rodin figures here is perhaps no surprise, since *Blue Nude* was generated from *Reclining Nude I (Aurora),* a small figurine started at the end of 1906; when the clay model broke in the studio, Matisse embarked instead on the painting and only returned to the sculpture after the painting was mostly complete (figs. 61 and 62). *Reclining Nude* is a work Matisse did, still, with Rodin in the back of his mind, one could say: despite his decision to work on a nonmonumental scale, and despite his insistence on working in terms of whole bodies versus Rodin's fragments, his teacher is still present in this work.[41] While Matisse does not present fragmented bodies as such—no hands, feet, or torsos disengaged from any other corporeal existence, as are found in abundance in Rodin's oeuvre—he manages to create a figure that is practically ripped apart as you move around it, such is the violence of its dissonant views. *Blue Nude* incorporates the bodily discontinuity of *Reclining Nude,* thanks to an exaggerated twist of the figure's torso that makes the buttock and thigh of the top leg seem almost to detach itself from the figure. And no wonder that part of the woman's anatomy seems so disjunctive: for this female figure's left haunch takes the form of the phallus, an organ that quite literally does not belong to her. It is only the insistent doubling of the emphatic curves of the body by the curving palm fronds and by the deep blue shadow—that material accumulation of painterly *stuff*—that surrounds her that keeps this nude figure

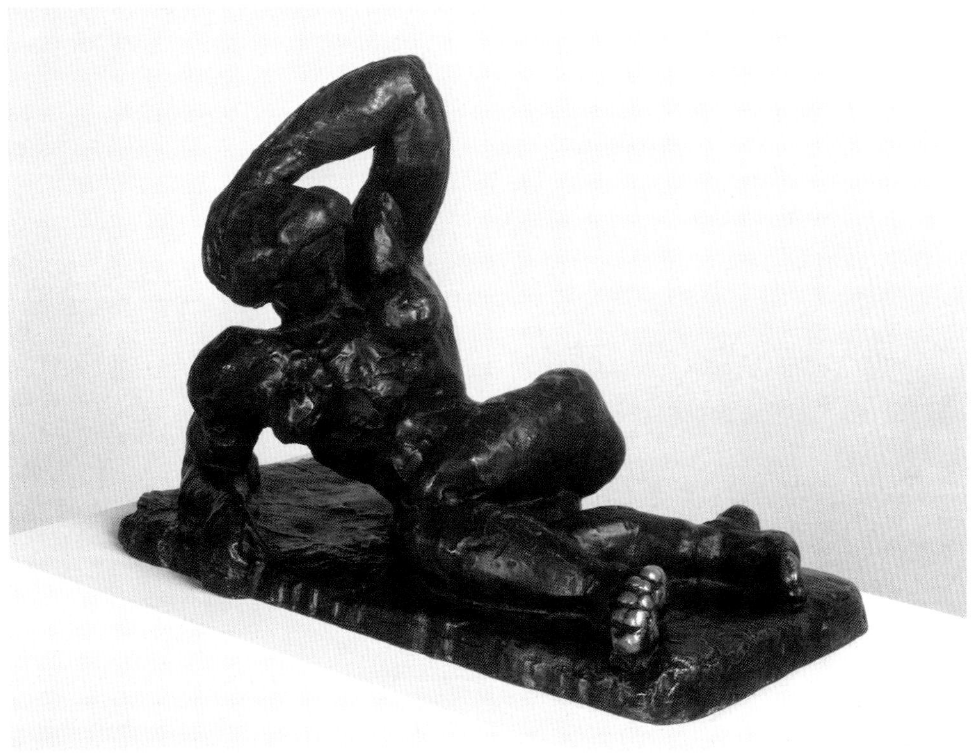

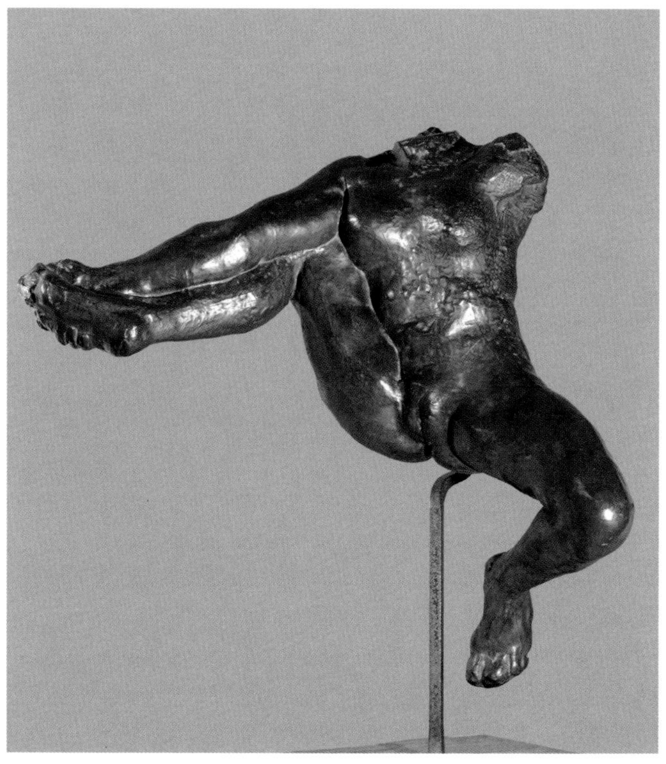

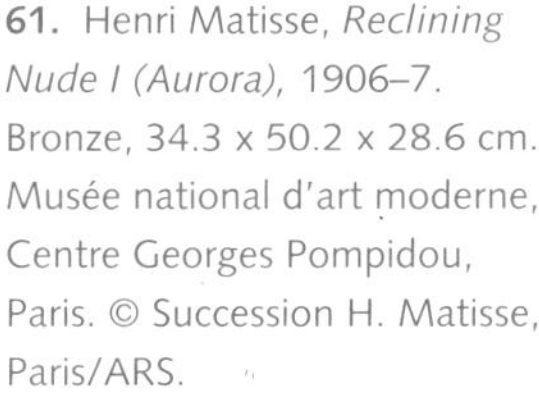

61. Henri Matisse, *Reclining Nude I (Aurora)*, 1906–7. Bronze, 34.3 x 50.2 x 28.6 cm. Musée national d'art moderne, Centre Georges Pompidou, Paris. © Succession H. Matisse, Paris/ARS.

62. Auguste Rodin, *Iris, Messenger of the Gods*, ca. 1890–95. Bronze, 82.7 x 69 x 63 cm. Musée Rodin, Paris.

from dispersing completely.[42] Indeed, Morice's complaints about the painting were based on just this threatened fragmentation: "despite the stammering simplicity of the drawing"—he refers here to the reworked contours, a mark of Matisse's debt to Cézanne—"one searches in vain for the unity of the 'Tableau,' for it is lost in the colliding planes, in the colors which refuse to harmonize."[43]

The violent dissonance of the picture, the sense of incoherence or of a kind of centrifugal force that wrenches apart the figure from within is a sign, I think, of the contradiction of these two positions, Rodin and Cézanne.[44] And Matisse's understanding of this incongruity is precisely what lies behind his "Notes of a Painter," written in the aftermath of his work on this painting and the violent critical reaction to it. For Matisse's comments about Cézanne—the comments that opened this chapter—were in fact framed by a criticism of Rodin and particularly of the anatomical disarray of Rodin's work:

> For me all is in the conception. I must therefore have a clear vision of the whole from the beginning. I could mention a great sculptor who gives us some admirable pieces: but for him a composition is merely a grouping of fragments, which results in a confusion of expression. Look, in contrast, at one of Cézanne's pictures: all is so well-arranged that no matter at what distance you stand or how many figures are represented you will always be able to distinguish each figure clearly and to know which limb belongs to which body. If there is order and clarity in the picture, it means that from the outset this same order and

clarity existed in the mind of the painter, or that the painter was conscious of their necessity. Limbs may cross and intertwine, but in the eyes of the spectator they will nevertheless remain attached to and help articulate the right body: All confusion has disappeared.[45]

Matisse is surely substituting a language of bodily integrity to speak about compositional imperative: when he speaks of Cézanne's figures and their anatomical coherence and clarity, he is clearly speaking, on the contrary, about the way in which Cézanne's facility for *arrangement* takes the place of the need to make the body cohere, and this in contrast to Rodin's penchant for fragmentation, for compositionless groupings, for parts that did not necessarily relate to an abstract whole.[46] But he is also speaking about two very different ways of communicating the erotic: two possibilities, within the modern idiom, for understanding how sensual pleasure could be coaxed from the inert matter of art. *Blue Nude* demonstrates Matisse's realization of the incompatibility of these two modes: of Rodin's eroticism produced by the visual metaphorization of the sculpted object—the creation of a painted figure that in some sense was meant to recall a real body in the world—and Cézanne's eroticism produced through other means than the body depicted—the creation of a painting whose materiality as such could be understood as the dislocated pleasures of the bodies depicted.[47] That is to say, the contradiction between the fetishization of the body through its presentation as a part-object versus the production of visual erotics outside the confines of the figure.

It is not that *Blue Nude* represents the first time these ideas would enter into Matisse's painted work. Matisse's early, "Cézannesque" forays—studio nudes like *Male Model* (ca. 1900), *Standing Model/Nude Study in Blue* (1900–1901), and *Nude with a White Towel* (ca. 1902–3)—demonstrate a relatively facile understanding of Cézanne, such that his presence is reduced to a kind of geometricization of the figure, bluish tonalities, faceted planes, and *passage*-like brushwork, contained within images that are otherwise utterly unlike Cézanne's *figurative* work, even as they may recall his landscapes or still lifes. However, it seems that by 1905 or so things were beginning to change. *Joy of Life* (fig. 63)—a painting done in the aftermath of Cézanne's retrospective exhibition at the Salon d'Automne and at the height of the controversy over the *salle des fauves*—shows us that Matisse is thinking about Cézanne. But in this case it is a Cézanne seen (no less than Denis's) through the lens of Ingres. It may well be that it was necessary for him come to Cézanne by way of Ingres in order to understand Cézanne's play with the body as something other than a sculptural one, in order to understand Cézanne's *déformations* as introducing an altogether new vision of the erotic based, if not on the arabesque, then on the fusion of the body with the formal and material elements of painting. And thus it is no coincidence that this canvas was read by contemporary critics as achieving a sensuality that had not been obvious in Matisse's earlier work; where Charles Morice could say that *Luxe, calme, et volupté* was devoid of life, let alone eroticism, *Joy of Life* was praised by the same critic for its pronounced sensual character.[48] This eroticism was not only embodied in the "languorous . . . creatures with lovely hips," as Louis Vauxcelles put it, nor simply in the seemingly primal melting of the lovers' bodies into each other's ecstatic embrace. It was embodied as well in the complex rhythmic pictorial organization, which depended as much on the interaction of contrasting and complementary hues as it did on formal arrangement. Yve-Alain Bois argues that this

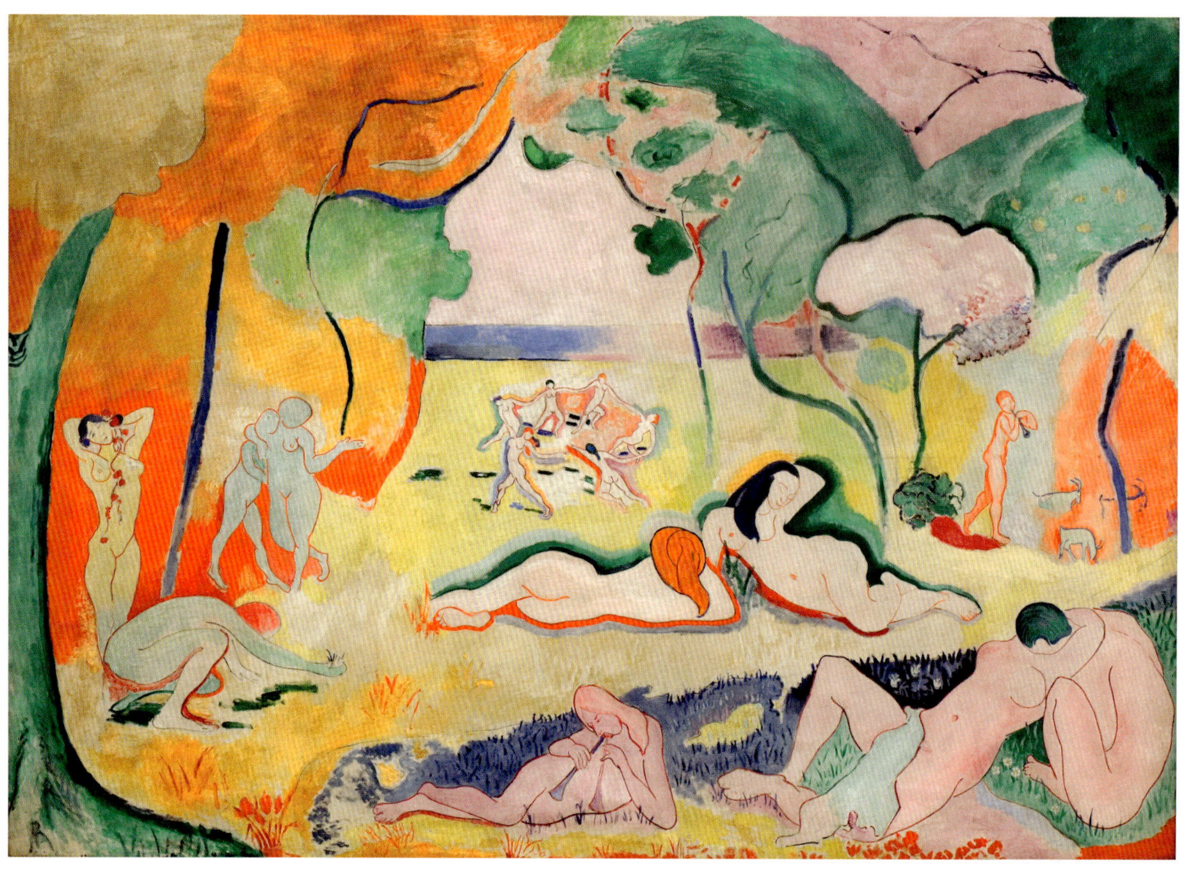

63. Henri Matisse, *Joy of Life,* 1906. Oil on canvas, 174 x 238.1 cm. Barnes Foundation, Merion, Pa. BF719. © Succession H. Matisse, Paris/ARS.

pulsional energy derives in large part from Matisse's desire to emulate Cézanne not in terms of any bodily or corporeal cohesion but in terms of the pictorial tautness that characterizes the latter's work, resulting in painting that is all surface. The outcome, an image in which the eye can only range over the tight, almost pneumatic expanse, is, according to Bois, analogous to the play of the desiring, voracious, erotic gaze over the skin of its object of desire.[49]

If *Blue Nude* instances Matisse entering into an argument put into play by Rodin on the one hand and Cézanne on the other, an argument between an abstraction of the body—and its erotics—through its fragmentation and an abstraction of the eroticized body through its synthesis with its composition, it was for the last time. *Blue Nude,* in other words, is the last painting that Matisse did under the sign of the eroticized body (as opposed to the erotics of paint). "Notes of a Painter" indicates which path Matisse would eventually choose. That this argument about visual erotics can and should be read into this text should be no surprise, since it is largely concerned with explaining—or even justifying—Matisse's figurative practice in the face of accusations that his paintings of women were ugly, lacking sensual interest, refusing of pleasure. Matisse writes:

Suppose I want to paint a woman's body: first of all I imbue it with grace and charm, but I know that I must give something more. I will condense the meaning of this body by seeking its essential lines. The charm will be less apparent at first glance, but it must eventually emerge from the new image which will have a broader meaning, one more fully human. The charm will be less striking since it will not be the sole quality of the painting, but it will not exist less for its being contained within the general conception of the figure.[50]

Though he would later recast this idea in terms of sublimation I do not believe that in 1908 Matisse was interested in either the suppression or the dissimulation of eroticism.[51] On the contrary, such passages need to be read in terms of his dawning understanding of the new conditions established for the painting of the nude in the wake of Cézanne's *Bathers.*[52] However clumsy the terms, Matisse was talking about the way that the erotic was to be communicated now, not bounded by bodies but articulated through the tensions and formal structures of the canvas as a whole.

The paintings of nudes that Matisse made in the wake of *Blue Nude* and "Notes of a Painter" are, not surprisingly, a more precise articulation of these ideas: *Le luxe I* (1907) (fig. 64), with its fragmented brushstroke and lack of finish, such that a great deal of white canvas shows through the thinned-out paint, and in the willfulness of the paint application—the touches of pink on the extremely thinly painted body of the standing nude, for example, which caress the rounded lower contour of the breasts and the hairless, infantile skin of the pubis; or *Bathers with a Turtle* (1908) (fig. 65), not solely in the pose of the crouching, blonde bather—a pose that refers to one of the central figures in Cézanne's Philadelphia *Bathers*—but in the very nature of the surface, the sticky, clotted, heavily scraped down and reworked skin of paint, in which flesh mingles in a muddied, primordial mess of pigment; or *Dance I* (1909) (fig. 66), where the bodies take on an elastic quality as they are stretched across the expanse of the canvas, their extremities fading out into nothingness and their reworked contours demonstrating the process of their construction.[53] In all of these examples, the very distortions and lack of idealization of the figures suggest not a refusal of sensual pleasure

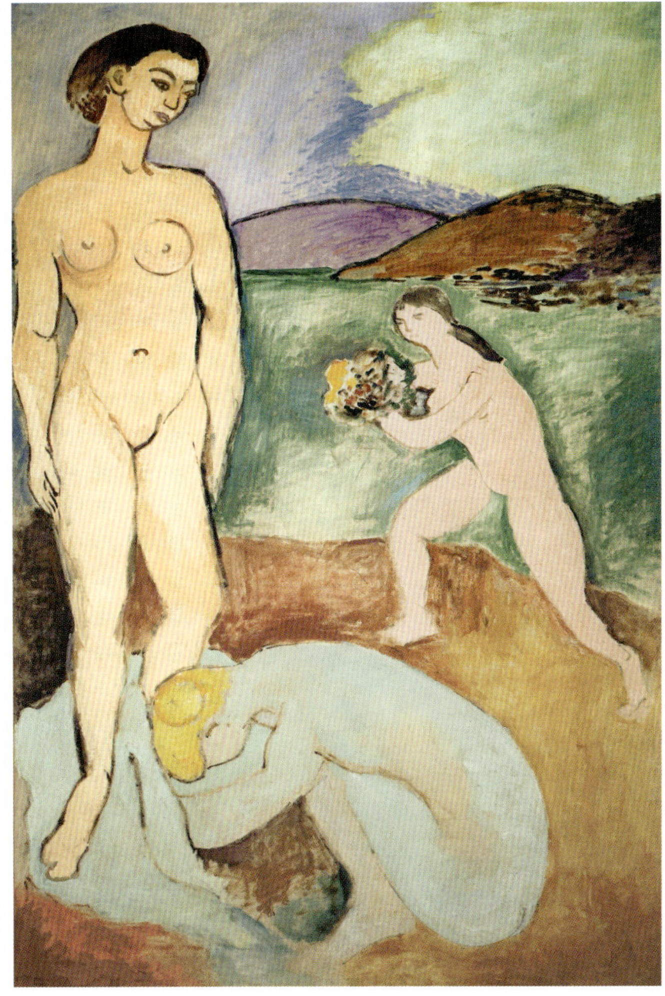

64. Henri Matisse, *Le Luxe I*, 1907. Oil on canvas, 210 x 138 cm. Musée national d'art moderne, Centre Georges Pompidou, Paris. © Succession H. Matisse, Paris/ARS.

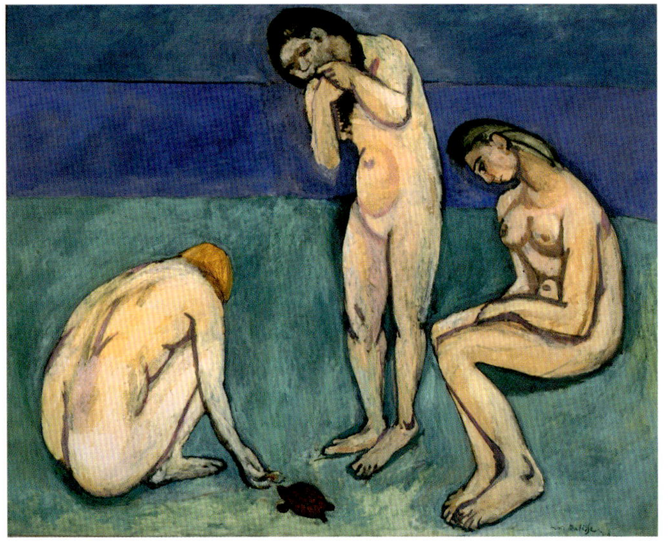

by the artist but the opposite: a sensual pleasure produced by the very medium of painting, outside of the conventions of the eroticized nude.

One only has to look at Matisse's *Standing Bather* (fig. 67), the result of his close study of *Three Bathers*, to see how much he learned, and in what terms, from Cézanne's conception of the nude: it is not simply the borrowing of a pose, not simply the gestural, reworked outlines left visible, not simply in the way the color of the surrounding field—that deep, impossible blue—infects the flesh of the bather that signal Matisse's debt to Cézanne. Rather, it is that breast, that curious appendage of flesh that never securely enough establishes this bather's gender; it is the way Matisse

65. Henri Matisse, *Bathers with a Turtle,* 1908. Oil on canvas, 179.1 x 220.3 cm. Saint Louis Museum of Art. © Succession H. Matisse, Paris/ARS.

66. Henri Matisse, *Dance I,* March 1909. Oil on canvas, 259.7 x 390.1 cm. Museum of Modern Art, N.Y., gift of Nelson Rockefeller in honor of Alfred H. Barr Jr. © Succession H. Matisse, Paris/ARS.

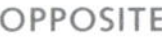

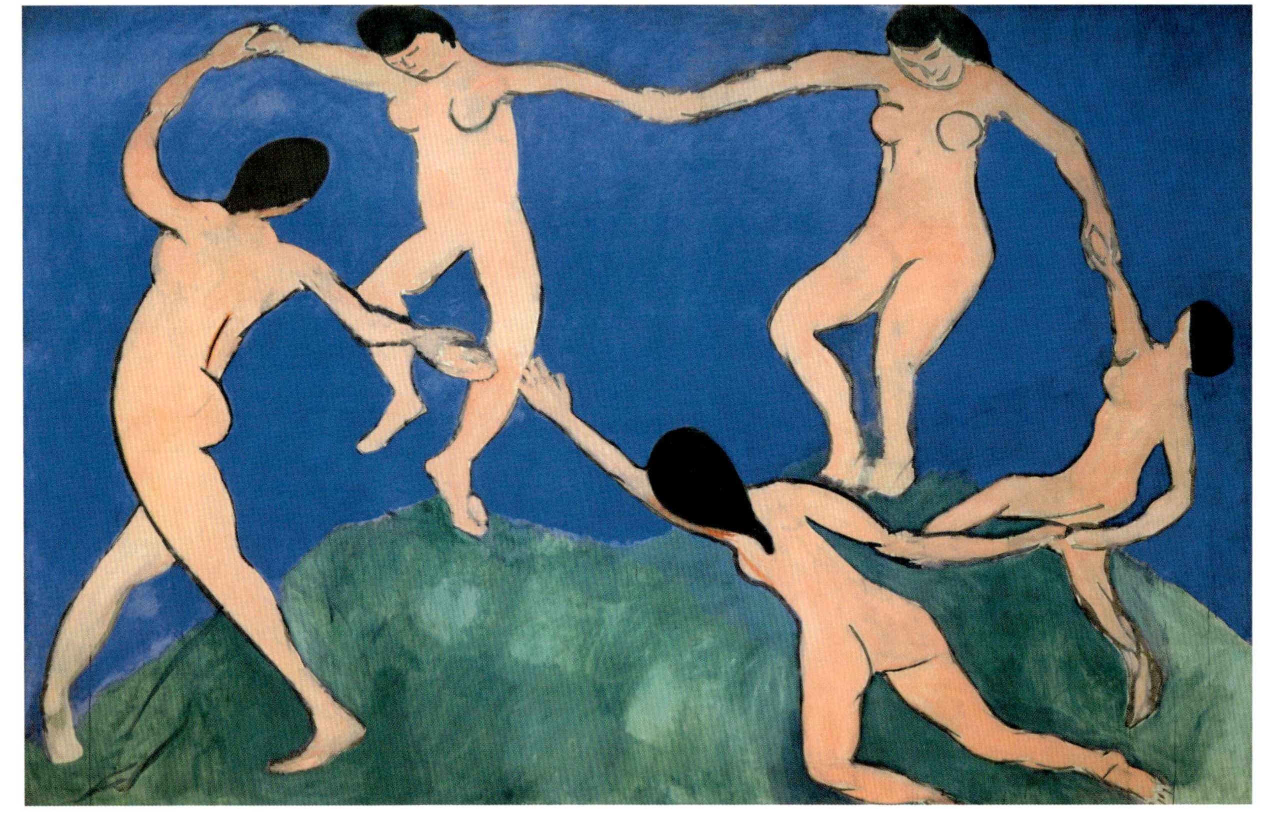

OPPOSITE
67. Henri Matisse, *Standing Bather,* 1909. Oil on canvas, 92.7 x 74 cm. Museum of Modern Art, N.Y., gift of Abby Aldrich Rockefeller. © Succession H. Matisse, Paris/ARS.

wrenches that appendage around so that it lies flat on the surface of the picture, rendering it a figure that has no front; it is the way this flattening of the figure makes her (it?) part of, continuous with, the picture surface; it is the way that, now, the body is made a function of the flatness of the canvas, of its span, of its saturation, of its skin of paint.[54] It is this way that Matisse understands Cézanne: it is in the way that now the depicted body and its erotics, the pleasure it produces, is a function of the paint out of which it is constituted.[55] For Cézanne—and Matisse shows us this—the nude as a category in painting would never again be able to function as it had in the past, because the pleasure it produced was not a matter of bodies seen but medium manipulated. It was a pleasure not of form but of substance, an erotics of paint that seeped beyond the body's contours, that constituted those body's contours, that collapsed the sensuality of medium with the sensuality of the body.

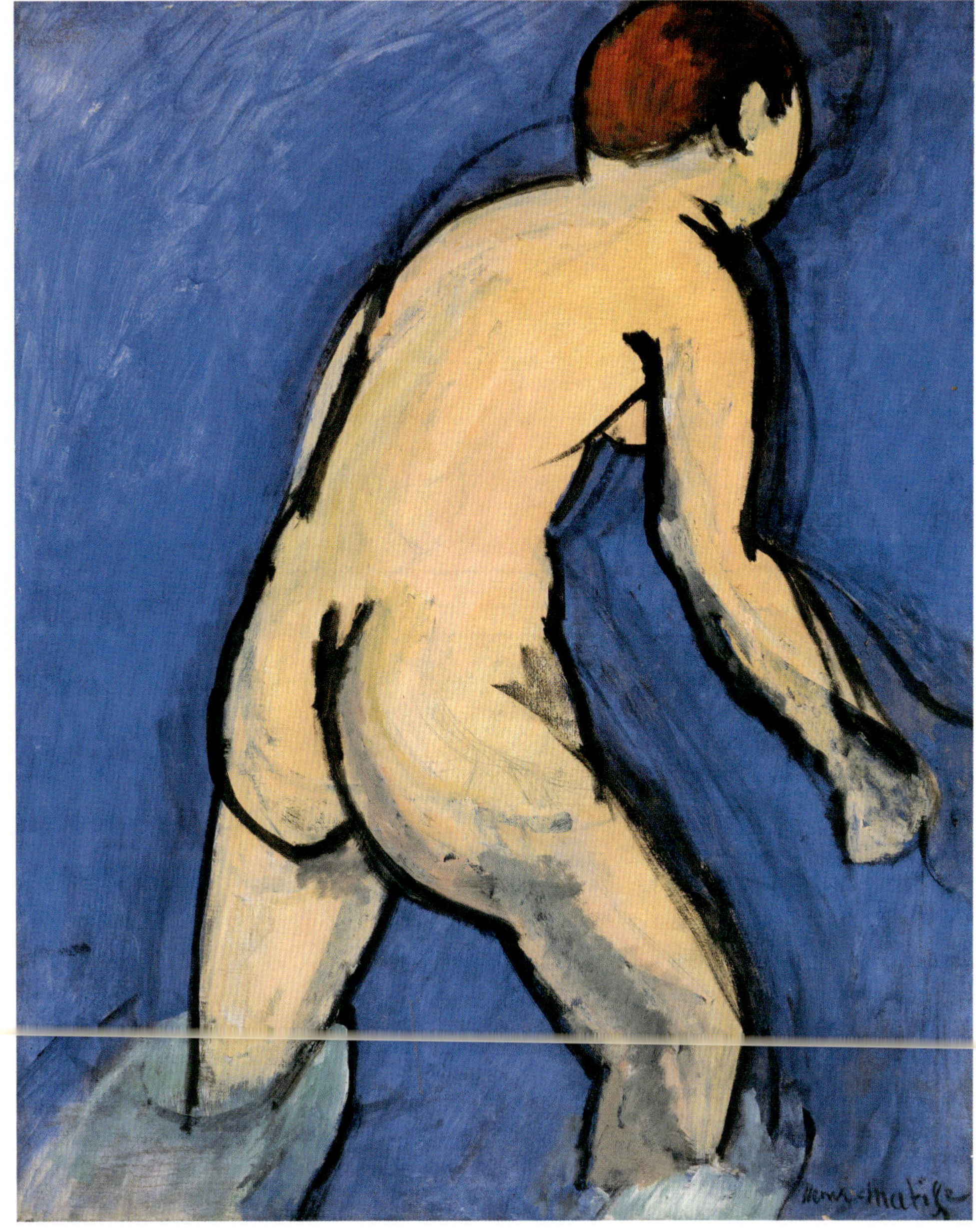

NOTES

INTRODUCTION

1. On the interpretation of Bernard's photograph as an imaging of the artist's creative, masculine authority, see Tamar Garb, *Bodies of Modernity: Figure and Flesh in Fin-de-Siècle France* (London: Thames and Hudson, 1998), 199–201. I do not at all disagree with Garb's interpretation of this image but merely suggest, in what follows, that it coexists with another one, one that is in some senses contradictory to the first.

A recent article suggests that this photograph by Bernard could have been the source for Picasso's earliest work on the *Demoiselles d'Avignon,* though the author admits that it would be difficult to prove Picasso's access to the photograph. However, the visual evidence is intriguing. If indeed Picasso did borrow this photograph for his imaging of femme fatale power and threat to masculinity, it would seem to suggest the veracity of my claim that this image is ambivalent, at least, in the portrayal of Cézanne as a figure of male power. See David Fraser Jenkins, "Baigneuses and Demoiselles: 'Bathers' in Cézanne, Picasso, and Matisse," *Apollo* 145, no. 421 (1997): 39–44.

CHAPTER 1

The epigraph to this chapter is drawn from Pablo Picasso, quoted in "Picasso 1930–35," *Cahiers d'Art* (1935): 42. All translations from the French are mine unless otherwise noted.

1. Émile Bernard, *Souvenirs sur Paul Cézanne, et lettres* (Paris: À La Rénovation Esthétique, 1921), 15. The work first appeared, in two parts, in *Mercure de France*, 1 October 1907, 385–404, and in *Mercure de France,* 16 October 1907, 606–27. Republished as a book in 1912.

2. Bernard, *Souvenirs,* 15.

3. Bernard, *Souvenirs,* 16.

4. Bernard, *Souvenirs,* 17.

5. Bernard, *Souvenirs,* 18–19.

6. Léo Larguier, "Le dimanche avec Paul Cézanne," in *Conversations avec Cézanne: Émile Bernard, Maurice Denis, Joachim Gasquet, Gustave Geffroy, Francis Jourdain, Léo Larguier, Karl-Ernst Osthaus, R. F. Rivière et J. F. Scherb, Ambroise Vollard,* ed. P. M. Doran (Paris: Macula, 1978), 10–11.

7. R. F. Rivière and J. F. Schnerb, "L'atelier de Cézanne," *La Grande Revue,* 25 December 1907, 811–17, reprinted in *Conversations avec Cézanne,* 85.

8. Nina Athanassoglou-Kallmyer points out, quite correctly, that a range of stereotypes of the Provençal, both negative and nationalistically positive, inflected these sorts of descriptions of Cézanne. Larguier was obviously drawing upon the latter tropes. See Athanassoglou-Kallmyer, *Cézanne and Provence: The Painter and His Culture* (Chicago: University of Chicago Press, 2003), 15–32.

9. Bernard himself refers to Cézanne's suspicion of people in his *Souvenirs sur Cézanne:* in that text, he claims that Cézanne said "I am a shy man, a bohemian[;] . . . people mock me. I don't have the power to fight back. People think I am crazy because I am isolated. *At least that way no one can get their hooks into me* [*personne ne met le grappin dessus*]" (24, my emphasis). This idea—and the particular phrase that Bernard attributed to Cézanne—would be adopted wholesale by other writers. See, for example, Georges Rivière: "The solitude to which Cézanne confined himself can, to a great degree, find its justification in the constant fear which he had always had of coming under someone else's influence, of seeing someone try to '*get their hooks into him,*' according to his familiar expression. His isolation was the fortress which protected him against a hypothetical enemy who might insinuate himself at certain moments under the guise of suggestions coming from his friends" (*Le maître Paul Cézanne* [Paris: Floury, 1923], 105, my emphasis).

10. Paul Cézanne, letter to Joachim Gasquet, 30 April 1896, in *Paul Cézanne: Letters,* ed. John Rewald, trans. Marguerite Kay, 4th ed. (New York: Da Capo Press, 1995), 245.

11. See the discussion in chapter 3. Terence Maloon suggests that one of the reasons for Bernard's change of position had to do with some damaging remarks that Cézanne had made about Bernard in letters that had surfaced in public ("Tableau/Peinture: Critical Responses to Cézanne's Unfinished Works," in *Cézanne: Finished, Unfinished,* ed. Felix Baumann, Evelyn Benesch, Walter Feilchenfeldt, and Klaus Albrecht Schröder, exh. cat. [Ostfildern-Ruit, Denmark: Hatje Cantz, 2000], 89). Although Maloon does not provide further details, he presumably refers to letters such as the one Cézanne wrote to his son on 26 September 1906, in which he refers to Bernard as "an intellectual constipated by recollections of museums, but who does not look enough at nature" (*Paul Cézanne: Letters,* 332).

12. Gasquet's account of Cézanne's life and approach to painting, in particular, has been treated with a measure of scholarly distrust because of the way in which the author attributes to Cézanne a poetic language that does not jibe with any other portrait of him and because of the author's liberal (and uncited) borrowings from others' accounts. John Rewald's study, *Cézanne, Geffroy et Gasquet* (Paris: Quatre-Chemins-Editart, 1959), has been most influential here. However, recent writings on Gasquet suggest that his writings might be more useful than has been thought; see especially Richard Shiff, introduction to *Joachim Gasquet's Cézanne: A Memoir with Conversations,* trans. Christopher Pemberton (London: Thames and Hudson, 1991), 15–24, and Nina Athanassoglou-Kallmyer, *Cézanne and Provence,* 5. Kallmyer writes that, despite Gasquet's reputation as an unreliable witness, "Gasquet's account of Cézanne appears to fit seamlessly and convincingly with its contemporary cultural setting. Historicized and contextualized, Gasquet not only makes sense but becomes an invaluable period voice on a par with his contemporaries Émile Bernard, Maurice Denis, and Ambroise Vollard (all of whose recollections on Cézanne, through some inexplicable historiographic inequity, enjoy greater respectability than Gasquet's)." Gasquet's book was first published in Paris in 1921.

13. Any discussion of biographical criticism in art history must be framed by the structural and poststructural critiques of that methodology that took place in the discipline in the 1980s, beginning with an article written by Rosalind Krauss in 1981, "In the Name of Picasso." Here Krauss contended that biographical criticism attempted to close off the fullness or multiplicity of meaning in a work by resorting to the false authority of the unknowable intentions of its maker ("In the Name of Picasso," in *The Originality of the Avant-Garde and Other Modernist Myths* [Cambridge: MIT Press, 1985], 23–41, originally published in *October* 16 [Spring 1981]: 5–22). Basing her argument on literary critiques of the author or "author function"—primarily Roland Barthes's "Death of the Author" and Michel Foucault's "What is an Author?" (Roland Barthes, "Death of the Author," *The Rustle of Language,* trans. Richard Howard [Berkeley and Los Angeles: University of California Press, 1989] and Michel Foucault, "What is an Author?" in *The Foucault Reader,* ed. Paul Rabinow [New York: Pantheon Books, 1984])—Krauss compares what she calls an "art history of the proper name" to a detective story, in which the only goal is to find "whodunnit." Thus, in this approach to art history, there is "a contraction of sense to the simple task of pointing, or labeling, to the act of univocal reference": "For the individual who can be shown to be the 'key' to the image, and thus the 'meaning' of the image, has the kind of singularity one is looking for. Like his name, his meaning stops within the bounds of identity" ("In the Name of Picasso," 28).

14. It may also, as Wayne Andersen proposes in a suggestive, if eccentric, study, tell us something of the historian's own investments in the figure of Cézanne: "By forcing enmity between Cézanne and women, and between him and his father, one is able to established a personal relationship to Cézanne—to love him, father him, mother him—each art lover wanting him for his or herself, wanting him to be devoted only to art and art history, his potency not in other ways expended. . . . To possess Cézanne, one must first isolate him, kill his father, refuse him the love of a woman, and assert that he had difficulty making friends" (*The Youth of Cézanne and Zola: Notoriety at its Source; Art and Literature in Paris* [Geneva: Éditions Fabriart, 2003], xix).

15. Émile Zola, "Peinture," *Le Figaro,* 2 May 1896, quoted in Françoise Cachin and Joseph Rishel, *Cézanne,* exh. cat., trans. John Goodman (Philadelphia: Philadelphia Museum of Art, 1996), 33; Bernard, *Souvenirs*; Ambroise Vollard, *En écoutant Cézanne, Degas, Renoir* (Paris: Bernard

Grasset, 1985), 56–64, originally published in 1938; Maurice Merleau-Ponty, "Cézanne's Doubt," in *Sense and Non-Sense,* trans. Hubert L. Dreyfus and Patricia Allen Dreyfus (Evanston, Ill.: Northwestern University Press, 1964), 9–25, originally published as "Le doute de Cézanne," *Fontaine* 8 (December 1945): 80–100.

16. Élie Faure, "Paul Cézanne," *Portraits d'Hier,* 1 May 1910, 119; Georges Rivière, *Le maître Paul Cézanne.* Faure's comments echo those of Charles Morice, which open this section ("Paul Cézanne," *Mercure de France,* 15 February 1907, 37), in their puzzlement over the simultaneously fecund and sterile quality of the Cézannian mythos.

17. Carol Duncan, "Virility and Domination in Early Twentieth-Century Vanguard Painting," *Artforum,* December 1973, 30–39.

18. On Degas's purported "artistic impotence," see Roy McMullen, *Degas: Life, Times, and Art* (Boston: Macmillan, 1984), and Carol Armstrong, *Odd Man Out: Readings of the Work and Reputation of Edgar Degas* (Chicago: University of Chicago Press, 1991). A point of clarification here: I am not trying to argue that these identifications are stable or that artists like Cézanne and Degas have not been portrayed simultaneously as fecund, powerful men with phallic paintbrush in hand ready to create—although I would, in the case of these two artists, suggest that these latter, heroic images are less common. Rather, these images have no problem existing parallel to each other. For an interesting example of the other, hypermasculinized representation of Degas for his British contemporaries, please see Andrew Stephenson's review of the Sickert exhibition, "Buttressing Bohemian Mystiques and Bandaging Masculine Anxieties," *Art History* 17 (June 1994): 269–78.

19. Faure, "Paul Cézanne."

20. Émile Zola, *L'Oeuvre* (Paris: Charpentier, 1886). I refer in the comments that follow to the Oxford Classics translation (*The Masterpiece,* trans. Thomas Walton, rev. Roger Pearson [Oxford: Oxford University Press, 1993], translation originally published in London by Elek Press in 1950); page references appear in parentheses in the text. The classic study of the Lantier-Cézanne connection is Robert J. Niess, *Zola, Cézanne, and Manet: A Study of "L'Oeuvre"* (Ann Arbor: University of Michigan Press, 1968). See also Patrick Brady, *"L'Oeuvre" d'Emile Zola: Roman sur les arts; Manifeste, autobiographie, roman à clef* (Geneva: Librarie Droz, 1967); John A. Frey, "The Artist as Failure—Two Brands of Naturalism: *Madame Sourdis* and *L'Oeuvre,*" *Emile Zola and the Arts,* ed. Jean-Max Guieu and Alison Hilton (Washington, D.C.: Georgetown University Press, 1988); and Jean-Luc Steinmetz, "*L'Oeuvre,*" in *Le naturalisme: Colloque de Cerisy,* ed. Pierre Cogny (Cerisy-la-Salle: Centre Culturel Internationale, 1978).

21. On *L'Oeuvre* as a condemnation of impressionism, see William J. Berg, *The Visual Novel: Emile Zola and the Art of His Times* (University Park: Pennsylvania State University Press, 1992), 40–44, and Brady, *"L'Oeuvre" d'Emile Zola.* For a study of *L'Oeuvre* as a roman à clef, see Niess, *Zola, Cézanne, and Manet.*

22. Quoted in John Rewald, *Cézanne: A Biography* (New York: Harry N. Abrams, 1986), 161.

23. Niess, *Zola, Cézanne, and Manet,* 82; Monet's letter is quoted in full in Rewald, *Cézanne: A Biography,* 169. Monet writes: "You were purposely careful to have none of your characters resemble any one of us, but, in spite of that, I am afraid lest our enemies amongst the public and the press identify Manet or ourselves as failures, which is not what you have in mind, I cannot believe it."

24. Rewald, *Cézanne: A Biography,* 166. Though Rewald explains the lack of recognition to be the result of Cézanne's being relatively unknown, a review that appeared in *La Revue Indépendante* late in 1886, the year of *L'Oeuvre*'s publication, suggests that Cézanne had, by this time, been acknowledged as a central figure in impressionism. See Teodor de Wyzewa, "L'art contemporain," in *La Revue Indépendante,* November–December 1886, quoted in Rewald's *Seurat* (New York: Harry N. Abrams, 1990), 104.

25. It was in 1896, for example, that Zola wrote of Cézanne as nothing more than a "great aborted genius" ("Peinture," quoted in Cachin and Rishel, *Cézanne,* 33). On the marketability of artistic biography, see Nicholas Green, "Dealing in Temperaments: Economic Transformation of the Artistic Field in France during the Second Half of the Nineteenth Century," *Art History* 10 (March 1987): 59–78.

26. Louis Vauxcelles, "Salon d'Automne, le vernissage," *Gil Blas,* 15 October 1904; Arsène Alexandre, "Claude

Lantier," *Le Figaro,* 9 December 1895, 5; Georges Lecomte, "Paul Cézanne," in the catalogue of the Collection Blot, Hôtel Drouot, Paris, May 1900, quoted in Rewald, *Cézanne: A Biography,* 166.

27. Niess, *Zola, Cézanne, and Manet,* 90: "Everything written on Cézanne of the years before 1890 has been based either on *L'Oeuvre* as a direct biographical source, on his letters to Zola, on Zola's letters, or on a small handful of testimonies written by men who knew him more or less well and who left descriptions of him, factual or fictional, which may perhaps—but do not surely—render some or part of the truth."

28. Émile Bernard, "Paul Cézanne," *Les Hommes d'Aujourd'hui* 8, no. 387 (1891): n.p., quoted in Cachin and Rishel, *Cézanne,* 29.

29. Joachim Gasquet, *Joachim Gasquet's Cézanne,* 68. Gasquet's liberal borrowings from Zola's text are all the more significant considering the fact that his biography was used as a source by such influential writers as Roger Fry, Merleau-Ponty, and Meyer Schapiro. See Shiff's introduction, 15–16.

30. Maurice Denis, journal entry from 1906, in *Conversations avec Cézanne,* 93.

31. I use the masculine pronoun throughout the rest of this discussion advisedly: the discourses of genius to which I refer were inseparable from discourses of masculinity and virility. According to these terms, the very possibility of feminine or female genius was inconceivable.

32. Eugène Delacroix, "Michel-Ange," *Revue de Paris* 15 (May 1830): 41 and *Revue de Paris* 16 (July 1830): 165, reprinted in *Écrits sur l'art,* ed. François-Marie Deyrolle and Christophe Denissel (Paris: Séguier, 1988), 89–124; Honoré de Balzac, *Le chef-d'oeuvre inconnu* (Paris, 1845).

33. The works in question are these: Jacques Joseph Moreau de Tours's *La psychologie morbide dans ses rapports avec la philosophie de l'histoire, ou de l'influence des névropathies sur le dynamisme intellectuel* (Paris: V. Masson, 1859); Bénédict Augustin Morel's *Traité des dégénérescences physiques, intellectueles, et morales de l'espèce humaine* (Paris: J. B. Ballière, 1857); Césare Lombroso's *Genio e follio* (1864); and Max Nordau's *Dégénérescence* (Paris: Alcan, 1894).

34. Quoted in Barbara Spackman, *Decadent Geneaologies: The Rhetoric of Sickness from Baudelaire to D'Annunzio* (Ithaca: Cornell University Press, 1989), 20.

35. Max Nordau, *Degeneration,* 6th ed. (New York: D. Appleton, 1895), 128, translation of *Entartung,* 2nd ed. (Berlin: C. Duncker, 1892–93), quoted in Spackman, *Decadent Genealogies,* 10–11. The "ignorance" of the judges comes from their failing to recognize that Verlaine was "degenerate"—i.e., physically and psychically "ill"—rather than merely a wrongdoer.

36. Nordau, *Degeneration,* 27, quoted in Spackman, 11.

37. Most important, of course, is Balzac's *Chef-d'oeuvre inconnu.*

38. From Émile Zola, Ébauche (preparatory notes for *L'Oeuvre*), Bibliothèque Nationale, Paris, MS N.A.F., fol. 265), quoted in Brady, "*L'Oeuvre*" *d'Emile Zola,* 19.

39. Thomas Zamparelli, "Zola and the Quest for the Absolute in Art," *Yale French Studies* 42 (1969): 147.

40. Émile Zola, "Le Naturalisme au Salon," *Voltaire,* 19 June 1880, 3, reprinted in *Les écrivains devant l'impressionisme,* ed. Denys Riout (Paris: Macula, 1989).

41. This notion of the link between generation and degeneration in the genius was echoed in the scientific literature of the day, specifically in the writings of Césare Lombroso, who argued that the artistic genius represented at once the highest evolutionary development and the most atavistic throwback of the species, since sterility was the inevitable outcome of an evolving intelligence. See Spackman, *Decadent Genealogies,* 21.

42. J.-K. Huysmans, "Trois peintres," *La Cravache,* 4 August 1888, republished in *Certains* (Paris: Tresse and Stock, 1889); Arsène Alexandre, "Le mouvement artistique: Claude Lantier," *Le Figaro,* 9 December 1895, 5; Joseph Rishel, "A Century of Criticism II: From 1907 to the Present," in Cachin and Rishel, *Cézanne,* 47; Rainer Maria Rilke, *Letters on Cézanne,* trans. Joel Agee (New York: Fromm International, 1985).

43. Cézanne was asked to respond to a questionnaire sent to a number of artists by a Parisian art periodical. Answering the question, "Which literary character do you most identify with?" Cézanne responded, "Frenhofer." On the questionnaire, see Jean-Claude Lebensztejn, "Les couilles de Cézanne," *Critique* 44 (December 1988): 1031–47. The full

questionnaire ("Mes confiances") is reproduced in Adrien Chappius, *The Drawings of Paul Cézanne: A Catalogue Raisonné* (Greenwich, Conn.: New York Graphic Society, 1973), 1:25–28. On Cézanne's anxieties about reaching his artistic goals, see his letter to Émile Bernard, 21 September 1906, in *Paul Cézanne: Letters* (329); for Bernard's account of Cézanne's identification with Frenhofer, see *Souvenirs.*

44. Linda Nochlin, "Cézanne: Studies in Contrast," *Art in America,* June 1996, 67.

45. See Henri Mitterand, "*L'Oeuvre:* Étude, notes et variantes," in Émile Zola, *Les Rougon-Macquart: Histoire naturelle et sociale d'une famille sous le Second Empire,* ed. Armand Lanoux (Paris: Gallimard, Bibliothèque de la Pléiade, 1996), 4:1338, for a transcription of the notebook page that indicates the various titles Zola considered for his work, most of which have to do with the notion of the creation of a work of art as being something like childbirth.

For a more precise, and historically specific, examination of the differences between the terms "oeuvre" and "chef-d'oeuvre," see Walter Cahn, *Masterpieces: Chapters on the History of an Idea* (Princeton: Princeton University Press, 1979).

46. Even the cemetery in which Lantier is buried reeks of this soon-forgotten quality: the plots are only granted for five years, "so there was a 'here-today-and-gone-tomorrow' feeling about the place, a sense of poverty, a cold, clean, bare look that made it as melancholy as a barracks or a charity ward" (*The Masterpiece,* 418).

47. Judith Wechsler argues that Zola's standards for finish or completion were less than purely formal: "What characterized a realized artist for Zola? One whose work exhibited sufficient 'finish' to be acceptable to the public. After all, finish and acceptability characterized Zola's own work and success" (*The Interpretation of Cézanne* [Ann Arbor, Mich.: UMI Research Press, 1972], 12.

48. Zola, "Le naturalisme au Salon," in *Écrits sur l'art,* ed. Jean-Pierre Leduc-Adine (Paris: Gallimard, 1991), 420.

49. Zola, "Le naturalisme au Salon," 422–23.

This view was shared by other critics at the time. Huysmans, for one, voiced his agreement with Zola thus: "Today the difficulty of transcribing light effects has been resolved, or at least restored to the only exact proportions possible. In short, off-the-cuff sketches have disappeared, in large part, in favor of finished and complete works; the system consisting of dropping a hardly-begun canvas, under the pretext that the impression desired is already there, of contenting oneself thus with too-facile rudiments, of avoiding from the start all the difficulties of painting—this impotence [*impuissance*], to give it a name, to place on its feet a solid and complete work, hardly exists today" ("L'Exposition des Indépendants en 1880," in *L'art moderne* [Paris: Charpentier, 1883], reprinted in *Les écrivains devant l'impressionisme,* 256.

50. Zola, "Le naturalisme au salon," 423.

51. That this may indeed have been the case was only made clear upon Rewald's publication, in 1936, of Cézanne's correspondence; no letters to Zola are extant after one written on 4 April 1886, in which Cézanne thanks Zola for sending him a copy of *L'Oeuvre:* "I thank the author of the 'Rougon-Macquart' for this kind token of remembrance and ask him to allow me to clasp his hand whilst thinking of bygone days." Cézanne signs off with the phrase "Ever yours under the impulse of past times" (*Paul Cézanne: Letters,* 183).

52. Vollard's encounter with Zola, and Cézanne's response, is described in Vollard's text on the artist originally published in 1914. I refer to the following translation: *Cézanne,* trans. Harold L. Van Doren (New York: Dover Publications, 1984), especially 96–107.

53. Zola laments: "Ah! why did he not also give me the great painter upon whom I counted so much! . . . His comrades were ready enough to set him down as a failure, but I told them over and over again: 'Paul has the genius of a great painter.' Ah! why was I not a good prophet? . . . Dear grand Cézanne had the divine spark! But, if he had the natural genius of a great painter, he did not have the persistence to become one. He lost himself too much in his dreams, dreams that were never fulfilled. To use his own words, he gave himself to be nursed by illusions!" (Vollard, *Cézanne,* 99–100).

54. Vollard, *Cézanne,* 100.

55. "No harsh words ever passed between us," Vollard recalls Cézanne saying. "It was I who stopped going to see Zola. I was not at my ease there any longer, with the fine rugs on the floor, the servants, and Emile enthroned behind a carved wooden desk. It all gave me the feeling that I was paying a visit to a minister of state. He had become . . . a dirty bourgeois" (Vollard, *Cézanne,* 103–4).

56. Vollard, *Cézanne,* 105.

57. Théodore Duret, "Cézanne," in *Histoire des peintres impressionistes* (Paris: H. Floury, 1906), 178–79.

58. As if in agreement with Duret, Maurice Denis reports that "Gauguin used to say, thinking of Cézanne: 'Nothing is so much like a *croûte* as a real masterpiece.' *Croûte* or masterpiece, one can only understand it in opposition to the mediocrity of modern painting." *Croûte* is used here in its figurative sense, as "bad painting" or "daub," both familiar usages in French ("Paul Cézanne—I," trans. Roger Fry, *Burlington Magazine* 16 [January 1910]: 208).

In Thadée Natanson's review of the 1895 Vollard exhibition, he cited a purely venal impulse behind the public's confusion of finish (the academic's standard of making a picture) and completeness (Cézanne's new, modern standard of aesthetic balance): "*Complete* [is] an epithet hypocritically synonymous with *advantageous* in exciting dealers or the cupidity of speculative buyers, eager to get the most of everything for their money." ("Paul Cézanne," *La Revue Blanche,* 1 December 1895, reprinted in *La promenade du critique influent,* ed. Jean-Paul Bouillon, Nicoele Dubreuil-Blondin, et al. [Paris: Hazan, 1990], 386.)

59. In *Cézanne and the End of Impressionism: A Study of the Theory, Technique, and Critical Evaluation of Modern Art* (Chicago: University of Chicago Press, 1984), Richard Shiff carefully delineates the differences among the various terms—*étude, ébauche, impression,* etc.—that could be used to describe a work that did not conform to academic standards of finish; he builds on the work of Albert Boime in *The Academy and French Painting in the Nineteenth Century* (New Haven: Yale University Press, 1986). Recently, an exhibition of Cézanne's work focused on the very issue of completion and its relation to the Cézannian notion of *réalisation:* see *Cézanne: Finished, Unfinished.* Terence Maloon's essay in the catalogue, "Tableau/Peinture: Critical Responses to Cézanne's Unfinished Works," is particularly relevant to my discussion here, especially 88ff.

60. My language here might suggest that the only viable point of comparison for Cézanne's practice was, in fact, academic notions of the development and construction of a painting. Certainly that was not the case. However, such a model was not entirely rejected by avant-garde painters—think, for example, of Manet's work on *Olympia* or the *Déjeuner sur l'herbe* or Seurat's long and carefully studied gestation of *Sunday Afternoon on the Island of the Grande-Jatte.* Moreover, while impressionism, as practiced by figures like Monet and Pissarro, did away with the idea of the study in favor of spontaneous work en plein air and the innocence of the unpremeditated view of the motif, it also largely did away with drawing and watercolor, two mediums closely associated with the patient, studied development of a final painting. It is precisely Cézanne's emphasis on these two mediums in his oeuvre that makes the issue of finish and unfinish—in the terms set by traditional, academic painting in France—a central question when faced with his work.

61. That the term *sensation* implied an encounter between self and nature—or subjective and objective "truth"—is a point argued by Shiff in *Cézanne and the End of Impressionism.* Shiff elaborates on this point in a later essay, maintaining that the artist's belief in an endlessly incomplete project of painting was one held by all the impressionist painters in opposition to the Symbolists: "Whereas Symbolists sought to discover universally meaningful visual configurations, complete in themselves, Impressionists believed it virtually impossible to give a picture definitive completion. The life of a picture should remain open, growing organically, just like 'real' life" ("Cézanne's Blur, Approximating Cézanne," in *Framing France: The Representation of Landscape in France, 1870–1914,* ed. Richard Thomson [Manchester: Manchester University Press, 1998], 63).

62. Gustave Geffroy, "Salon de 1901," in *La vie artistique* (Paris: H. Floury, 1903), 8:376.

63. Yve-Alain Bois, "Cézanne: Words and Deeds," *October* 84 (Spring 1998): 39.

64. Richard Shiff, "Cézanne's Blur," 67.

65. R. F. Rivière and J. F. Schnerb describe Cézanne's working method in detail in "L'atelier de Cézanne," which appeared in *La Grande Revue* in 1907: "Cézanne did not seek to represent forms by line. The contour did not exist for him in the sense of being the site where one form ended and another began. Looking at his unfinished canvases, objects in the background are often left blank, and their silhouettes are indicated only by the ground against which their profiles

come into view. Form only exists through its proximity to neighboring forms, not strictly through line. The black lines which often delineate his paintings were not for Cézanne an element to which color was intended to be added, but were simply the most efficient way of reestablishing the whole form through means of contour before modeling it through means of color" (reprinted in *Conversations avec Cézanne,* 87).

66. Vollard remarks that "Cézanne used to fly into a passion for the most absurd reasons—sometimes for no reason at all. Suddenly seizing a portrait of himself he tried to tear it to pieces; but his palette knife had been mislaid, and his hands were trembling violently. So he rolled the canvas up, broke it across his knee, and flung it in the fireplace" (*Cézanne,* 105). Vollard captures the scene of Cézanne returning to a canvas as follows: "Cézanne had tossed [a still-life painting] out of the window, but it had caught in the branches of a cherry tree, and had hung there a long time. Inasmuch as they [Cézanne's household staff] had seen Cézanne armed with a long pole prowling about the tree, they decided that he intended to recover the canvas, and consequently they left it severely alone. I was present when the canvas was rescued. We were walking in the garden, Cézanne, young Paul, and I. The painter, who was a few paces in advance, his head slightly bent, turned around suddenly and said to the young man: 'Son, we must get down the *Apples;* I think I'll work on that study some more'" (*Cézanne,* 63).

Rivière and Schnerb also comment on Cézanne's tendency to abandon his canvases, but they seem to attribute this more to the fact that the artist placed little emphasis on the finished product of his efforts: "He never cared about his works and there were canvases dragged into corners, still on stretchers or rolled up. His studios . . . were in great disarray, in a beautiful disarray" (reprinted in *Conversations avec Cézanne,* 86).

67. Carol Armstrong notes a similar equation between a process-oriented, serial method of working and charges of artistic impotence in critical responses to Degas's work. For example, Paul Valéry writes of Degas's drawings that "a work was for Degas the result of an indefinite quantity of studies and then a series of operations. I really believe that he thought that a work could never be said to be finished . . . [;] certain artists . . . work over, attack, correct, and imprison themselves. They cannot leave the game or get out of the circle of their gains and losses." Armstrong sees in this statement a charge of "draughtsmanly impotence" (*Odd Man Out,* 224).

She comments elsewhere that "the problem with Degas was an obsessiveness that could not be placed—then or now—noted by critics who suspected that his concerns were trivial. Indeed, more famous critics and writers . . . —namely, the Goncourt brothers and Manet's critic Zola—overtly described Degas's elusiveness as a function of artistic impotence" (*Odd Man Out,* 15).

68. These "secrets" revolve around Christine's shy refusal to reveal the details of her sexual history. Claude's response is extremely troubled: "For the first time, that day, Claude felt that they were still strangers to each other. He felt chilled by the cold from another body. Could it be impossible, he wondered, for each to become part and parcel of the other when they lay breathless in each other's arms, each clinging tighter and tighter to the other in their burning desire to attain something beyond mere possession?" (*The Masterpiece,* 164–65). Laurie Milner points out this connection in her dissertation ("Modernism's Absent Father: Constructions of Cézanne and His Art in Paris, 1886–1901" [Ph.D. diss., Northwestern University, 1994], 13).

69. Laura Mulvey states the problem succinctly: "Fetishism, Freud first pointed out, involves displacing the sight of woman's imaginary castration onto a variety of reassuring but often surprising objects . . . which serve as *signs* for the lost penis but have no direct connection with it. . . . It is man's narcissistic fear of losing his own phallus, his most precious possession, which causes shock at the sight of the female genitals and the subsequent fetishistic attempt to disguise or divert attention from them" ("Fears, Fantasies, and the Male Unconscious, or 'You Don't Know What is Happening, Do You, Mr. Jones?'" in *Visual and Other Pleasures* [Bloomington: Indiana University Press, 1989], 10–11; essay originally published in 1973).

70. Mulvey, "Fears, Fantasies, and the Male Unconscious," 10.

71. Tamar Garb, "Cézanne's Late Bathers: Modernism and Sexual Difference," in *Bodies of Modernity: Figure and*

Flesh in Fin-de-Siècle France (London: Thames and Hudson, 1998), 204.

72. Tamar Garb imagines Renoir's psychic investments in his images of women as such: "Like the infant at the breast of the fecund and ever-nurturing mother, Renoir looked to a mythic Woman to shelter him from the ravages of modernity. Painting was the space for the elaboration of that phantasmatic plentitude which is associated with early infancy. The mother exists for the infant only as a projection of his or her psychic and physical need. The withdrawal of the mother and the gradual realization of her separateness produces immense psychic pain for the infant, but a pain that is necessary in order to enter into the symbolic languages of culture. Renoir's art amounts to an elaborate defense against the pain of separation. For Renoir produced an art in which the exploration of conflict, of pain, of alienation, of separation itself, had no place. In his art, Woman as mother, as nature, as goddess was to function as the sign of eternal reparation in a painterly practice which became increasingly a defense against the ravages of adulthood. Infantile in the most profound sense, Renoir's art remained locked into the pursuit of pleasure, a pleasure symbolized in the rapacious suckling of the infant at the mother's breast. It never moves therefore to an art of desire, for it remains fatally locked in the realm of wish-fulfillment and the gratuitous gratification of appetite" ("Painterly Plenitude," in *Bodies of Modernity,* 176).

CHAPTER 2

1. Matisse, letter to the French state on the occasion of his donation of *Three Bathers* to the Petit Palais (1936), *Matisse on Art,* ed. Jack D. Flam (New York: Phaidon, 1973), 75; Matisse, "Notes of a Painter" in *Matisse on Art,* 37–38, originally published as "Notes d'un peintre," *La Grande Revue*, 25 December 1908, 731–45.

2. Émile Bernard, "Paul Cézanne," *Les Hommes d'Aujourd'hui* 8, no. 387 (1891): n.p., quoted in translation in Françoise Cachin and Joseph Rishel, *Cézanne,* trans. John Goodman (Philadelphia: Philadelphia Museum of Art, 1995), 29; Émile Bernard, "Réflexions à propos du Salon d'Automne," *La Rénovation Esthétique,* December 1907, reprinted in Émile Bernard, *Propos sur l'art,* ed. Anne Rivière (Paris: Séguier, 1994), 179.

3. These numbers were culled from John Rewald, *The Paintings of Paul Cézanne: A Catalogue Raisonné,* 2 vols. (New York: Harry N. Abrams, 1996). Where confusion might arise in the endnotes over which painting with the same title I am referring to, I will include the catalogue numbers to distinguish them (e.g., R251).

4. Curiously, at the Salon d'Automne, panels of photomechanical reproductions of Cézanne's work were shown alongside the paintings; so, in effect, a larger number of bather images were visible in this exhibition than the number of canvases shown would suggest. See Robert Boardingham, "Cézanne and the 1904 Salon d'Automne: 'Une chef d'une école nouvelle,'" *Apollo* 142 (October 1995): 31–39.

5. Though the bathers were not readily available to the public in these years, they did make their way into the collections of a number of artists, including Gustave Caillebotte (*Bathers at Rest III*), Camille Pissarro and Auguste Renoir (each owned a version of *The Battle of Love*), Edgar Degas (*Bather with Outstretched Arms*), Claude Monet, and Maurice Denis. See Mary Louise Elliot Krumrine, *Paul Cézanne: The Bathers*, exh. cat. (Basel: Kunstmuseum Basel, 1990), 34.

6. The examples of this interpretation of Cézanne's project are numerous, and it should come as no surprise that it was driven largely by a generation of Symbolist artist-critics such as Émile Bernard and Maurice Denis, although not by any means exclusively. For an overview of the contemporary criticism, see Cachin and Rishel, "A Century of Cézanne Criticism," in *Cézanne,* 24–75.

7. Indeed, by the time that Vollard asked Cézanne to produce a lithographic version of *Bathers at Rest III* in the late 1890s for inclusion in an album of prints published by the gallery, the painting had quite possibly emerged as the artist's most famous work: it had been exhibited in the 1877 impressionist exhibition, had been part of the 1893 Caillebotte bequest to the French state museums (at which time it was rejected), was the subject of an important article by Gustave Geffroy in 1894, and had been displayed in Vollard's window during the 1895 exhibition. See Douglas Druick, "Cézanne's Lithographs," in *Cézanne: The Late Work,* ed. William S. Rubin (New York: Museum of Modern Art,

1977), 119–38. Melvin Waldfogel has suggested that it was the controversy around the Caillebotte bequest—and Cézanne's displeasure at the painting's rejection by the state—that inspired his decision to turn it into a color lithograph. See Melvin Waldfogel, "Caillebotte, Vollard, et Cézanne's *Baigneurs au repos*," *Gazette des Beaux-Arts* 65 (February 1965): 113–20.

With respect to the male nude, while historians such as Margaret Walters and Abigail Solomon-Godeau have argued that it largely "disappeared" as a major genre in painting over the course of the nineteenth century, recent scholars have questioned that view, arguing that the male nude was simply relegated to other forms of visual culture and other types of "gazes," such as the medical gaze. See Walters, *The Nude Male: A New Perspective* (London: Paddington Press, 1978) and Solomon-Godeau, *Male Trouble: A Crisis in Representation* (London: Thames and Hudson, 1997); for an example of a critique of such a position, see Anthea Callen, "Doubles and Desire: Anatomies of Masculinity in the Later Nineteenth Century," *Art History* 26 (November 2003): 669–99.

8. For a tentative suggestion on Courbet's erotics of landscape, see Paul Galvez, "Courbet's Touch," in *Soil and Stone: Impressionism, Urbanism, and Environment,* ed. Frances Fowle and Richard Thompson (Aldershot, U.K.: Ashgate, 2003), 17–31.

9. For a useful compendium of literature (and critical positions) vis-à-vis Manet's painting, see Paul Hayes Tucker, *Manet's "Le Déjeuner sur l'herbe"* (Cambridge: Cambridge University Press, 1998).

10. For an excellent discussion of Puvis's interventions into late-nineteenth-century conventions of academic theories of the nude, see Jennifer Shaw, *Dream States: Puvis de Chavannes, Modernism, and the Fantasy of France* (New Haven: Yale University Press, 2002), especially 13–42. The words quoted are Shaw's, 18.

11. See the discussion in chapter 3, 95ff.

12. Here I diverge significantly from Shaw's illuminating reading of Puvis: she argues that in fact Puvis's paintings found their modernity in the same kinds of disruptive strategies as his avant-garde colleagues and finds that the rough surfaces of Puvis's canvases assert their materiality in ways akin to Manet's or Courbet's nudes. I do not believe this to be the case with Puvis; more importantly, as Shaw goes some way to demonstrate through her reading of the contemporary literature on Puvis, this is not how his work was generally understood to operate in the late nineteenth century either.

13. Both Puvis de Chavannes and Cézanne were honored with retrospective exhibitions at the 1904 Salon d'Automne. At that time, conservative critics such as Élie Faure, wanting to ally Cézanne to a nationalist project of rebuilding French culture in the decadence of the fin-de-siècle, were eager to align his work with that of Puvis de Chavannes, despite clear formal dissimilarities: "Puvis and Cézanne are side by side at the Salon d'Automne. And here is an admirable and decisive lesson. I do not know, in the history of art, two artists as different on the surface and coming from such opposite directions who have marched toward the same horizon with so much steadfastness. . . . [T]he idealist [Puvis] has encountered life, the realist has glimpsed the dream: reason coming down from the heights and instinct coming up from the plain have joined in the middle. . . . Both are pure primitives, and archaic primitives" ("Le Salon d'Automne," *Les Arts de la Vie* [November 1904]: 293–94, quoted in translation in Margaret Werth, *The Joy of Life: The Idyllic in French Art, circa 1900* [Berkeley and Los Angeles: University of California Press, 2002], 203).

The literature on the relationship between the art of Cézanne and Poussin stems largely from a symposium held on the occasion of the exhibition curated by Richard Verdi, *Cézanne and Poussin: The Classical Vision of Landscape* (Edinburgh: National Galleries of Scotland, 1990). The symposium included papers by Richard Shiff and Richard Kendall, both of whom presented revisionist accounts of Poussin's impact on Cézanne. Shiff argued that the comparisons between Poussin and Cézanne, commonplace since the turn of the twentieth century, are red herrings: they were based in large part not on any specific formal comparison of the work of the two artists but on the critics' attempts to position Cézanne in relation to emerging modernist painting and in relation to a French (and specifically Mediterranean) tradition. Kendall, on the other hand, argued that while Poussin's influence is normally sought in Cézanne's landscapes, it in fact is more properly sought in the latter's figurative works, including the bathers. See Shiff, "Cézanne and Poussin: How the Modern Claims the Classic," 51–68, and Kendall, "The Figure in the Landscape," 88–108, in *Cézanne and Poussin: A Symposium,* ed. Richard Kendall (Sheffield, U.K.: Sheffield Academic Press, 1993). See also Katia Tsiakma, "Cézanne's and Poussin's Nudes," *Art Journal* 37 (Winter 1977–78): 120–32. On Poussin's importance vis-à-vis Cézanne's interest in Arcadia and a Virgilian notion of idyll, see Nina Athanassoglou-Kallmyer, *Cézanne and Provence: The Painter in His Culture* (Chicago: University of Chicago Press, 2003), 190–207, and Werth, *Joy of Life,* 202–8.

14. This is not to imply that these were the only two modes available for the painting of the nude in the later years of the nineteenth century, but that these were the two most relevant modes is certain. One might speak of an eroticized academicism—exemplified by the work of William Bouguereau and Alexandre Cabanel, for example—but Cézanne hardly seems to have been interested in such a practice. The other important touchstone in Cézanne's exploration of the genre—one that must have seemed especially relevant in the early years of the twentieth century and certainly was crucial to understanding Cézanne's notion of *déformation*—was the eroticized classicism of Ingres, which I discuss in the final chapter of the present volume.

15. The most important of the iconographic studies is Gertrude Berthold, *Cézanne und die alten Meister* (Stuttgart: W. Kohlhammer, 1958). See also Guila Ballas, "Unknown Sources for Cézanne's Women Bathers," in *Norms and Variations in Art: Essays in Honour of Moshe Barasche* (Jerusalem: Magnes Press, 1983). There are some conspicuous exceptions to ahistoricism in the treatment of Cézanne. Nina Athanassoglou-Kallmyer's article "An Artistic and Political Manifesto for Cézanne" (*Art Bulletin* 72 [September 1990]: 483–92) and her recent book *Cézanne and Provence* both argue for a political and contextual reading of Cézanne's practice. Robert Simon's "Cézanne and the Subject of Violence" (*Art in America,* May 1991, 120–35, 185–86) likewise offers a reading of Cézanne's early subject matter as fully in concert with contemporary visual culture. More recently, T. J. Clark's reading of Cézanne and the work of his student Kathryn A. Tuma have attempted to locate Cézanne's work in the context of late-nineteenth-century intellectual thought; see Clark, *Farewell to an Idea* (New Haven: Yale University Press, 1999), and Tuma, "Cézanne and Lucretius at the Red Rock," *Representations* 78 (Spring 2002): 56–85.

16. Of course, I am painting the situation with a broad brush: one might quite rightly note that the characterization of the "cool formalism" of some of his later work, especially his portraits, is itself a critical construct meant to justify a canonical narrative rather than an intrinsic quality of the work.

17. Kurt Badt, *The Art of Cézanne,* trans. Sheila Ann Ogilvie (Berkeley and Los Angeles: University of California Press, 1965), 155.

18. Roger Fry reminds us of the disparity of these two portraits of Cézanne:

> We are so familiar with the picture which those who knew him have given us of Cézanne as an old man, that we think of him inevitably in that light. We picture him in his retirement in Aix, disillusioned, shy, living in obscurity, avoiding all contact with the world—for all his timidity, capable of a sudden sally if attacked in his den—half-conscious of the immensity of his genius and yet ridiculously humble before accepted authority, or exaggeratedly pleased with any recognition—we know all this so well, it composes for us so striking a portrait that it is difficult to picture Cézanne as a young man contemptuous of authority, full of Mediterranean exuberance, confident of success, bursting with ambition and assurance but already devoured by the purist passion for his art. Such was, however, the young Cézanne who came up from Provence to conquer Paris, who was recognized as the *enfant terrible* of the youngest group. . . . He seemed the most extreme, the most impossible of revolutionaries. (*Cézanne: A Study of His Development* [Chicago: University of Chicago Press, 1989], 3–4, originally published in 1927 by the Hogarth Press)

19. Roger Fry's classic monograph, *Cézanne: A Study of His Development,* is but one example of this impulse. It paints a portrait of Cézanne as a young man, profoundly misreading Manet's *Déjeuner sur l'herbe:* rather than following the lead of Manet, whose "imagination was purely visual," Cézanne "believed himself to be a visionary. His imagination, nourished on poetry, aimed at something besides the plastic interpretation of actual appearances. He worked, above all, to find expression for the agitations of his

inner life, and . . . he sought to express himself as much by the choice and implications of his figures as by the plastic exposition of their forms" (9). The works that resulted were failures, according to Fry, for "he did not possess the special gifts for such a gestation of poetical ideas, and for transmuting them into coherent plastic images" (10), but Cézanne took a long time to recognize them as such. Eventually, such "extravagances of invention and expression" (24) give way to "a complete suppression of his subjective impulses," a condition necessary to allow his true genius to emerge. An apprenticeship to Pissarro in Auvers in 1873–74 "cooled [Cézanne's] Provençal impetuosity" (35).

20. Badt's idea of Cézanne's "conversion" is subtended by an argument about the artist's submission to a state of loneliness, which the author understands to be a fundamental condition of modernity; Cézanne reaches this state of acceptance partly through disappointments in his erotic life, his isolation and rejection by his intellectual colleagues (Zola, most importantly), and his reinvolvement with religion (*The Art of Cézanne,* 131–81). While I have characterized Badt's approach as formalist, it would be more correct to say that he privileges the visual (or the formal) in his interpretative strategy, which is inflected by a phenomenological impulse as well.

21. Freud defined sublimation as the redirection, even "purification," of the libidinal drive through its transformation into artistic (or other culturally reified) pursuit. An elusive concept in his writing, it is presented as the original impulse for all creative activity, and an artist like Leonardo—whose ego transmuted a latent homosexual desire into Renaissance masterworks—typified the power of this psychic process. Subject to a childhood influenced by an "overaffectionate" mother and a distant father, Leonardo's personality was, according to Freud, marked by an emotional disinterest: "in an age which saw a struggle between sensuality without restraint and gloomy asceticism," Freud writes, "Leonardo represented the cool repudiation of sexuality—a thing that would scarcely be expected of an artist and a portrayer of feminine beauty." But this sensual renunciation was far from unproductive, for in fact his somatic, sexual drive was converted into something far more valuable: "In reality Leonardo was not devoid of passion. . . . He had merely converted his passion into a thirst for knowledge; he then applied himself to investigation with the persistence, constancy and penetration which is derived from passion, and at the climax of intellectual labor, when knowledge had been won, he allowed the long restrained affect to break loose and flow away freely, as a stream of water drawn from a river is allowed to flow away when its work is done." Freud's language here makes explicit the way in which Leonardo's artistic and scientific investigations were fully sexualized in this process of sublimation: it is a description of the sexual act, otherwise conceived. And after climax, when "the long restrained affect [breaks] loose and [flows] away freely," we are perhaps permitted to wonder if we are witnessing, finally, the satisfaction of this instinctual drive ("Leonardo da Vinci and a Memory of his Childhood," in *The Freud Reader,* ed. Peter Gay [New York: W.W. Norton, 1989], 443–81).

22. For a discussion of the problem posed by Cézanne's early output for writers on his work, see Roger Cranshaw and Adrian Lewis, "Wilful Ineptitude," review of Lawrence Gowing, ed., *Cézanne: The Early Years, 1859–72, Art History* 12 (March 1989): 129–35, and Griselda Pollock, "What Can We Say About Cézanne These Days?" *Oxford Art Journal* 13, no. 1 (1990): 95–101.

23. Meyer Schapiro, *Paul Cézanne,* 3rd ed. (1965; repr., New York: Harry N. Abrams, 1988), 44.

24. Theodore Reff, "Painting and Theory in the Final Decade," in *Cézanne: The Late Work,* 39.

25. Theodore Reff, "Painting and Theory in the Final Decade," in *Cézanne: The Late Work,* 39. See also Theodore Reff, "Cézanne's *Bather with Outstretched Arms,*" *Gazette des Beaux-Arts* 59 (March 1962): 173–90. The latter essay, focused on one of Cézanne's single-figure male nudes, is a critical expression of Reff's views of Cézanne's formal "progress" toward a purification of unavowable desires: he interprets the painting as the result of Cézanne's arduous repression of homoerotic impulses.

26. Fritz Novotny, "The Late Landscape Paintings," in *Cézanne: The Late Work,* 111.

27. As Jacques Lacan noted in his gloss on Freud's concept, the paradox of sublimation is that it implies a satisfaction of the libidinal drive even though the drive is displaced

or redirected via its transformation through art. To other commentators, such as Leo Bersani, Freud's notion of sublimation would seem to suggest that complete, unproblematic, and sustained repression is possible. The problem in both cases, of course, is that Freud's other writings on the drives tell us that they are not so easily dissipated. This ambiguity is inherent in Freud's essay on Leonardo itself, which seems to argue for sublimation as a productive form of repression at the same time as it suggests sublimation is (in Bersani's words) "coextensive with sexuality, as an appropriation and elaboration of sexual impulses rather than as a special form of renunciation of such impulses." Freud hints at, but never admits, the possibility that sublimation is "not a transcendence of desire, but rather a kind of extending of desire" (again I quote Bersani). Thus, in any account that uses sublimation as its organizing term, desire necessarily resurfaces *as a structural condition of the argument,* and must, as a consequence, be accounted for. For Lacan's gloss on Freud's notion of sublimation, see "The Deconstruction of the Drive," in *Four Fundamental Concepts of Psycho-Analysis,* ed. J.-A. Miller, trans. Alan Sheridan (New York: W. W. Norton, 1981). Leo Bersani discusses the lacunae in Freud's discussion of sublimation vis-à-vis Leonardo in *The Freudian Body: Psychoanalysis and Art* (New York: Columbia University Press, 1986), especially 43–47 and 108–10.

For a more detailed discussion of the problem of sublimation in Freud and Lacan in relation to Cézanne scholarship, see the excellent dissertation by Michio Hayashi, "Paul Cézanne: The Resistance of Painting" (Ph.D. diss., Columbia University, 1999). Hayashi, who wrote his dissertation at the same time I wrote mine and completed it in the same year I completed mine, comes to a number of sympathetic conclusions, although the material we cover is often quite different, and our arguments diverge at crucial points.

28. Krumrine, *Paul Cézanne: The Bathers.*

Another account, whose method and conclusions mirror Krumrine's to an uncanny degree, is Guila Ballas's *Cézanne: Baigneuses et Baigneurs* (Paris: Adam Biro, 2002). My comments about Krumrine's analysis would seem applicable, too, to Ballas's.

29. Krumrine, *Paul Cézanne: The Bathers,* 33.

30. In fact, Meyer Schapiro famously challenged Freud's interpretation of Leonardo's *Virgin and Child with St. Anne* in "Leonardo and Freud: An Art Historical Study," *Journal of the History of Ideas* 17 (April 1956): 147–78, reprinted in *Theory and Philosophy of Art: Style, Artist, and Society,* vol. 4 of *Selected Papers* (New York: George Braziller, 1994): 153–92. Schapiro argues there that "Freud's theory provides no bridge from the infantile experience and the mechanisms of psychic development to the style of Leonardo's art" and furthermore contends that if psychoanalysis is to be useful to art historical analysis, it must incorporate a degree of social, cultural, and art historical knowledge. Despite this, Schapiro demonstrates a willingness to accept sublimation as a viable explanatory model and in fact proposes that Leonardo's sublimation occurred most productively in the realm of scientific investigation, rather than art.

31. Theodore Reff, "Cézanne's Constructive Stroke," *Art Quarterly* 25 (Autumn 1962): 214–26.

32. Reff, "Cézanne's Constructive Stroke," 219.

33. Reff, "Cézanne's Constructive Stroke," 224. Reff notes that his interpretation is "analogous to—and inspired by—Meyer Schapiro's interpretation of the *Grandes baigneuses* as an 'overdetermined' composition."

34. Reff, "Cézanne's Constructive Stroke," 221.

35. To briefly summarize the arguments about dating these works: both Lawrence Gowing and Douglas Cooper discussed the emergence of the constructive stroke in Cézanne's work in the 1870s (Gowing, "Notes on the Development of Cézanne," *Burlington Magazine* 98 [June 1956]: 185–92, and Cooper, "Two Cézanne Exhibitions," *Burlington Magazine* 96 [November 1954]: 344–49, and *Burlington Magazine* 96 [December 1954]: 378–83). Gowing dates the constructive stroke's appearance quite precisely to 1878, on the basis of two still life paintings. Cooper, on the other hand, suggests that the constructive stroke appeared over the years 1875–77, in a view of L'Estaque (R256, 1876) and in three bather compositions: *Bathers* (R256, which Cooper dates to 1875 and Rewald dates to 1875–76), *Five Bathers under the Trees* (R257, which Cooper dates to ca. 1876 and Rewald dates to ca. 1875), and *Five Bathers* (R365, which Cooper dates to ca. 1877 and Rewald dates to ca. 1877–78). (Though I, too, will argue that the constructive stroke emerged in paint-

ings of bathers, I do so based on an entirely different set of images. This, too, is a matter of chronology.) Reff's own contribution to the dating of these works is to argue that the three imaginative compositions—*The Battle of Love, The Eternal Feminine,* and *The Temptation of St. Anthony*—should be prioritized, citing the "generally accepted" dating of these works to ca. 1875. This date seems to derive from Lionello Venturi's original dating of the paintings in his catalogue raisonné of 1936. Venturi later revised the dating of these works to around 1880.

The whole notion of the "constructive stroke" as a way of describing Cézanne's facture after this brief moment in the 1870s has been questioned by Kathryn Tuma ("Cézanne and Lucretius at the Red Rock").

36. On the idea of subjectivity and the painted mark, see Richard Shiff, *Cézanne and the End of Impressionism: A Study of the Theory, Technique, and Critical Evaluation of Modern Art* (Chicago: University of Chicago Press, 1984).

37. Garb's argument is elaborated in two slightly different versions: "Visuality and Sexuality in Cézanne's Late Bathers," *Oxford Art Journal* 19, no. 2 (1996): 46–60, and "Cézanne's Late Bathers: Modernism and Sexual Difference," in *Bodies of Modernity: Figure and Flesh in Fin-de-Siècle France* (London: Thames and Hudson, 1998), 196–218. The second version of the essay sets out to answer a major problem in the first essay—namely, that the author speaks of the pictures of bathers as if they had been done from life, as a project of capturing optical sensation—but does so in a way that renders the argument slightly contradictory. As a consequence, I focus my remarks on the first version of the essay, which is coherent, if flawed, with the caveat that Garb has herself acknowledged the criticisms of her argument, even if the second version does not fully resolve them. My critique of Garb, I think, obtains even in light of the essay's revision.

38. Garb, "Visuality and Sexuality," 47.

39. Garb, "Visuality and Sexuality," 47.

40. Maurice Merleau-Ponty, "Cézanne's Doubt," in *Sense and Non-Sense,* trans. Hubert L. Dreyfus and Patricia Allen Dreyfus (Evanston, Ill.: Northwestern University Press, 1964), 9–25, originally published as "Le doute de Cézanne," *Fontaine* 8 (December 1945): 80–100. Galen Johnson provides a useful introduction to the essay in *The Merleau-Ponty Aesthetics Reader*, ed. Galen Johnson and Michael B. Smith (Evanston, Ill.: Northwestern University Press, 1993), 3-13.

41. Merleau-Ponty, "Cézanne's Doubt," 11. For all that Merleau-Ponty's phenomenological account supplies a third path for Cézanne scholarship, his essay on Cézanne ends with a discussion of Freud's essay on Leonardo, and the possibilities of a psychoanalytic explanation of creative expression. "Whatever is arbitrary in Freud's *explanations,*" he concludes, "cannot in this context discredit *psychoanalytic intuition*. . . . How can we deny that psychoanalysis has taught us to notice echoes, allusions, repetitions from one moment of life to another—a concatenation we would not dream of doubting if Freud had stated the theory correctly?" (24).

42. Garb, "Visuality and Sexuality," 48.

43. Garb, "Visuality and Sexuality," 53.

44. Garb, "Cézanne's Late Bathers," 202.

45. Garb, " Cézanne's Late Bathers," 205.

46. Roger Fry, *Cézanne*, 78. "The point of departure is the pyramid given by the inclined tree trunks on either side. The poses of the figures are clearly dictated by this—too clearly, too obtrusively indeed do they adapt themselves to this elementary schema. In spite of the marvels of his handling and the richness and delicacy of the color transitions he has not escaped the effect of dryness and willfulness which so deliberate a formula arouses."

47. Garb, "Visuality and Sexuality," 54 (my emphasis).

48. Garb, " Cézanne's Late Bathers," 218.

49. Maurice Denis, "Cézanne—II," trans. Roger Fry, *Burlington Magazine* 16 (February 1910): 275.

50. R. F. Rivière and J. F. Schnerb, "L'atelier de Cézanne," *La Grande Revue,* 25 December 1907, reprinted in *Conversations avec Cézanne,* ed. P. M. Doran (Paris: Macula, 1978), 87.

51. Forty-odd years after Denis and his contemporaries, and forty-odd years before Garb, Clement Greenberg would enter into this argument about the unintended nature of Cézanne's gaucheries by painting him as an *accidental* revolutionary in his essay "Cézanne and the Unity of Modern Art" (*Partisan Review* 18, no. 3 [1951], reprinted in *Affirmations and Refusals, 1950–1956,* vol. 3 of *Clement Greenberg: The Collected Essays and Criticism,* ed. John O'Brian

[Chicago: University of Chicago Press, 1993], 82–91). There, he argues that it was not simply the inadvertent dissonance of conceptual project and formal method that produced works of such striking modernity. Rather,

> The problematic quality of his art—the source, perhaps, of its unfading modernity—and of which he himself was aware, came from the ultimate necessity of revising his intentions under the pressure of a style that evolved as if in opposition to his conscious aims. He was making the first—and last—pondered effort to save the intrinsic principle of the Western tradition of painting: its concern with an ample and literal rendition of the illusion of the third dimension. . . . Like Manet and with almost as little appetite as he for the role of revolutionary, he changed the course of art out of the very effort to return it by new paths to its old ways. (83–84)

There is a shift here—from Denis et al.'s proposal that Cézanne's insufficiencies were the result of his almost-too-sincere commitment to *sensation* to Greenberg's contention that Cézanne's radical formal discoveries were the unintentional by-product of his sincere attempt to paint tradition. Garb conflates these two positions (inadvertently, perhaps?) in her argument.

52. T. J. Clark, "Freud's Cézanne," *Representations* 52 (Fall 1995): 94–122, revised in *Farewell to an Idea*. I cite the version in *Farewell to an Idea*. See also his essay "Phenomenality and Materiality in Cézanne," in *Material Events: Paul de Man and the Afterlife of Theory,* ed. Tom Cohen (Minneapolis: University of Minnesota Press, 2001), 93–113.

53. Clark, *Farewell to an Idea,* 165.

54. Clark, *Farewell to an Idea,* 149.

55. Clark, *Farewell to an Idea,* 152 and 162.

56. Clark, *Farewell to an Idea,* 149.

57. Clark, *Farewell to an Idea,* 154.

58. For example: "I take the Barnes painting to be a staging of some ultimate sexual material" (147); "The script, as I say, is easy to write" (150); "We should not be surprised if the effort [to have the existence of the body in fantasy be literalized] finally opens onto a scene and dramatis personae which seem almost to illustrate 'On the Sexual Theories of Children' or the 'Analysis of a Phobia in a Five-Year-Old Boy'" (150); "I would say the setting [of the Philadelphia Bathers] confirms the unreality of the figural scene below: that is, its quality of intense generalization, the insistent rhyming and redundancy of its key shapes, the look the figures all have of obeying a strict but obscure choreography" (152).

59. *Acheronta movebo* is a Latin phrase that translates roughly as "the release from the powers of hell." It derives from Virgil's *Aeneid,* and is used by Freud as the epigraph to *The Interpretations of Dreams.* In Clark's words, "The more the material of phantasy bubbles to the surface—and the tortured surface of the actual oil paint is itself a kind of literalization of this *Acheronta movebo*—the more the representation insists on phantasy's inhering in a world of bodies, sensations, sights, shocks, touches, *coups de pied dans le cul,* 'quantitatively determined states'" (151).

60. "This is the truth to which the Philadelphia picture naively returns. The being-in-the-eye of a body—that is, the full and adequate representation of its purely optical existence—will be, if we manage it, the representation of the body as it is, in its plenitude, in all its irrevocable separateness from us" (159). Elsewhere he writes that Cézanne's painting of the bathers was informed by the notion that "our representation of bodies—our own and other people's—just is some such process of interchange and duplication, of unstoppable weird empathy, of our somehow putting an internal sense of what being in the body feels like into our picture of how another body looks" (157).

61. Although referring to Poussin and Rubens, not Titian, Georges Braque's comments remind us that the mode of address of the Old Masters, to which Cézanne would constantly refer in other ways in his work, was inoperative in Cézanne's pictures: "Poussin and Rubens confused composition with staging. It was opera and stage directing. But with Cézanne, composition is really painting," quoted in Terence Maloon's introduction in *Classic Cézanne,* exh. cat. (Sydney, Australia: Art Gallery of New South Wales, 1998), 11.

62. While it has been suggested that the second of the Auvers landscapes exhibited at the 1874 exhibition was in fact a landscape study from the Philadelphia Museum of Art (R198, *Quartier Four, Auvers-sur-Oise,* ca. 1873)—see for example Henri Loyrette's entry on *The House of the Hanged Man* in Cachin and Rishel, *Cézanne,* 139—Rewald's catalogue raisonné suggests, instead, that the painting shown was *The*

House of Père Lacroix (1873), now owned by the National Gallery in Washington. Rewald bases his identification primarily on the fact that *The House of Père Lacroix* is prominently signed in the lower left corner, which is often an indication that Cézanne intended the work for public exhibition. See Rewald, *The Paintings of Paul Cézanne*, 1:151–52.

That said, my comments that follow—regarding the stylistic opposition between Cézanne's two landscape submissions to the exhibition—would seem to apply whether he sent the Philadelphia or the Washington painting.

63. Cézanne's early career was characterized, generally, by a self-conscious attempt to claim an avant-garde identity for himself. See Athanassoglou-Kallmyer, "An Artistic and Political Manifesto for Cézanne," Simon, "Cézanne and the Subject of Violence," and Cranshaw and Lewis, "Wilful Ineptitude."

64. Gasquet, *Cézanne* (Paris: Éditions Bernheim-Jeune, 1921), 31, quoted in translation in Cachin and Rishel, *Cézanne*, 133.

65. Cézanne's dependence on Delacroix's composition in both *A Modern Olympia* and in *The Eternal Feminine* has been discussed by Sara Lichtenstein in her article, "Cézanne and Delacroix," *Art Bulletin* 46 (March 1964): 55–67.

66. My reading this painting as somewhat comical or satirical is starkly at odds with Roger Fry's assessment of Cézanne's artistic temperament. Describing *The Pasha*, Fry writes: "The naïvely erotic inspiration of this picture has suggested to the artist an operatic phantasmagoria so absurd, so unconvincing, that, if the art of Cézanne admitted the possibility of irony, we might imagine it to be a parody of Baroque pretentions. But, not only does the concentrated vehemence, the fanatical determination of his handling contradict such an interpretation at every point, everything brings us the conviction that such ideas were foreign to his nature. . . . He had indeed much of the sly malice of the Southern peasant; but the kind of sophisticated wit which would lead to ironical compositions, the wit of the Parisian, was not his" (*Cézanne: A Study of His Development*, 16).

67. Cited in Theodore Reff, "Courbet and Manet," *Arts Magazine* 54 (March 1980): 98–102.

68. See Mona Hadler, "Manet's *Woman with a Parrot* of 1866," *Metropolitan Museum Journal*, 1973, 115–22.

69. Apparently, at a dinner party at Dr. Paul Gachet's house in Auvers, "Gachet's frank admiration [of Manet's painting *Le Bon Bock*, which was a great success at the Salon of 1873] stung the self-regard of Cézanne, who responded quite vigorously that the invention of an Olympia, even a recast one, was for him a mere bagatelle. He resolved to prove it. And, on a '10' canvas, there appeared almost immediately *A Modern Olympia*, exceptionally dashed-off, dazzlingly fresh despite [being created in] an usually dark period, in short a 'marvelous sketch' on which Gachet subsequently placed an embargo, fearing that Cézanne would wreck it by setting out to 'take it further'" (Paul Gachet *fils*, *Deux amis des impressionistes, le docteur Gachet et Murer* [Paris: Éditions des Musées Nationaux, 1956], 56–57, cited in Cachin and Rishel, *Cézanne*, 132).

70. See Hollis Clayson, *Painted Love: Prostitution in French Art of the Impressionist Era* (New Haven: Yale University Press, 1991), for a reading of Cézanne's *A Modern Olympia* through the lens of this particular cultural history.

71. Clark's notion of the narrative content of the *Large Bathers* is perhaps more complicated than my characterization would suggest. Clark wants to see the Barnes and London bathers as Cézanne's attempt "to escape from narration, and from the dream-space—the invitation to come inside, to circulate easily and identify at will—which narration in pictures was supposed to bring with it." Cézanne did not succeed in setting aside narrative in the development from Barnes to London—in fact, he says that the multiplication of figures and rhyming of bodies and space simply turned the London picture into one "great narrative machine . . . even if disengaged from a readable plot." But for Clark, the change in format from London to Philadelphia made a crucial difference: "It was not until the Philadelphia picture that a narrative of sexual difference (sexual difference actually happening, as if it had never happened before) gave way to a kind of tragic positing of sexuality as fate" (*Farewell to an Idea*, 161–62). But if narrative is dispensed with in Philadelphia, it is only because the drama has reached its resolution: we are seeing the climax of the play, or perhaps its dénouement, frozen in momentariness. It is curious the extent to which Clark's thesis echoes that of William Rubin's discussion of the eventual rejection of narrative in the work of

Picasso under the influence of Cézanne. See William Rubin, "From Narrative to 'Iconic' in Picasso: The Buried Allegory in *Bread and Fruitdish on a Table* and the Role of *Les Demoiselles d'Avignon*," *Art Bulletin* 65 (December 1983): 615–49.

72. The following reading of Manet's *Olympia* is indebted to two different accounts: T. J. Clark, "Olympia's Choice," in *The Painting of Modern Life: Paris in the Art of Manet and His Followers* (Princeton: Princeton University Press, 1984), 79–146, and Charles Bernheimer, "Manet's *Olympia:* The Figuration of Scandal," in *Figures of Ill-Repute: Representing Prostitution in Nineteenth-Century France* (Durham, N.C.: Duke University Press, 1997), 89–128.

73. See the technical analysis of *A Modern Olympia* done in conjunction with the exhibition of the collection of Dr. Paul Gachet that took place in Paris, New York, and Amsterdam in 1999 in Anne Distel and Susan Alyson Stein, *Cézanne to Van Gogh: The Collection of Dr. Gachet* (New York: Metropolitan Museum of Art, 1999), 39–43.

74. The full quotation is as follows: "Investment in the look is not as privileged in women as in men. More than other senses, the eye objectifies and masters. It sets at a distance, and maintains a distance. In our culture the predominance of the look over smell, taste, touch and hearing has brought about an impoverishment of bodily relations. The moment the look dominates, the body loses its materiality." Luce Irigaray, interview in *Les femmes, la pornographie et l'érotisme,* ed. M.-F. Hans and G. Lapouge (Paris: Seuil, 1978), 50, quoted in translation in Griselda Pollock, "Modernity and the Spaces of Femininity," in *Vision and Difference: Femininity, Feminism, and Histories of Art* (New York: Routledge, 1988), 50.

75. Luce Irigaray, "This Sex Which Is Not One," originally published as "Ce sexe qui n'en est pas un," *Cahiers du Grif* 5 (1975) and published in translation in *This Sex Which Is Not One,* trans. Catherine Porter with Carolyn Burke (Ithaca: Cornell University Press, 1985), 23–33. See also her essay, "Psychoanalytic Theory: Another Look," originally published as "Retour sur la théorie psychanalytique," in *Encyclopédie medico-chiurgicale, gynécologie* 3 (1973), and published in translation in *This Sex Which Is Not One,* 34–67.

76. Irigaray, "This Sex Which Is Not One," 25–26.

77. Irigaray, "This Sex Which Is Not One," 29–30. Compare this to Irigaray's articulation of her notion of *écriture féminine,* a radical mode of writing that would function to subvert patriarchal discourse: "This 'style,' or 'writing,' of women tends to put the torch to fetish words, proper terms, well-constructed forms. This 'style' does not privilege sight; instead, it takes each figure back to its source, which is among other things, *tactile*" ("The Power of Discourse and the Subordination of the Feminine," originally published as "Pouvoir du discours/subordination du féminin," in *Dialectiques* 8 [1975], and published in translation in *This Sex Which Is Not One,* 79). While my argument might suggest—through this invocation of the French feminist philosopher—that I am seeing Cézanne as a "feminist" painter, this is not the case, although I am proposing something that might be even harder to swallow: that the history of modern art is punctuated by a series of radical interruptions or eruptions of the language of painting (Cézanne's nudes being one of the most important), and that these moments of discursive illegibility are moments in which female sexuality is freed from its usual censored position in the languages of Western culture.

78. I am certainly not the first scholar to invoke French feminist psychoanalysis in relation to Cézanne's painting, although those who do treat genres other than the bathers. Paul Smith's essay, "Cézanne's Maternal Landscape and Its Gender" (in *Gendering Landscape Art,* ed. Steven Adams and Anna Greutzner Robins [New Brunswick, N.J.: Rutgers University Press, 2001], 116–32), for example, deploys Melanie Klein's models of infantile psychic development to read Cézanne's images of Provence as, quite literally, the painter's "motherland." Tamar Garb's recently published book on nineteenth-century portraiture includes a chapter that analyzes Cézanne's portrait of his wife, Hortense Fiquet, in relation to Irigarayan notions of tactility and sexuality (*The Painted Face: Portraits of Women in France, 1814–1914* [New Haven: Yale Univerity Press, 2007]. This book was published after completion of the present volume.) And, most importantly for the clarification of my argument here is Carol Armstrong's examination of Cézanne's approach to still life that argues for a bodily, and not merely a visual, address in these works, for a material practice that develops out of the manual experience of making. What is most remarkable

about this account is precisely the way that it demotes vision as the privileged plane of Cézanne's investigations—refutes, that is to say, the idea of Cézanne as the "optical" painter (*Cézanne in the Studio: Still Life in Watercolors* [Los Angeles: Getty Publications, 2004]).

79. In the terms of Freudian and Lacanian psychoanalysis, to imagine a moment in which bodies find their logic in an incoherent, empathetic relation to other bodies requires a retreat into a moment prior to Oedipus. For Irigiray, by contrast, the overemphasis on Oedipus within classical psychoanalysis erases the operations of female sexuality, which cannot be represented according to such a scenario. One need not, in other words, imagine Cézanne's bathers as the evidence of his desire to erase femininity or gender from the discussion, simply because the pictures formally propose a dissolute body.

CHAPTER 3

1. For an important articulation of this notion of the "erotics of paint," albeit in an earlier historical period, see Ewa Lajer-Burcharth, "Pompadour's Touch: Difference in Representation," *Representations* 73 (Winter 2001): 54–88.

On Cézanne's sources from rococo images of the *fête galante,* see Mary Tomkins Lewis, *Cézanne's Early Imagery* (Berkeley and Los Angeles: University of California Press, 1989), 83–112.

2. Karl Ernst Osthaus, "Une visite à Paul Cézanne," *Das Feuer* (1920–21), reprinted in *Conversations avec Cézanne,* ed. P. M. Doran (Paris: Macula, 1978), 99 (my emphasis).

3. Julius Meier-Graefe, "Paul Cézanne," in *Entwicklungsgeschichte der modernen Kunst* (Stuttgart: Verlag Julius Hofmann, 1904), 167, translated by Florence Simmonds and George W. Chrystal as *Modern Art, Being a Contribution to a New System of Aesthetics* (London: Heinemann, 1908), 268, quoted in *Cézanne: Finished, Unfinished,* ed. Felix Baumann, Evelyn Benesch, Walter Feilchenfeldt, and Klaus Albrecht Schröder, exh. cat. (Ostfildern-Ruit, Denmark: Hatje Cantz Publishers, 2000), 244. Interestingly, Walter Feilchenfeldt points out in his note that the English-language translation of Meier-Graefe's text omitted the last sentence of this passage, with its simultaneous expression of revulsion and desire.

4. Fry, *Cézanne: A Study of His Development* (Chicago: University of Chicago Press, 1989), 78.

5. Émile Bernard, "Réflexions à propos du Salon d'Automne," *La Rénovation Esthétique,* December 1907, reprinted in Émile Bernard, *Propos sur l'art,* ed. Anne Rivière (Paris: Séguier, 1994), 179.

6. Émile Bernard, *Souvenirs sur Paul Cézanne, et lettres* (Paris: À La Rénovation Esthétique, 1921), 51.

7. Gustave Coquiot, *Paul Cézanne* (Paris: Ollendorff, 1919), 144–45, first published in 1914.

8. Émile Bernard, "Paul Cézanne," *Les Hommes d'Aujourd'hui* 8, no. 387 (1891): n.p., quoted in translation in Françoise Cachin and Joseph Rishel, *Cézanne,* exh. cat., trans. John Goodman (Philadelphia: Philadelphia Museum of Art, 1996), 29.

9. Émile Bernard, "Paul Cézanne," *Le Coeur,* 9 December 1894, reprinted in Bernard, *Propos sur l'art,* 53.

10. Émile Bernard, *Le Petit Dauphinois,* 25 October 1905, quoted by Ambroise Vollard, *Cézanne* (Paris: Galerie A. Vollard, 1914), 168, quoted in translation in George Heard Hamilton, "Cézanne and His Critics," in *Cézanne: The Late Work,* ed. William S. Rubin (New York: Museum of Modern Art, 1977), 148n14.

According to MaryAnne Stevens, the change in Bernard's artistic attitudes generally around 1904 corresponded with his return from Egypt: "Now his devotion to the classical ideal in art, his horror at the aesthetic anarchy which he believed had been wrought by Impressionism, Synthetism and Socialism, left little space for praising Toulouse-Lautrec, Gauguin, Pissarro, Van Gogh, or even the Nabis. Even Cézanne receives only qualified praise" (*Émile Bernard, 1868–1941: A Pioneer of Modern Art/ Ein Wegbereiter der Moderne Kunst* [Mannheim: Städische Kunsthalle; Amsterdam: Van Gogh Museum, 1990], 21–22).

11. Bernard, *Souvenirs,* 28, quoted in translation in Cachin and Rishel, *Cézanne,* 498 (my emphasis).

Bernard reinforces his claim of Cézanne's irrational fear of women by recounting an anecdote supposedly told to him by the artist: Cézanne's gardener brought his two daughters to the Jas de Bouffan to meet his employer; Cézanne, having agreed to the meeting and expecting to see two young children was instead faced with "two magnificent creatures around eighteen or twenty years old." Terrified by the possibility of having to converse with these strange women, Cézanne creates a ridiculous diversion so that he can escape, slipping into his house and locking himself into his studio.

12. Élie Faure, "Paul Cézanne," *Portraits d'Hier,* 1 May 1910, 119.

13. *Joachim Gasquet's Cézanne: A Memoir with Conversations,* trans. Christopher Pemberton (London: Thames and Hudson, 1991), 76. Coquiot had, in fact, claimed that Cézanne had become "as misogynist as he was misanthropic" in his old age (*Paul Cézanne,* 219). Rivière repeats this sentiment when he writes that the reason for the lack of beauty in Cézanne's women lay in his ferocious misogyny, which "explains, in part, why Cézanne availed himself so rarely of the live model in order to paint his nude women" (*Le maître Paul Cézanne* [Paris: Floury, 1923], 143–44).

14. Vollard, *Cézanne,* 96, quoted in translation in Cachin and Rishel, *Cézanne,* 498.

15. Vollard, *Cézanne,* 96, quoted in translation in Cachin and Rishel, *Cézanne,* 498.

16. *Standing Female Nude,* 1898–99, and *Standing Female Nude,* 1898–99, private collection, R897.

In Georges Rivière's 1923 biography, he identified the model for these compositions as a certain Marie-Louise, who was a "rare female model used by Cézanne" according to the artist's son (*Le maître Paul Cézanne,* 222). Venturi later questioned this assertion and proposed that they represented Cézanne's wife (*Cézanne, son art, son oeuvre* [Paris: P. Rosenberg, 1936], cat. no. 710). Götz Adriani maintains that it is highly unlikely that Mme. Cézanne did any posing for her husband after 1892 (*Cézanne Paintings* [New York: Harry N. Abrams, 1993], 225). Rewald, in his catalogue raisonné, agrees (*Paintings of Paul Cézanne*), 1: 527.

Curiously, another witness to Cézanne in this period, Léo Larguier, claims that Cézanne declared his preference for the figure of a mature woman, since "a woman's body is at its plenitude between forty-five and fifty years of age." Good old Cézanne. Léo Larguier, *Le dimanche avec Paul Cézanne: Souvenirs* (Paris: L'Édition, 1925), 112. Larguier was recounting conversations that took place around 1901–2, when he was stationed in Aix during his military service. He met Cézanne through his friend Joachim Gasquet.

17. The words of Camille Pissarro, from a letter to Théodore Duret in 1873, suggest that the issue of the difficulties in working from the live model were not his alone and thus should not so readily be linked to his eccentric personality or working method but treated as a larger problem within contemporary painting. He writes: "What has prevented me for a long time from painting directly from nature is simply the ability [*facilité*] to have models readily available, not only for the actual painting, but in order to make serious studies. However, I will soon try to do it again, [but] it will be difficult, because you shouldn't assume [*douter*] that you can count on always doing these paintings from nature, that is, outdoors; it will be very difficult" (*Correspondance de Camille Pissarro,* ed. Janine Bailly-Herzberg [Paris: Presses universitaires de France, 1980], 1:88; quoted in translation in Joel Isaacson, "Pissarro's Doubt: Plein-air Painting and the Abiding Questions," *Apollo* 136 [November 1992]: 320–24).

18. In addition to the twenty-odd painted portraits of his wife, Hortense Fiquet, there exist about fifteen portraits of female subjects in Cézanne's oeuvre, many of them, such as *Woman with a Coffee Pot* (ca. 1895, Musée d'Orsay, Paris, R781) and *Young Italian Woman* (ca. 1900, private collection, R812), major and highly finished works.

19. Bernard, *Souvenirs,* 49–50. Interestingly, this passage speaks to another issue that cannot be treated here but is the subject of a further study: here we see an early appearance of the anxiety over mechanical reproduction, later expressed by Valéry and Benjamin. In Bernard's explanation, the machine intervenes (negatively) in the artist's vision, such that Cézanne is not afflicted with a biological defect of the eye (as Huysmans would have it) but is subject to a defect of the mechanized eye.

To speak of the mechanized eye, of course, brings up another issue of technology: Bernard never mentions the possibility that Cézanne could have worked from photographs, such as the one we know he used as a model for his MoMA *Bather* or any of the pictures in Armand Silvestre's *Le nu au Louvre* (published 1891), a book Cézanne owned and that quite possibly was a source of images for the artist. See Alicia Faxon, "Cézanne's Sources for *Les Grandes Baigneuses,*" *Art Bulletin* 65 (June 1983): 320–23.

20. A recently published letter from Bernard to his mother, dated 5 February 1904 (Paris, private collection, reprinted in Rodolphe Rapetti, "L'inquiétude cézannienne: Émile Bernard et Cézanne au début du XXè siècle," *Revue de L'Art* 144, no. 2 [2004]: 49–50), illuminates both the ways in which Bernard viewed Cézanne through the lens of provincial stereotypes as well as his notion that Cézanne was ignorant of art's history:

> I found him a bit maniacal, worn out from diabetes, with a lot of provincial ideas and prejudices of all kinds. . . . In short, he struck me as misanthropic and deranged of spirit. . . . I have come to believe that Cézanne speaks of the masters (Michelangelo, Raphael) in the way that many writers speak of Homer, of Dante, of Milton: without having ever read them. If he believes that he saw Raphael in the Louvre, he is wrong, because there are are only two or three paintings by him among those which are in the museum, and even those are ruined by cleaning and retouching. . . . Not ever having been to Italy, despite being only steps away, he only knows Michelangelo, Raphael, or Tintoretto by hearsay or through bad engravings. Down deep, Cézanne is a good man, extremely ignorant about art, a sort of peasant of painting [*paysan de la peinture*] who returns to thick impastos like rich soil, but who cannot grow anything there but poor grass.

On the various stereotypes of the provincial, and particularly the Provençal, in the later nineteenth century as well as an account of how those stereotypes were exploited both by writers on Cézanne as well as by Cézanne himself, see Nina Athanassoglou-Kallmyer, *Cézanne and Provence: The Painter and His Culture* (Chicago: University of Chicago Press, 2003), especially chapter 1.

21. Terence Maloon notes that "When [Cézanne] drew from classical sculpture in the Louvre, it was not the ideal proportions and regular features that he aimed to imitate. Rather, he set out to seize the individualizing characteristics, the quirks of style, the irregularities that contradict the bland correctness and impersonality of the academic ideal. Cézanne's many drawings after other artists' work in the Louvre take this approach so consistently that it must be assumed to have been part of a conscientiously anticlassical stance" ("Classic Cézanne," in *Classic Cézanne,* exh. cat. [Sydney: Art Gallery of New South Wales, 1998], 36).

22. Bernard, *Souvenirs,* 55. It is worth referring back here to the original French. "Il ne savait pas dessiner sans le modèle, obstacle sérieux à toute création valide": here, Bernard seems to refer to an academic practice of drawing in which the artist's memory was cultivated, through close observation and study of the human form, such that the artist would be able to render the human figure without having the model standing in front of him or her. The academician Horace Lecocq de Boisbaudrin was a well-known advocate of this pedagogical method. "L'imagination de Cézanne était pauvre, il n'avait qu'un goût très fin d'arrangement": the French *arrangement* seems to imply the composition of objects, as in still life, versus that of people. In other words, Cézanne was fine as long as he was painting apples or mountains.

23. Guila Ballas, "Unknown Sources for Cézanne's Women Bathers," in *Norms and Variations in Art: Essays in Honor of Moshe Barasche* (Jerusalem: Magnes Press, 1983), 179. All translations are Ballas's.

In an interesting, if bizarre, passage, Joachim Gasquet explains Cézanne's inadequacy by claiming that "Perhaps Cézanne's excitable, disorderly imagination came from his mother, who, I have been told, was of Creole descent" (*Joachim Gasquet's Cézanne,* 42). Gasquet probably derived this information on Mme Cézanne's heritage from Vollard, who mentions that she was "of a family of remote Creole origin" (*Cézanne*, trans. Harold L. Van Doren [New York: Dover Publications, 1984], 16). The idea is not repeated in other writings on the artist. Gasquet's hypothesis is followed by a claim that it was Cézanne's father's "Latin" heritage that counteracted, or kept in check, the other, unruly tendency, and in fact Gasquet's account of Cézanne's work is structured around this racially-based opposition between passion and discipline.

24. Bernard, "Paul Cézanne," *L'Occident,* July 1904, 17–30, reprinted in Bernard, *Propos sur l'art,* 91–92.

25. In this, of course, Bernard was hardly original. Paul Bergon and René Le Bègue, for example, in a book on nude photographs called *Le nu et le drapé en plein air* (1898), relied on the claims to disinterestedness of the aesthetic ideal in painting to elevate the moral qualities of their photographs:

"Beauty imposes itself on every artistic eye, without regard for any notion of morality or of modesty, by the happy accord of lines, of the medium, and of values; and the closer that harmonious ensemble approaches ideal perfection, the more every idea of sensual animality disappears," quoted in James D. Herbert, *Fauve Painting: The Making of Cultural Politics* (New Haven: Yale University Press, 1992), 68; see also Herbert's discussion of the sexual disavowal embodied in the discourse of the ideal, 65ff.

On this point, see the discussion of the ideology of the life class in Tamar Garb, *Sisters of the Brush: Women's Artistic Culture in Late Nineteenth-Century Paris* (New Haven: Yale University Press, 1994), 88–91. Representation of the nude was, in this discourse, a means to achieve "transcendence" over the material aspects of the model.

26. He would not be the last to see this in his master's painting: Joachim Gasquet delicately stated some years later that "the more [Cézanne's] affections were involved, the more inhibited he was and the more his technique failed to measure up to his aspirations"(*Gasquet's Cézanne,* 48).

27. While the majority of Bernard's bathers are conventionally dated 1889–90 and others are thought to have been done sometime around 1904 (coinciding with Bernard's visit to Cézanne in Aix-en-Provence in the early months of that year), neither the chronology of Bernard's oeuvre nor the circumstantial evidence that would allow the reconstruction of such a chronology are secure enough to support the dating provided by Jean-Jacques Luthi in his catalogue raisonné (*Émile Bernard: Catalogue raisonné de l'oeuvre peint* [Paris: Éditions Side, 1982]). The biggest problem arises because Luthi takes at face value the artist's dating of the works in question, which is not the most prudent course. These years coincided with his friendship and then break with Gauguin, and Bernard was determined to rewrite his own history, redating works so that he would always be the antecedent of their shared artistic innovations. Stylistic evidence is not a useful guide, either, because Bernard worked in multiple styles at once. According to MaryAnne Stevens, this situation "complicate[s] an analysis of the artist's own stylistic evolution during this period. Bernard did not habitually sign and date his works on their completion. Rather, given the evidence of a changing style of handwriting, it is possible to assert that in very many cases, paintings were signed and dated after a lapse of several years. Thus a date taken from a canvas cannot necessarily be accepted as clear evidence of that work having been actually executed in that year" (*Émile Bernard, 1868–1941,* 106). Please see note 28 for my objections to certain of Luthi's proposed dates.

28. Bernard had first encountered Cézanne's work in Tanguy's shop in 1886 and might have seen any of the *baigneuses* that are known to have passed through there at some point, including *Three Bathers* (1874–75, Musée d'Orsay, Paris, R258) and *Bather Seen from the Back* (1877–78, Kazumasa Nakagawa, Tokyo, R368). He may also have had access to those paintings of female bathers that had entered the collections of Victor Choquet, Camille Pissarro, and Henri Rouart. These included *Three Bathers* (which Choquet purchased from Tanguy), *Standing Bather, Drying Her Hair* (ca. 1869, private collection, R114), *La Baignade* (1875–77, private collection, R250), and *Five Bathers* (1877–78, Barnes Foundation, Merion, Pa., R364).

In addition, he may also have seen the infamous large reclining nude which Cézanne submitted unsuccessfully to the Salon of 1870 and is now known only through a Stock caricature (before 1870, R140) as well as *Sketch of Bathers* (1888–90, Ny Carlsberg Glyptotek, Copenhagen, R667) exhibited at Les XX in Brussels in the spring of 1890 (Stevens, *Émile Bernard, 1868–1941,* 164). Bernard described the lost Salon submission, commonly called *La femme du vidangeur,* as "a nude woman reclining who, although quite ugly, was a masterly piece. Stretched out her entire length, this truly immense woman stands out in light against the background of a gray wall where a simple image remained. In the foreground blazed a red cloth thrown across a crude chair" ("Julien Tanguy, dit le 'Père Tanguy,'" *Mercure de France,* 16 December 1908, 609, quoted in translation in Rewald, *The Paintings of Paul Cézanne: A Catalogue Raisonné,* 2 vols. [New York: Harry N. Abrams, 1996], 1:120). Bernard dates his discovery of this work to around 1890.

This list, however, is hardly complete, if we trust what we see in Bernard's paintings. Bernard's *Three Bathers,* thought to have been done around 1890 (according to Luthi, *Émile Bernard,* no. 263), is his only picture that might legitimately be called a copy after Cézanne. Bernard reproduces the general pyramidal composition of the latter's series of female bathers of the late 1870s as well as the poses of specific figures. In light of this, it seems likely that by the time he completed certain of his compositions he must have been familiar with not only works like the Barnes *Five Bathers* and others from this 1876–77 series but also Cézanne's *Five Bathers under the Trees* (ca. 1875, private collection, Paris, R257), from which he lifted the raised arm pose of his central figure.

The case of Bernard's *Three Bathers* brings up some complicated issues regarding the dating of these paintings by Luthi in the catalogue raisonné of the artist's work. According to Rewald, who bases his contention on the evidence contained in Vollard's stock books, *Five Bathers under the Trees* was obtained by the art dealer directly from the artist before it was sold to Auguste Pellerin. This means that the earliest that Bernard could have seen the work is 1895, the year that Vollard began dealing Cézanne's paintings, since Bernard had not yet met Cézanne or been to his studio by that time. (The Cézanne is not known to have been exhibited before that date.) As such, we are left with three possible explanations: that a date of 1890 for Bernard's *Three Bathers* is untenable (although one must keep in mind that after 1895 Bernard was spending most of his time in Cairo, where he lived until 1904); that the Cézanne work (or a similar one that included a similarly posed figure) was available for Bernard to see prior to 1895, perhaps at Tanguy's shop; or that the resemblance between the two figures is the result of happenstance rather than premediatated emulation on Bernard's part. This last explanation seems rather less attractive to me, for the specificity of the central figure's pose and the uncharacteristic brushwork (much more Cézanne-like than Bernard-like) makes it unlikely that the similarity to the Cézanne work is merely a coincidence.

29. Stevens, *Émile Bernard, 1868–1941,* 159.

30. These included *Seven Bathers* (ca. 1889, private collection), *Bathers, Four Bathers,* and *Three Bathers.* Bernard continued to paint the motif after 1908, at which point his manner of painting consistently reverted to a Renaissance-inspired academicism; I do not address these later works.

31. My choice of Cézannes is, of course, arbitrary: it would be difficult to claim these specific works as verifiable sources for the Bernard, since one cannot imagine where Bernard might have seen either of them prior to his completion of *Seven Bathers.*

32. The relationship between Cézanne's striding figure—who is almost always shown full length—and Bernard's truncated woman is perhaps more convincing when one notes the clear resemblance between Bernard's figure and Matisse's *Standing Bather* (1909, Museum of Modern Art, New York; fig. 46), which was definitely based on the figure from *Three Bathers,* formerly in Matisse's collection (John Elderfield, *Matisse in the Collection of the Museum of Modern Art* [New York: Museum of Modern Art, 1978], 60).

33. It was in the spring of 1881 that Gauguin came into contact with Cézanne, through their mutual friend Camille Pissarro. Gauguin was interested in Cézanne's color and facture and remarked facetiously to Pissarro: "Has Monsieur Cézanne found the exact *formula* for a work acceptable to everyone? If he discovers the prescription for compressing the intense expression of all his sensations into a single and unique procedure, try to make him talk in his sleep by giving him one of those mysterious homeopathic drugs and come immediately to Paris to share it with us" (quoted in Rewald, *Cézanne: A Biography* [New York: Harry N. Abrams, 1986], 130). The effects of Cézanne's *passage* first came to be felt in Gauguin's work during the latter's stay in Pont-Aven, in his *Still Life with an Iridescent Glass,* which is dated 1884 (Françoise Cachin, *Gauguin,* trans. Bambi Ballard [Paris: Flammarion, 1988], 28.) Cézanne, for his part, was highly suspicious of Gauguin's interest in his art and accused Gauguin of having "nicked his little number" and "hawked it round the Tropics" (Cachin, *Gauguin,* 28).

34. Bernard's *Seven Bathers* measures 61 x 63 cm, while Cézanne's *Three Bathers* measures 60 x 73 cm and *Five Bathers under the Trees* measures 50 x 61 cm.

35. Émile Bernard, "Paul Cézanne," *Le Coeur,* 9 December 1894): 4–5, reprinted in Bernard, *Propos sur l'art,* 1:53; Maurice Denis, "Paul Cézanne—I," trans. Roger Fry, *Burlington Magazine* 16 (January 1910): 207–19, and "Paul Cézanne—II," trans. Roger Fry, *Burlington Magazine* 16 (February 1910): 275–80; Roger Fry, *Cézanne: A Study of His Development* (Chicago: University of Chicago Press, 1989), 57, originally published in 1927 by the Hogarth Press. Vollard mentions, in a rather cryptic passage, a fact that may well

contradict the veracity of the tale that Cézanne's *baigneurs* were based on bathing soldiers: "Timid and helpless in the ways for the world, Cézanne rather distrusted soldiers on leave. But these same soldiers, kept well in hand, and ready without cavil to march against enemies from without as well as from within, seemed to him a blessing from on high" (*Cézanne,* 93).

36. Mentions of Cézanne's unidentified study of male bathers exhibited at the 1877 impressionist exhibition are listed in *The New Painting: Impressionism; Documentation,* ed. Ruth Berson, 2 vols. (San Francisco: Fine Arts Museums of San Francisco), 2:71. See 1:182 for the remark by Rivière.

37. Gustave Geffroy, "Paul Cézanne," *Le Journal,* 25 March 1894, reprinted in *La vie artistique,* 3rd ser. (Paris: Dentu, 1894), cited from Gustave Geffroy, *Paul Cézanne et autres textes,* ed. Christian Limousin (Paris: Séguier, 1995), 52.

38. See chapter 2, 35.

39. Renoir actually painted his *Young Boy with Cat* in Bazille's studio, possibly using the same model that Bazille used for *Nude Reclining on the Grass;* on this see Gary Tinterow and Henri Loyrette, *Origins of Impressionism* (New York: Metropolitan Museum of Art, 1994), cat. no. 75. It has also been suggested that the same model was used by Bazille for one of his figures in *Summer Scene* (Gabriel Sarrante, *Bazille* [Paris: Galerie Wildenstein, 1950]). I would like to thank John Goodman, whose ideas about this constellation of work has influenced my own.

40. Whitney Davis, "Erotic Revision in Thomas Eakins's Narratives of Male Nudity," *Art History* 17 (September 1994): 317. The literature on the male nude, primarily focusing on the nineteenth century, includes: Margaret Walters, *The Nude Male: A New Perspective* (New York: Paddington Press, 1978); Alex Potts, *Flesh and the Ideal: Winckelmann and the Origins of Art History* (New Haven: Yale University Press, 1994); Abigail Solomon-Godeau, *Male Trouble: A Crisis in Representation* (London: Thames and Hudson, 1997); and Anthea Callen, "Doubles and Desires: Anatomies of Masculinity in the Later Nineteenth Century," *Art History* 26 (November 2003): 669–99.

41. On Caillebotte's often transgressive treatment of the male nude, see Tamar Garb, "Gustave Caillebotte's Male Figures: Masculinity, Muscularity and Modernity," in *Bodies of Modernity: Figure and Flesh in Fin-de-Siècle France* (London: Thames and Hudson, 1998), 24–53. On Courbet's *Wrestlers,* see Klaus Herding, "Les Lutteurs Détestables," in *Courbet: To Venture Independence,* trans. John W. Gabriel (New Haven: Yale University Press, 1991), 11–43.

Georges Seurat's *Bathers at Asnières* provides an interesting, though slightly later, counterpoint to Bazille's image. The fact that Seurat's painting could be taken for what it was—simply, an image of (primarily) working-class men enjoying a few moments of sporting leisure by the banks of the Seine—must have had to do, in part, with Seurat's complicated choice and treatment of art historical references, which were as much anticlassical as classical, and also with the distancing and disinterested effect of his mechanized brushstroke.

42. See James Saslow, "The Tenderest Lover: Saint Sebastian in Renaissance Painting; A Proposed Iconology for North Italian Art 1450–1550," *Gai Saber: Journal of the Gay Academic Union* 1 (Spring 1977): 58–66. For a discussion of nineteenth-century revivals of Sebastian imagery, see Richard A. Kaye, "Losing His Religion: Saint Sebastian as Contemporary Gay Martyr," in *Outlooks: Lesbian and Gay Sexualities in Visual Cultures,* ed. Peter Horne and Reina Lewis (New York: Routledge, 1996), 86–105.

43. For an overview of this idea, see Tamar Garb, "Painterly Plenitude: Pierre-Auguste Renoir's Fantasy of the Feminine," in *Bodies of Modernity,* 145–77.

44. Chaplin was often cited as a foil to the group of painters with which Bazille was associated, and the fashionable portraitist appeared opposite Courbet, Monet, and other avant-garde painters in Bertall's caricatures of the 1860s. See Dianne W. Pitman, *Bazille: Purity, Pose, and Painting in the 1860s* (University Park: Pennsylvania State University Press, 1998), 41–42.

45. Bertall's use of the word *"ton"* of course has multiple meanings: in addition to the artistic connotation (gradations of color and value), it may also refer to the physical appearance of the men (as in well-toned muscles, which Bertall suggests Bazille's figures lack) as well as to their comportment (as in one's behavior in accord with the rules of high society) (Pitman, *Bazille,* 43).

46. One might say, in fact, that Bertall's intervention was the necessary prerequisite for understanding the activity

of Bazille's men as homosocial, for the term implies a female entity through which the relations between men are negotiated. In other words, without Chaplin's lady's maid, the Bazille painting speaks to something akin to the homoerotic; with the addition of this female presence, it can be understood as a comforting depiction of male homosociality.

47. Quoted in Tinterow and Loyrette, *Origins of Impressionism*, 324.

48. Quoted in Valérie Bajou-Charpentreau, *Frédéric Bazille, 1841–1870* (Aix-en-Provence: Edisud, 1993), 181.

49. Tamar Garb, in a discussion of the nude figures of Gustave Caillebotte, states the problem succinctly: "The male nude had traditionally been used as a vehicle to signify abstract truths and lofty aspirations, not the mundane day-to-day functions of contemporary men. Naturalism posed a threat to a heroic image of masculinity, depriving it of its conventional props and epic significance. In this context, it was the body itself which alone had to become the locus of men's manliness, the site for an elaboration of an invigorated modern masculinity" ("Gustave Caillebotte's Male Figures," 28).

50. Bernard Dorival, "La *Scène d'été* de Bazille et Cézanne," *Bulletin des Musées de France* 4 (May 1949): 94. Nancy Locke notes that Cézanne was living in Paris at the time of the Salon of 1870, and that Bazille's painting was exhibited at the same time as the La Caze donation—an object of much study by Cézanne—at the Louvre. See Nancy Locke, "Cézanne's Bathers, Watteau, and the Idea of Fantasy," *Bulletin of the Detroit Institute of Arts* 77, nos. 1–2 (2003): 29.

51. Mary Louise Krumrine's *Paul Cézanne: The Bathers* (Basel: Kunstmuseum, 1989) is the most sustained investigation of art-historical sources for these images. Her work builds on Gertrude Berthold's broad-based study, *Cézanne und die alten Meister* (Stuttgart: W. Kohlhammer, 1958). Theodore Reff's "Cézanne's *Bather with Outstretched Arms*" (*Gazette des Beaux-Arts* 59 [March 1962]: 173–90) posits sources for Cézanne's single-figure compositions.

52. Adrien Chappuis, among others, finds a source for the central figure seen from behind in this composition in an antique marble of Cleomenes's *Roman Orator,* in the Louvre, as well as in Signorelli's drawing (*The Drawings of Paul Cézanne: A Catalogue Raisonné* [Greenwich, Conn.: New York Graphic Society, 1973], cat. nos. 428 and 949).

53. The shorts were apparently "de rigueur for male models in mixed or female life classes" and thus may be less a "realist" marker (i.e., the sign of contemporaneity and pleinairism) than an indication of the source of these images in the studio (Kathleen Adler, "Cézanne's Bodies," *Art in America,* April 1990, 277).

54. Gustave Geffroy, "Paul Cézanne," *Le Journal,* 16 November 1895, reprinted in Geffroy, *La vie artistique,* 6th series (Paris: H. Floury, 1900), cited from Gustave Geffroy, *Paul Cézanne et autres textes*, 58–60. The original French reads as follows: "Le meme souci de beauté puissante, le même désir de l'équilibre des grandes oeuvres, on les retrouvera dans ces indications, ces ébauches de figures nues en plein air: des baigneurs, des baigneuses au bord de l'eau, silhouettes grandies, ayant la noblesse et la grace rudes de la force, dréssées en statues sur des paysages admirables, aux ciels bleus et chaleureux, aux verdures violemment jaillies, vivaces et délicates, libres et épanouies comme des produits de nature, et en même temps, par le sortilège de l'art, voulues et stylées comme les arrangements d'un parc idéal."

55. This tendency to treat Cézanne's male bathers as either childhood memories or studies of live models does not apply to his images of single male figures, such as *Bather with Outstretched Arms* (1877–78, private collection, R370) or *Large Bather* (ca. 1885, Museum of Modern Art, R555). These latter paintings are much more likely to be seen as "projections of Cézanne himself, images of his own solitary condition," to paraphrase Theodore Reff's formulation. See Reff, "Cézanne's *Bather with Outstretched Arms,*" 174.

56. In a letter to his son dated 12 August 1906, Cézanne writes: "Two days ago the sieur Rolland came to see me, he made me talk about painting. He offered to pose for me as a bather on the shores of the Arc.—That would please me, but I am afraid that the gentleman simply wants to lay hands on my sketch; in spite of that I almost feel inclined to try something with him" (*Paul Cézanne: Letters,* ed. John Rewald, trans. Marguerite Kay, 4th ed. [New York: Da Capo Press, 1995], 322).

Joseph Rishel, writing in the catalogue for the 1995 retrospective of Cézanne's work, claims that "[Cézanne's] letters also record his pleasure, later in life, in watching soldiers swimming in the same Arc River, just south of Aix" (*Cézanne,* 350). As far as I can tell, no such letter or reference appears in any of the artist's published correspondence.

Lionello Venturi, in his catalogue raisonné of the artist's work, reproduces a drawing which he contends was a life study of soldiers bathing by the river Arc (cat. no. 1265); Adrien Chappuis, finding no basis for such a claim, disputes the identification of this drawing as a life study (*Drawings of Paul Cézanne*, cat. no. 352).

57. Gustave Geffroy, writing in 1894, succinctly described just how limited this group of Cézanne devotees was: "What were his paintings like? Where could you see them? The response was that there was a portrait at Émile Zola's, two trees at Théodore Duret's, four apples at Paul Alexis's, or even that the previous week a canvas was seen at Père Tanguy's . . . but that one needed to rush to see it, since, for a Cézanne painting, there were always amateurs quick to jump on such infrequent prey. We spoke, too, of collections we had heard about, of a number of different canvases: to find them, it was necessary to search out M. Choquet in Paris, or M. Murer in Rouen, or Doctor Gachet in Auvers, near Pontoise" ("Paul Cézanne," *Le Journal*, 25 March 1897, reprinted in *La vie artistique*, 3rd series [Paris: Dentu, 1894], 249–60, cited from Gustave Geffroy, *Paul Cézanne et autres textes*, 46.

58. Theodore Reff ("Painting and Theory in the Final Decade," in *Cézanne: The Late Work*, 41) locates the origin of this reading in the words Joachim Gasquet attributes to Cézanne: "I have tried, when the soldiers are bathing, going along the Arc and observing the contrasts, the colors of the flesh against the greens" (*Joachim Gasquet's Cézanne*, 78).

Gasquet's book, however, while undeniably influential on subsequent study of Cézanne, was only published in 1921. Already in 1914, Gustave Coquiot declared that "for male models, the soldiers stationed at the garrison at Aix who often bathed in the Arc as soon as the weather was warm enough were sufficient 'indications'" (*Paul Cézanne*, 219). And as early as 1910, Élie Faure, hardly an important source for documentary evidence on the artist, could refer to Cézanne's difficulty finding models to pose for him: "He could only find male models with great difficulty. In the summer, he went to watch the soldiers bathing in the Arc" ("Paul Cézanne," *Portraits d'Hier*, 119).

59. *Paul Cézanne: Correspondance*, ed. John Rewald (Paris: Grasset, 1937), 5. The letter was exhibited shortly afterward, at the Orangerie's Cézanne retrospective in 1939.

60. See Henri Mitterand, "*L'Oeuvre:* Etude, notes et variantes," in Émile Zola, *Les Rougon-Macquart: Histoire naturelle et sociale d'une famille sous le Second Empire*, ed. Armand Lanoux (Paris: Gallimard, Bibliothèque de la Pléiade, 1966), 4:1337–486.

61. Emile Zola, *The Masterpiece*, trans. Thomas Walton, rev. Roger Pearson (Oxford: Oxford University Press, 1993), 35, translation originally published in London by Elek Press in 1950.

62. As Linda Nochlin points out, a similar story is to be found in Antonin Proust's recollections of conversations he had with Manet; such repetitions within the context of the impressionist circle suggest that these recollections should be understood as something akin to "screen memories," in the psychoanalytic sense. Proust claims that the origins of Manet's *Déjeuner sur l'herbe* derive from an actual experience he and Manet had shared in the country. "Right before he painted the *Dejéuner sur l'herbe*," Proust reminisces in 1890, "we spent a Sunday at Argenteuil, stretched out on the river bank, watching the white yawls making a wake in the Seine, striking a light note on the dark blue of the water. Some women were bathing. Manet fixed his eyes on the flesh of those who came out of the water. 'It seems' he said to me, 'that I have to make a nude. Okay, I'll make them one. When we were in the atelier I copied Giorgione's women, the women with musicians. It's dark, that painting. . . . I want to redo it and make it in the transparency of the atmosphere, with people like those whom we see over there'" (*Édouard Manet: Souvenirs* [Paris: H. Laurens, 1913], 171–72, originally published in 1897). Nochlin made the point in "Manet's *Le Bain*: The *Déjeuner* and the Death of the Heroic Landscape," in *Bathers, Body, Beauty: The Visceral Eye* (Cambridge, Mass.: Harvard University Press, 2006), 55–94. I thank her for the reference.

63. Faure, "Paul Cézanne," 101–2. This English translation is a modification of that provided in Élie Faure, *Cézanne*, trans. Walter Pach (New York: Association of American Painters and Sculptors, 1913), 14–15.

64. Alfred Neumeyer, *Paul Cézanne. Die Badenden* (Stuttgart: Philip Reclam, 1959); Kurt Badt, *The Art of*

Cézanne, trans. Sheila Ann Ogilvie (Berkeley and Los Angeles: University of California Press, 1965); Dorival, "La *Scène d'été* de Bazille et Cézanne"; Meyer Schapiro, *Paul Cézanne* (New York: Harry N. Abrams, 1952).

65. Krumrine, *The Bathers,* passim. It is interesting that while Krumrine is one of the few commentators on the *Bathers* who has been interested in finding the continuities between the male and female compositions, she still insists, in the end, on a distinction between the male and female versions of this particular pose, calling it the pose of the temptress when exhibited by a female figure and the pose of the tempted when exhibited by a male.

66. J.-K. Huysmans, *Certains* (Paris: Tresse and Stock, 1889), quoted in translation Cachin and Rishel, *Cézanne,* 27. The original French reads as follows: "des baigneuses nues, cernées par des lignes insanes mais emballées, pour la gloire des yeux, avec la fougue d'un Delacroix, sans raffinement de vision et sans doigts fins, fouettées par une fièvre de couleurs gâchées, hurlant, en relief, sur la toile appesantie qui courbe!"

67. Robert Ratcliffe, "Cézanne's Working Methods and Their Theoretical Background" (Ph.D. diss., University of London, 1960), cited in Rewald, *The Paintings of Paul Cézanne,* cat. no. 261. According to Rewald, "Ratcliffe is certainly right in suggesting that J.-K. Huysmans referred to this painting when he devoted a short chapter to Cézanne in his book *Certains* (1889). Even though Huysmans speaks of *Baigneuses* rather than *Baigneurs,* his description fits this picture (and he does mention the 1877 exhibition, though not in connection with it)."

68. This same elision of male and female is present in Camille Mauclair's vituperative commentary on Cézanne's contributions to the Salon d'Automne: "Signs for fairground stalls, seen in the sun, can be diverting, but placed within frames they're unspeakable—and here I'm thinking of several small paintings of nudes that seem to be made out of hatred for the flesh, grace, light, and love by some baroque image maker" ("La peinture et la sculpture au Salon d'Automne," *L'Art Décoratif* 75 [December 1904], quoted in translation in Cachin and Rishel, *Cézanne,* 40). The only *baigneuses* picture on view at this exhibition was *Three Bathers,* which Matisse had lent specially for the occasion; there were, however, two additional male bathers on display.

69. Reff, "Painting and Theory," 38.

70. Dorival, "La *Scène d'été* de Bazille et Cézanne," 80–81.

71. Richard Kendall, "A Test-Case of Modern Art: Cézanne's *Bathers,*" *Apollo* 130 (November 1989): 337–38.

72. Schapiro, *Paul Cézanne,* 116.

73. In other words, they cannot be the object of Cézanne's (or our) gaze because they are, in effect, the subjects of the gaze themselves: a situation made literal in two small paintings, both entitled *La Baignade* (both 1875–77, both in private collections, R250 and 251), in which three men on a river bank, one hiding behind a tree, gaze surreptitiously on female bathers in the river beyond.

74. Gasquet, *Gasquet's Cézanne,* 78.

CHAPTER 4

The epigraph to this chapter is drawn from Henri Matisse, "Notes of a Painter," in *Matisse on Art,* ed. Jack D. Flam (New York: Phaidon, 1973), 37–38, originally published as "Notes d'un peintre," *La Grande Revue,* 25 December 1908, 731–45. It is necessary from the outset to thank Ellen McBreen, whose work on Matisse (in "The Pinup and the Primitive: Matisse's Sculpture from 1900–1909" [Ph.D. diss., New York University, Institute of Fine Arts, 2007]) has guided my own explorations of the subject. Our very early conversations about the strangeness of this particular passage in Matisse's writings, and on the general misreading of Cézanne's influence on Matisse, have very much shaped my thoughts, and her continued advice has been most valuable to me.

1. For a summary of Matisse's first contacts with the work of Cézanne, see Isabel Monod-Fontaine, "Cézanne chez Matisse," in *Cézanne aujourd'hui: Actes du colloque organisé par le musée d'Orsay 29 et 30 novembre 1995,* ed. Françoise Cachin, Henri Loyrette, and Stéphane Guégan (Paris: Réunion des Musées Nationaux, 1997), 165–73.

We know that Matisse acquired *Three Bathers* from Vollard on 7 December 1899 for twelve hundred francs, but the date of Matisse's first exposure to Cézanne's work is uncertain. Matisse himself recalled that he first saw a Cézanne when the Caillebotte bequest was shown publicly in Paris in March

1897, and that he managed to study paintings at both Vollard's gallery and Durand-Ruel's in the 1890s; he may or may not have seen the 1895 Vollard show as well as the one there in 1898. Prior to the retrospectives of 1904 and 1907, Cézanne had begun showing works at the Salon des Indépendants as well. Matisse had met Pissarro in 1897 and could well have had a chance to study the canvases that Pissarro possessed (around twenty in all). See also Roger Benjamin, *Matisse's "Notes of a Painter": Criticism, Theory, and Context, 1891–1908* (Ann Arbor, Mich.: UMI Research Press, 1987), 66.

2. Émile Bernard, *Souvenirs sur Paul Cézanne* (Paris: Société des Trente, 1912), 28.

3. Harold Bloom, *The Anxiety of Influence: A Theory of Poetry,* 2nd ed. (New York: Oxford University Press, 1997).

4. Henri Matisse from a 1925 interview with Jacques Guenne, in *Écrits et propos sur l'art,* ed. Dominique Fourcade (Paris: Hermann, 1972), 87.

5. Charles Morice, "Le XIX Salon des Indépendants," *Mercure de France,* June 1903, 404, quoted in translation in Benjamin, *Matisse's "Notes of a Painter,"* 114.

6. Camille Mauclair, "La crise de la laideur en peinture," in *Les trois crises de l'art actuel* (Paris: Fasquelle, 1906), 296–97, quoted in translation in Roger Benjamin, "Expression, Disfiguration: Matisse, the Female Nude, and the Academic Eye," in Terry Smith, ed., *In Visible Touch: Modernism and Masculinity* (Chicago: University of Chicago Press, 1997), 92.

7. Louis Vauxcelles, "Le Salon des Indépendants," *Gil Blas,* 20 March 1907, quoted in translation in Benjamin, *Matisse's "Notes of a Painter,"* 180.

8. Charles Morice, "Art moderne. Le XXIIe Salon des Indépendants," *Mercure de France,* 15 April 1907, 735, quoted in translation in Benjamin, "Expression, Disfiguration," 75.

9. I depend tremendously, in this chapter, on the work of Roger Benjamin, especially his essay "Expression, Disfiguration: Matisse, the Female Nude, and the Academic Eye," which, along with his book *Matisse's "Notes of a Painter,"* does the hugely valuable service of gathering an important range of contemporary criticism on Matisse and especially his treatment of the nude. However, I do disagree, often, with his reading of those sources and especially of the motivations behind certain of Matisse's utterances.

See also James D. Herbert, *Fauve Painting: The Making of Cultural Politics* (New Haven: Yale University Press, 1992), especially chapter 2 ("Mirroring the Nude"), for another discussion of Fauve painting of the nude in relation to academic conventions of the genre.

Both Herbert and Benjamin make a lot of the attempt by the painters in question (Fauves generally, but especially Matisse) to use academic discourse to *dissimulate* sexual interest in their motifs. To my mind, whatever Matisse's writings claim, his paintings do nothing to dissimulate their erotic motivations; rather, his writings are at purposeful odds with the painted work.

10. Maurice Denis, "Le Salon d'Automne de 1905," in *Du symbolisme au classicisme: Théories,* ed. Olivier Revault D'Allonenes (Paris: Hermann, 1964), 110.

11. Maurice Denis, "Définition du néo-traditionnisme," in *Le ciel et l'arcadie,* ed. Jean-Paul Bouillon (Paris: Hermann, 1993), 5.

12. See, for example, his article "De la gaucherie des Primitifs," in *Les Arts de la Vie* (July 1904), reprinted in *Théories, 1890–1910: Du symbolisme et de Gauguin vers un nouvel ordre classique* (Paris: Bibliothèque de *L'Occident,* 1912), 167–73. "The ideas of *gaucherie* and that of the Primitive are so inseparable that when a modern artist draws with a true naïveté, when he paints as he feels, and throws out accepted formulae—which themselves do not imply that he will create Beauty—one accuses him of both anarchism and *gaucherie*"; "The *gaucherie* of the Primitives consists thus of painting objects according to the normal knowledge that they have of those objects, instead of painting them, as modern artists do, according to preconceived ideas of the picturesque or the aesthetic."

13. Maurice Denis, "Cézanne," *L'Occident,* September 1907, reprinted in *Théories,* 237–53.

14. See, for example, Roger Benjamin, *Matisse's "Notes of a Painter,"* and Jean-Paul Bouillon, "Denis/Matisse/Kandinsky,"in *Wallraf-Richartz Jahrbuch* 57 (Cologne: DuMont, 1996), 263–75.

15. See Jean-Roch Bouiller, "Probité de l'art, rappel à l'ordre et retour à Ingres au début du XXe siècle," in *Picasso, Ingres,* exh. cat. (Paris: Réunion des Musées Nationaux, 2004), 50–51.

16. On Cézanne's relationship to Ingres, see Nina Athanassoglou-Kallmyer, "An Artistic and Political Manifesto for Cézanne," in *Art Bulletin* 72 (September 1990): 482–91, and Lawrence Gowing, *Cézanne: The Early Years, 1859–1872,* exh. cat. (New York: Harry N. Abrams, 1988), 70.

17. Lawrence Gowing describes the panels as such: "These have usually been regarded as the earliest works by Cézanne that we know, on the assumption that their plain clear color and innocent drawing were merely ignorant. It now seems, on the contrary, that they represent a serious and creditable, indeed rather able, amateur's attempt to capture the character of Renaissance painting" ("The Early Work of Paul Cézanne," in *Cézanne: The Early Years,* 6). Gowing goes on to link the works to Tintoretto, Granet, Boticelli, and other venerable masters. How mercurial critical opinion could be, it seems: to go from "ignorant" to "serious and creditable, indeed rather able," in the description of these panels suggests the ways in which art history has failed to take sufficient account of the role of humor and parody in Cézanne's work. From Gowing's perspective, the significance of these paintings lay only in their art historical import and technical prowess; however, Cézanne, I suspect, only made these paintings to launch a good-natured and broad-humored rebellion against authority (parental—his father, who did not know what to make of the pictures that now adorned his house—and artistic—Ingres, who was the butt of Cézanne's visual joke).

18. Émile Bernard, "Paul Cézanne," *Propos sur l'art,* ed. Anne Rivière (Paris: Séguier, 1994), 93.

19. The exception to this devalorization of Ingres by vanguard painters of the period is, of course, Degas (and to a lesser extent, Cassatt), whose debts to the classicist are equivocal but apparent. Degas was, in fact, a student of Ingres's pupil Louis Lamothe in the 1850s, and his collection was richer in works by Ingres than any other artist. It is perhaps, then, not surprising that Denis invoked the name of Degas in order to link Cézanne to a classical strain of French art. On Degas's debts to Ingres, see Theodore Reff, "'Three Great Draftsmen': Ingres, Delacroix, and Daumier," in Ann Dumas, Colta Ives, Susan Alyson Stein, and Gary Tinterow, *The Private Collection of Edgar Degas,* exh. cat. (New York: Metropolitan Museum of Art, 1997), 137–76, and Jean-Paul Bouillon, "Degas, Bracquemont, Cassatt: Actualité de l'Ingrisme autour de 1880," *Gazette des Beaux-Arts* 111 (January–February 1988): 125–27.

For an extremely valuable accounting of the Ingres retrospective at the 1905 Salon d'Automne, see Roger Benjamin, "Ingres chez les fauves," *Art History* 23 (December 2000): 743–71.

20. Charles Morice, "Le Salon d'Automne," *Mercure de France,* 1 December 1905, 392, quoted in *Picasso, Ingres,* 163.

21. For a summary of this criticism, see Benjamin, "Ingres chez les fauves," and Alastair Wright, *Matisse and the Subject of Modernism* (Princeton: Princeton University Press, 2004), 93–129.

22. Maurice Denis, "Les élèves d'Ingres," *L'Occident,* July, August, and September 1902, reprinted in *Théories,* 86.

See also Maurice Denis, "Le Salon de la Société Nationale des Beaux-Arts," *La dépêche de Toulouse,* 22 and 28 April and 6 May 1901, reprinted in *Théories,* 55–73. If Denis was becoming the spokesman for a *retour à l'ordre* classicism, he was doing it by becoming a spokesman for Ingres—quite literally, in the case of the article cited here, in which he takes a stroll with the ghost of the late great artist through the Salon de la Société Nationale des Beaux-Arts of 1901 and has him comment on current trends in art. When Charles Morice published his "Inquiry into Current Trends in the Plastic Arts" in the *Mercure de France* in September 1905, before the Salon d'Automne was in full swing, Denis was one of only a handful of respondents to mention Ingres at all.

23. Denis, "Salon d'Automne de 1905," 106.

24. Denis, "Salon d'Automne de 1905," 106.

25. For a complete listing of the works on exhibition, see *Société du Salon d'Automne: Catalogue de la 3è exposition, 1905* (Paris: Société du Salon d'Automne, 1905), 185–89. Roger Benjamin estimates the number of studies for *The Turkish Bath* as follows: "The catalogue includes *Le Bain turc,* a *Fragment du Bain turc* (surely the *Femme aux troix bras*) and nine separate listings of *Etudes pour le Bain turc.* If each of these included at least two works, there must have been at least eighteen studies for the painting on display" ("Ingres chez les fauves," 768n24).

26. Gustave Kahn, "Ingres et Manet," *La Nouvelle Revue* 33 (1905): 556, quoted in translation in Benjamin, "Ingres

chez les fauves," 753. On the identification of Ingres's arabesque and anatomical distortions with erotic pleasure, see Carol Ockman, "Half Octopus, Half Tropical Flower: Modernist Criticism," in *Ingres's Eroticized Bodies: Retracing the Serpentine Line* (New Haven: Yale University Press, 1995), 111–26.

27. Henry Lapauze, "Le '*Bain turc*' d'Ingres," *La Revue d'Art Ancien et Moderne* 18 (1905): 386, quoted in translation in Benjamin, "Ingres chez les fauves," 754.

28. Louis Vauxcelles, "Le Salon d'Automne, le vernissage," *Gil Blas,* 15 October 1905, quoted in translation in Benjamin, *Matisse's "Notes of a Painter,"* 105.

29. Vauxcelles, "Le Salon d'Automne" quoted in translation in Benjamin, "Ingres chez les fauves," 753.

30. Denis was certainly not alone in his desire to create Cézanne as an inheritor of France's classicist past; even Charles Camoin—one of the Fauves himself—contributed to the idea of Cézanne's Poussinesque intentions. See John Elderfield, *The "Wild Beasts": Fauvism and Its Affinities* (New York: Museum of Modern Art, 1976), 118.

31. Bernard, *Souvenirs,* 28. This text, which is the origin of the by now canonical idea that Cézanne did not paint from the live model because of his sexual anxiety, was published in *Mercure de France* on 15 and 16 October 1907. Matisse surely knew these articles, since he derives much of the theoretical material of his 1908 text, "Notes of a Painter," from Bernard's report of Cézanne's approach to painting.

32. Charles Morice, "Art Moderne: Exposition Henri Matisse," *Mercure de France,* August 1904, 553, and Charles Morice, "Le XXII Salon des Indépendants," *Mercure de France,* 15 April 1906, 536, quoted in translation in Benjamin, "Expression, Disfiguration," 83.

33. Maurice Denis, "Sur les Indépendants," *La Grande Revue,* 10 April 1908, quoted in Benjamin, *Matisse's "Notes of a Painter,"* 97. It is remarkable that, as far as I can tell, no one has recognized that Denis's "black triangle" obviously refers to a woman's sex.

34. The theme of the subject's relation to the painted mark that runs through Alastair Wright's book, *Matisse and the Subject of Modernism* but is most interestingly argued in the second chapter, " 'Trouble Rétinien': Fauvism, Madness, and the Schizophrenic Eye," 55–90.

35. Denis, "Salon d'Automne of 1905," 106.

36. *Blue Nude* was based on the small sculpted figure, *Reclining Nude I,* which was, in turn, based on a photograph. On Matisse's use of photographs as the basis of his sculptures from this period, see Isabelle Monod-Fontaine, *The Sculpture of Henri Matisse* (London: Arts Council of Great Britain, 1984), and Ellen McBreen's dissertation. Many of the photographs were culled from a soft-porn-slash-"artistic" review called *Mes modeles.*

37. An interesting discussion of the painting appears in Alaistair Wright, *Matisse and the Subject of Modernism,* 163–91. Wright argues that Matisse's *Blue Nude,* while engaged in certain widespread anxieties about creolization and miscegenation, and while understood as "primitive" in some general sense, was not in fact recognized as a North African figure, nor was it specifically conceived or received in terms of colonial politics. Much of Wright's argument is convincing, but I take issue with the gender ambiguity that he (and many other critics) want to see in this painting: though Matisse certainly may have transgressed certain expectations for the depiction of an erotic nude, the emphasis on the massive, bulbous breasts and the juicy haunches seem to make this figure clearly—even threateningly—female.

In relation to this notion of the *Blue Nude's* femininity as not ambiguous but threatening, Gertrude Stein's response to the picture, which she owned, is revealing: "Gertrude enjoyed the shock effect [*Blue Nude*] had on their visitors and recalled with relish how the five-year-old son of their concierge had jumped into her arms when he first saw it and 'cried out in rapture, oh là là what a beautiful body of a woman.' Gertrude liked to tell this story, she wrote, 'when the casual stranger in the aggressive way of the casual stranger said, looking at this picture, and what is it supposed to represent'" (Jack D. Flam, *Matisse and Picasso: The Story of Their Rivalry and Friendship* [Cambridge, Mass.: Westview Press, 2003], 36). Stein's response, in other words, to the aggression of the casual stranger, was to tell a story that did not allow the observer to turn away from the emphatic femininity on display—a woman's body so obvious (and so beautiful) that even a five-year-old could recognize it as such.

38. Walter Pach, *Queer Thing, Painting: Forty Years in*

the World of Art (New York: Harper, 1938), 125, quoted in Wright, *Matisse and the Subject of Modernism,* 166.

39. The first quotation is taken from Albert Elsen, "The Sculpture of Matisse, Part I: A New Expressiveness," *Artforum,* September 1968, 28, and the second from Jack Flam, "La Sculpture de Matisse," *Cahiers du Musée National d'Art Moderne* 30 (Winter 1989): 28. On the idea that Cézanne was the source of the painting's sculptural address, see also William Tucker, "Matisse's Sculpture: The Grasped and the Seen," *Art in America,* July–August 1975, 62–66, and John Elderfield, *The "Wild Beasts,"* 118 and 137 especially.

40. See, for example, Albert Elsen, "Rodin et Matisse: Différences, affinités, et influences," in *Rodin et la sculpture contemporaine* (Paris: Ed. du Musée Rodin, 1983), 65–87; Roger Benjamin, "L'arabesque dans la modernité: Henri Matisse sculpteur," in *De Matisse à aujourd'hui: La sculpture du XXe siècle dans les musées et le fonds regional d'art contemporain du Nord-Pas de Calais* (Lille: Association des Conservateurs des Musées du Nord-Pas-de-Calais, 1992), 15–22; and William Tucker, "Matisse's Sculpture," 62–66.

41. Jack Flam, on the other hand, sees the sculpture as far more indebted to Maillol (*Matisse: A Man and His Art, 1869–1918* [Ithaca: Cornell University Press, 1986], 191).

42. See, for example, Jack Flam's description of the painting in *Matisse: A Man and His Art,* 195.

43. Charles Morice, quoted in Benjamin, *Matisse's "Notes of a Painter,"* 119.

44. Why speak of Rodin, though, in relation to a sculpture and a painting that are most often thought of in relation to Matisse's newfound interest in African art? Beyond the equivocal role that African art might have played in these works, it may be that for Matisse this foreign tradition was one that stressed (in his reading of it) the need to *abandon* the anatomical body as such in his sculptural practice. Recalling the African figurines he used to see in a curio shop on the rue de Rennes, Matisse later said that "I was astonished to see how they were conceived from the point of view of sculptural language, how close it was to the Egyptian. That is, compared to European sculptures, which always depend on musculature, primarily on the description of the object, these Negro statues were made in terms of their material, according to invented planes and proportions" (quoted in Flam, *Matisse: The Man and His Art,* 174). If *Reclining Nude* and *Blue Nude* retain any tie to the sculptural body, it is not because of Matisse's interest in African art—a tradition, in other words, that suggested a more material practice in which the body was a function of "invented planes and proportions" and a response to the conditions of the medium.

On *Blue Nude* as a synthesis of Cézanne and African art, see James D. Herbert, "Woman, Cézanne, and Africa," in *Fauve Painting: The Making of Cultural Politics,* 146–73; on *Blue Nude* in relation to a primitive reading of Western culture, see Alastair Wright, *Matisse and the Subject of Modernism,* 163–91; on *Blue Nude* in relation to African sculpture and Matisse's own sculptural practice, see Ellen McBreen's dissertation, "The Pinup and the Primitive."

45. Matisse, "Notes of a Painter," in *Matisse on Art,* 37–38. Translation slightly modified.

46. Contrast this with Matisse's complaint, made late in life, about Rodin's method of composition: "I could not . . . understand how Rodin was able to work on his Saint Jean by cutting off the hand and fixing it onto a pin. It seems he worked at the hand's details by holding it in his own left hand, or at least by keeping it detached from the whole. He would then fix the hand back onto the wrist, and try to give it a direction related to the general movement. Already, for myself, I could only envisage working towards a general architecture, replacing the explanatory details with a living and suggestive synthesis" (quoted in Raymond Escholier, *Matisse, ce vivant* [Paris: Fayard, 1956], 362, cited in translation in Benjamin, *Matisse's "Notes of a Painter,"* 200). Benjamin points out that this critique of Rodin's method was current in artistic circles at the moment.

Nor does it seem coincidental, as Yve-Alain Bois points out, that Matisse bought Cézanne's *Three Bathers* immediately after reading Paul Signac's treatise, *De Delacroix au néo-impressionisme,* in which Cézanne's *tache* was defined "as a perfectly nonmimetic element," important solely for its coloristic quality. See Bois, "Matisse and 'Arche-drawing,'" in *Painting as Model* (Cambridge, Mass.: MIT Press, 1990), 10–11.

47. Compare William Tucker's assessment: "The originality of Matisse's vision of the figure-in-sculpture may be judged by comparing his figures with those of Rodin and

some of Rodin's contemporaries—Maillol, Bourdelle, Lehmbruck—who took on the challenge of the extended figure rather than the figure-as-object. However far Rodin and these followers may depart from the norms of proportion and anatomical truth, however much they idealize or expressively distort, they always work from a conception of the human figure that is at bottom imitative. Rodin himself never pretended otherwise. There is here no distinction in feeling, no distance, between the figure-in-sculpture and the sculpture. The structure of the sculpture *is* the attitude of the figure. But Matisse deliberately employs the most banal and familiar academic poses to separate our experience of the figure itself from our experience of the sculpture, and this abstract presentation of the figure allows a liberation of direct feeling for the figure—notably *the expression of an intense sexuality that Rodin and Maillol could only achieve by illustration or implication*" ("Matisse's Sculpture: The Grasped and the Seen," 66).

48. For Morice's comments on *Luxe, calme, et volupté,* see Benjamin, *Matisse's "Notes of a Painter,"* 98; for his comments on *Joy of Life,* see Benjamin, "Expression, Disfiguration," 103.

49. Bois, "On Matisse: The Blinding," *October* 68 (Spring 1994): 68–121. Bois's citation of Matisse's eroticization of the picture plane—an eroticization that he came to, in part, through Cézanne—is part of a larger study of *Joy of Life* as a painting that kills its relation to art historical tradition in an Oedipal fashion.

John Elderfield *(Pleasuring Painting: Matisse's Feminine Representations* [London: Thames and Hudson, 1995]) offers a remarkably similar account of the way in which Matisse's visual erotics works, although he focuses more on the Nice period. Elderfield's account, however, is fully invested in sublimation as a structural principle of the work, and in fact his account is deeply problematic in a number of ways, not least because of his dismissal of feminist accounts of pleasure.

50. Matisse, "Notes of a Painter," in *Matisse on Art,* 36.

51. "The emotional interest aroused in me by them [his models] does not appear particularly in the representation of their bodies, but often rather in the lines or the special values distributed over the whole canvas or paper, which form its complete orchestration, its architecture. But not everyone perceives this. It is perhaps sublimated sensual pleasure, which may not yet be perceived by everyone" ("Notes of a Painter on His Drawing, 1939," quoted in translation in *Matisse on Art,* 82).

52. Though for entirely different reasons, Bois also suggests that, around this time, Matisse's understanding of the implications of Cézanne's practice changed radically, from a concentration on the usages of *passage* to assist in the creation of form to a focus on issues of compositional synthesis ("Matisse and 'Arche Drawing,'" 49–51).

53. Yve-Alain Bois, "Un silence de pierre: *Baigneuses à la tortue* (1908) de Henri Matisse," *Les Cahiers du Musée Nationale d'Art Moderne* 65 (Autumn 1998): 23–37.

54. While it seems to me that the Matisse *Bather* is a "complicated" female figure, so to speak, John Elderfield sees the ambiguity working in the opposite direction: "It is usually assumed that the *Bather* is a male figure. Certainly the hair is much shorter than that of the *Pink Nude* . . . and the body and legs are much broader. Although it seems unlikely that the *Bather* was painted directly from the model, indication of what seems to be a breast beneath the right arm renders the gender ambiguous" (*Matisse in the Collection of the Museum of Modern Art* [New York: Museum of Modern Art, 1978], 60).

55. The sculptures that Matisse produced in conjunction with this painting—the series of *Backs*—show the extent to which he was thinking about making the body continuous with the surface, outside of any notions of sculptural presence: his backs are figures without fronts, figures that absolutely deny any possibility of a body even as they depict an anatomical feature. Their dorsal views are fully and completely bounded by their material substrate, which does not read as a metaphor for the emergence of figure from ground, as a matter of primordial creation, as in the work of Medardo Rosso, for example, but rather is a mute wall into which the figure is embedded, a mass that offers no possibility of symbolic readings.

INDEX

Page numbers in *italics* refer to illustrations.

continued from front

Cézanne's Bathers proposes a new way of reading Cézanne's biography—not simply as a form of myth-making, but also as a form of art criticism. At the same time, it proposes a reading of Cézanne's images of bathers that accounts for their strangenesses and for the pleasures they produce. The book is fiercely engaged with arguments that have come before, mining the writings of figures such as Meyer Schapiro, Tamar Garb, and T. J. Clark to discover a new way of looking at these works.

Aruna D'Souza is Assistant Professor of Art History and Women's Studies at Binghamton University, State University of New York. She is the editor of *Self and History: A Tribute to Linda Nochlin* (2000) and *The Invisible Flâneuse? Gender, Public Space, and Visual Culture in Nineteenth-Century Paris* (2006).